Moving at the Speed of Wealth

Moving at the Speed of Wealth

*Discover the 17 Closely Guarded
Wealth-Building Secrets of the Super-Rich*

Wayde M. McKelvy

Cagan Publishing, LLC

Moving at the Speed of Wealth
Discover the 17 Closely Guarded Wealth-Building Secrets of the Super-Rich
Copyright © 2009 by Wayde M. McKelvy
Published by Cagan Publishing, LLC

All rights reserved. No part of this book may be reproduced (except for inclusion in reviews), disseminated or utilized in any form or by any means, electronic or mechanical, including photocopying, recording, or in any information storage and retrieval system, or the Internet/World Wide Web without written permission from Cagan Publishing, LLC and Wayde M. McKelvy.

For further information, please contact:
Cagan Publishing, LLC
6855 S. Havana Street, Suite 150
Centennial, CO 80112

Book design by Arbor Books, Inc.
www.arborbooks.com

Printed in the United States of America

Moving at the Speed of Wealth
Discover the 17 Closely Guarded Wealth-Building Secrets of the Super-Rich
Wayde M. McKelvy

1. Title   2. Author   3. Personal Finance, Retirement Planning, Wealth-Building Strategies, Alternative Investment Strategies

Library of Congress Control Number: 2008941683

ISBN 10: 0-9822475-0-8
ISBN 13: 978-0-9822475-0-1

This publication is designed to provide competent and reliable information regarding the subject matter covered. However, it is distributed with the understanding that the author and publisher are not engaged in rendering legal, tax, or other professional advice that the author is not qualified or licensed to provide. Laws and practices often vary state to state and if legal or other expert assistance is required, the services of a professional should be sought. The author and publisher specifically disclaim any liability that is incurred from the use or application of the contents of this text.

Table of Contents

Foreword xiii

Introduction
Secret of the Super-Rich #1
Super-Rich People Create Their Own Personal Banking System xvii
   Figure 1   Lost Purchasing Power xix
Chapter One
The Big Lie—Conventional Wisdom is Not Working 1
   Figure 2   Equity acceleration chart 17

Chapter Two
Secret of the Super-Rich #2
Super-Rich People Create a Personal Banking System
to Accelerate the Growth on Their Money Using a Properly
Designed Life Insurance Contract 21
   Figure 3   Lapsing policy 29
   Figure 4   Minimum Funding..33
   Figure 5   Target Premium 34
   Figure 6   Maximum Funding 35
   Figure 7   Reducing DB and SCV 36
   Figure 8   Returns with arbitrage 41
   Figure 9   Returns with no policy crediting......................................42
   Figure 10 Advantages of a life insurance contract
                 over traditional savings vehicles 43
Chapter Three
Secret of the Super-Rich #3
Super-Rich People Understand the Power of Compounding
Returns and How to Use Them Coupled with Simple Interest......45
   Figure 11 Penny Doubled Everyday 46
   Figure 12 Penny Doubled Everyday and Taxed 46
   Figure 13 Penny Doubled Everyday After Initial Penny is Taxed 47
   Figure 14 Rule of 72 vs. Rule of 108 48

Chapter Four
Secret of the Super-Rich #4
Super-Rich People Understand the Power of Arbitrage
and Get Stinking, Filthy Rich on Small Returns 53

Figure 15 Saving $500 in a life insurance policy 55
Figure 16 Maximum funding same $500 per month
to pay loan payment 56
Figure 17 SCV balances when maximum funding a plan 57
Figure 18 Unlock Your Equity and Increase Your Net Worth 58

Chapter Five
Secret of the Super-Rich #5
Super-Rich People Know About The Best-Kept Secrets
in the Investing Community 61
Figure 19 Banker slide 62
Figure 20 Borrow from policy to invest in private loans 70
Figure 21 Comparison of private loans with
and without an insurance policy 71
Figure 22 IRA vs. using an insurance policy
to make private loans 71
Figure 23 S&P 500 Index compared to 17%
private loans last ten years 75

Chapter Six
Secret of the Super-Rich #6
Super-Rich People Use Home Equity to Build Empires..................77
Figure 24 Your home has up to seven accounts
associated with it 79
Figure 25 Pulling home equity increases your net worth 87
Figure 26 Net worth when property depreciates 88
Figure 27 Growth over thirty years at 12% on lump sum 92
Figure 28 Periodic payments by twin brother 93
Figure 29 Reinvesting savings between interest
only and amortized loan 99
Figure 30 Spread of money and equity arbitrage 105
Figure 31 Compounding vehicle 106
Figure 32 Equity arbitrage at only 8% returns 107
Figure 33 Compounding vehicle 108
Figure 34 Spread of money..109
Figure 35 Policy Makes House Payment 111
Figure 36 On the Right Side of the Fence................................112

Chapter Seven

Secret of the Super-Rich #7

Super-Rich People Know How to Pay off
Their Home Loans Early with No Change in Lifestyle
and No Out-of-Pocket Money, but Choose Not to 115

Figure 37   Prepaying loan IRR in year seven....................................120
Figure 38   Spread of returns HELOC and hard money loans..........121
Figure 39   Side account IRR in year seven..122
Figure 40   IRR in seven years on scheduled 30-year
amortized loan 123
*Figure 41   **Figure Title needed**...124*

Chapter Eight

Secret of the Super-Rich #8

Super-Rich People Understand that Lump Sums of Money Grow
Larger than Monthly Periodic Payments!......................................127

Figure 42   IRA contribution limits 128
Figure 43 $417 periodic monthly payments growing
at 8% for thirty years..132
Figure 44 $83,333 lump sum growing at 8% for thirty years 134
Figure 45 $83,333 lump sum growing at after-tax rate of 13.6% for
thirty years 136
Figure 46 $417 periodic monthly payment growing
at 17% for thirty years tax-deferred 138
Figure 47   83,333 lump sum growing at 17%
for thirty years tax-deferred..140
Figure 48   Lump sum versus period payment at 8%
compounding tax-deferred 148
Figure 49   Lump sum versus period payment at 12%
compounding tax-deferred..149
Figure 50   Lump sum versus period payment at 15%
compounding tax-deferred 149

Chapter Nine

Secret of the Super-Rich #9

Super-Rich People Have a Great Understanding
of Opportunity Costs 151

Figure 51   Opportunity cost at 8%
on $30,000 paying cash for car 153

Figure 52	*Opportunity cost of buying five cars over thirty years for $30,000*	153
Figure 53	*Costs of financing a $30,000 car to someone with no cash in bank*	153
Figure 54	*Reinvesting residual value of car at 8% compounding tax-deferred*	155
Figure 55	*Using equity to purchase your cars*	156
Figure 56	*Repositioning cash to maximum fund a life insurance policy to pay cash for cars*	159
Figure 57	*Same policy 33 years later after borrowing from policy to buy five cars over thirty years*	160
Figure 58	*Opportunity cost of a cheap college education*	162
Figure 59	*Saving for college tuition starting when child is born using life insurance*	164
Figure 60	*Maximum funding insurance policy at age 40 to pay for college tuition*	165
Figure 61	*Growth of policy without paying back policy loan made for college tuition at age 50*	166

Chapter Ten
Secret of the Super-Rich #10
Super-Rich People Understand that You Must Absolutely, Positively Own Your Own Business to Build Tremendous Wealth 169

Figure 62	*List of some tax-deductible items when you own your own home-based business*	175

Chapter Eleven
Secret of the Super-Rich #11
The Super-Rich Create Tax Shelters, Pay Less Tax and Set up Tax-Free Retirement Income Streams 189

Figure 63	*Example of tax deductions for a home-based business with a family of four earning $75,000 a year in income*	192
Figure 64	*Traditional IRA withdrawals vs. Roth IRA withdrawals: all factors in the future remaining the same as they are today, they are the same*	198
Figure 65	*Required minimum distribution example*	201

Chapter Twelve
   Secret of the Super-Rich #12
      Super-Rich People Know How to Maximize
      Their Qualified Retirement Plans 207
      Figure 66 401(k) arbitrage spreadsheet, one-time loan 222
      Figure 67 401(k) arbitrage spreadsheet, rolling loans.....................223
      Figure 68 Better returns beat 401(k) matching contribution
                  spreadsheet...224

Chapter Thirteen
   Secret of the Super-Rich #13
      Super-Rich People Thoroughly Understand
      the Effects of Inflation and Use it to Their Advantage 225
      Figure 69 True inflation chart...227
      Figure 70 Inflation erodes your wealth 231

Chapter Fourteen
   Secret of the Super-Rich #14
      Super-Rich People Understand the Reality of Money 235

Chapter Fifteen
   Secret of the Super-Rich #15
      Super-Rich People Do Not Invest Where You Do; They Do Not
      Accept Returns Below Twelve to Fifteen Percent 241

Chapter Sixteen
   Secret of the Super-Rich #16
      Super-Rich People Own Nothing but Control Everything; They
      Protect Their Assets 257

Chapter Seventeen
   Secret of the Super-Rich #17
      Super-Rich People Do Not Procrastinate;
      They Take Immediate and Decisive Action 273

Foreword

"Forward"
(Mantria Corporation's Tagline)

Wayde McKelvy changed my life… As someone who understands finance—having executed on over $100 million dollars in real estate and finance transactions and graduating at the top of my class from Temple University with a triple major in finance, real estate and risk management— I knew that there wasn't anyone out there in the marketplace teaching people "true finance," not the run-of-the-mill, conventional "textbook finance." I owned and operated two multi-million-dollar companies during college, so I had great insight into the ins and outs of the market from an academic and professional standpoint. I knew that people were in trouble.

All I could think then was, "What are people going to do when it is time for them to retire and they haven't the slightest net worth to do it with?" It would pain me to think about all of the people that needed true direction in their wealth- and life-building strategies. I was reaching out to everyone I could, including my own family, about basic principles to help their financial future and overall life condition. However, I was far too busy building a series of real estate and finance companies to devote my attention to this issue. Instead, I decided with my partner, Amanda Knorr, that early on we would take a reduction on our margins and personal profits in an effort to create incredible investment offerings for all investors who worked with us—investments that have all of the elements of true wealth building: above average interest, secured 100% by real estate at a low loan to value, providing steady cash flow on a monthly basis, and backed by fundamental business initiatives, not pie-in-the-sky ideas. Mantria is, without question, the first "life" brand ever established. Everything we do is focused on helping our partners, consumers and stakeholders enhance and improve their lives. Every one of our products and services has unique life-building and wealth-building elements already implemented into the very DNA of that product.

Still, we weren't reaching people fast enough. With Middle America comprising seventy-five percent of the United States, I knew we were in grave financial jeopardy as a country, given that people are just not being taught the right information, are taking the wrong advice, and are losing the battle every day—the battle against their retirement future. Every day I saw people failing around me from making poor investments and from taking the advice of a conventional financial planner. My own grandparents even fell victim to this vicious cycle of believing that conventional wisdom would work.

Then, I met Wayde McKelvy... When I first started talking with Wayde, it was like looking into a mirror. It still is. Finally, there was someone who had dedicated his life to the same causes that we believe in: building wealth and improving life for your average, everyday investor and buyer. Yet, what makes Wayde so powerful is that he reaches out to the masses. There is not a single person alive whom he won't talk to; therefore, it is fair to say that there is not a single person alive whom he can't help. Wayde can help you; it is your choice to help yourself. While I could talk about Wayde's entrepreneurial and financial acumen all day, this book is about so much more than just making money. Wayde McKelvy understands that true success is defined by how much you build in life and by how much you help people achieve their dreams.

Financial wisdom is gained by experience—a lot of it. And getting your fingers burned several times is inevitable. What separates people who build great wealth and those who fail is, quite simply, listening and keeping an open mind. While you have to be very cautious about whom you listen to, listening carefully and believing there is always a better way of doing something is what separates the classes. As you will learn from Wayde, wealthy people just think differently. I would stake my reputation on this fact. Listening to Wayde McKelvy will change your life, just as it changed mine.

If there is anything I want you to remember it is that people, by nature, are bad at planning. We wait until the last minute for everything and then finally, when doomsday comes, we say, "Oh my gosh, I need to fix this!" Ladies and gentlemen, by the time most of you say this, it's already too late to move at the

Foreword

speed that you need to ensure you will correct the issue (that is, unless you're "Moving at the Speed of Wealth"™).

When reading this book, think of your future. Take every line as a pathway that will benefit your future and the future of your loved ones, every paragraph as growing a better net worth and every page as another day of a comfortable retirement life. I urge you to really take the time and let the messages sink in. The benefits to you and your family will be life altering.

Wayde and I have been friends for a long time and he's always been kind enough to call me a genius and a great partner; however, I have learned so much more from Wayde than probably even he knows. Being friends and partners with Wayde has truly been a life-altering experience. If he helped my partner and me, and our $40-million-dollar company, as much as he did, imagine what he can do for you. If you absorb even a small portion of the seventeen key principles of building wealth that you find in this book, it won't be long before you'll find the success you've always been after. You'll finally be able to sleep comfortably at night knowing your retirement future is bright.

I look forward to the opportunity to meet each and every one of you.

> With best personal regards,
> Troy Wragg
> Founder, Chairman & CEO
> Mantria Corporation
> May 17, 2008

INTRODUCTION

Secret of the Super-Rich #1:

Super-Rich People Create Their Own Personal Banking System

Every reader of this book has his or her own idea of what it takes to grow wealthy. Notice that I said, "grow wealthy." I stress this because, unless you fall into a huge inheritance or win a big lawsuit, you are going to need a plan to *grow* wealthy. Despite what you may think, there really is no true "get rich quick" scheme out there. However, there are strategies that will help you get rich much faster!

Two key words used in the above paragraph are "plan" and "strategies." Most Middle Americans use some plan passed to them by the media, financial planner or government to grow their retirement savings without any real idea of what it is they are doing. Sure, you may move your money around from one mutual fund to another and read the *Wall Street Journal* but for the most part, we are going through life with blinders on when it comes to our money. This is the out of sight, out of mind mentality.

You may think you are going to grow rich by buying real estate properties, fixing them up and selling them immediately (fix-n-flips). Your strategy may be to buy single-family residences, rent them out and hold them for years to come. You may think that beating the market is your best way to riches (although depending on who you listen to, it has been reported by Morningstar and *20/20* that most professional mutual fund managers cannot outperform the S&P 500 index®. But, hey, you're smarter than those professionals with thousands of team members doing research on companies!).

Look around you. Do you see a real estate mogul on every street corner? Do you see a stock market mogul on every street corner? No. What you see is a bank on every major intersection across America and then some. This should be a good indication to you that banks make a lot of money. And why not? They prey on your lack of a sound financial education to get richer, so it is not only in their best interest, but in all of Wall Street's, to keep you uninformed.

Doesn't it just make sense that if you want to build tremendous wealth then you need to create your very own banking system? *Sure it does, Wayde, but I don't know the first thing about being a banker.* Folks, I am not recommending that you go out and buy a bank. That would be foolish and it could take ten years to be approved.

No, I am talking about creating a "banking system" that you and your family will benefit from for years to come. But first, let's start off by explaining in layman's terms how banks are so darn profitable.

How many of you put money in a bank? How many of you put money in a bank Certificate of Deposit (CD), money market fund or other low interest-bearing account? I would bet that a whole lot of you raised your hands because you perceive that your money is safe.

Essentially, when you make a deposit into a bank, you are lending the bank money and in return they are going to pay you interest on your loan. These banks are generous; at the time of this writing, you could probably receive 3.5-4% on your money.

You say, "That's fine…my money is safe and not at risk." That is total brain-washing. Your money is at a huge risk because the risk you take is already happening the minute you make your deposit. You are losing purchasing power on a daily basis.

You see, the returns they are paying you are not keeping up with *true* inflation. I'm not talking about the inflation rate that the government publishes using the Consumer Price Index (CPI). This is totally fabricated. I will explain more about this in a later chapter but for now, would you please go along with me and agree that the true inflation rate is closer to 6% (I actually believe it is closer to 8%, especially when you have a declining dollar, but I will be conservative).

If you put $1,000 in a bank CD outside of an IRA or Qualified Retirement Plan (more on these vehicles later), not only are you receiving a pathetic return but the interest you earn is taxed as well. Let's say you are in only the 20% effective

Introduction

tax bracket (that is, the average you are paying in taxes is 20% of your income). Also assume that the bank is paying you 4% for your loan. After paying taxes on the interest you earn at the end of the year, your true effective return is only 3.2%.

The chart to the right shows how your $1,000 loses purchasing power over thirty years. Looking at this chart, you will see an initial deposit of $1,000 and the bank is paying you 4% on your money. After factoring in taxes on interest earned, your true net return is closer to 3.2%. Lo and behold, inflation is at 6% so you are truly receiving a negative return on your money of 2.80%.

By looking at the chart, you will see that what you could have bought for $1,000 today will only purchase $972.00 worth of goods just one year from now. If you stretch it out to ten years, what you could buy today for $1,000 will only buy $752.77 in the future.

Lost Purchasing Power When Returns Do Not Outpace Inflation.	
Deposit:	$1,000.00
Interest Paid to You:	3.20%
Inflation Rate:	6.00%
True Return:	-2.80%

Year	Purchasing Power of Initial Deposit
1	$972.00
2	$944.78
3	$918.33
4	$892.62
5	$867.62
6	$843.33
7	$819.72
8	$796.76
9	$774.46
10	$752.77
11	$731.69
12	$711.21
13	$691.29
14	$671.94
15	$653.12
16	$634.83
17	$617.06
18	$599.78
19	$582.99
20	$566.66
21	$550.80
22	$535.57
23	$520.38
24	$505.81
25	$491.65
26	$477.88
27	$464.50
28	$451.50
29	$438.86
30	$426.57

Figure 1

Look all the way down to year thirty and you will find that you can only buy $426.57 worth of goods and services with that $1,000. This is after the returns you received. Granted, your bank account will look as if it has grown but all that matters is the purchasing power of your dollars.

That's how inflation erodes your purchasing power. In reality, when you put money into an account that does not return interest at the same pace as inflation, you are essentially losing principal even though that is not what it looks like on paper.

This is no longer about "risk"—this is happening right now!

I recognize the appeal of loaning money to a bank. When I am in front of a live crowd presenting my seminar, I ask the attendees, "What is your collateral when you loan money to the bank?" I typically receive two answers:

1. Your collateral is money in the bank. Buzz—wrong! The bank can loan up to twenty times the reserves they hold. This means they have more outstanding loans than deposits. On top of that, who wants something that is not real as collateral? Money is fake, folks! Money is fiat. There is nothing backing money but the "good faith and credit of the United States government." This is one of the reasons we have inflation. Whenever the government needs to spur the economy, they turn to the Federal Reserve Bank (which, by the way, is not a branch of the U.S. government) to print more money. More money in print means more circulation, equals inflation. Money is not collateral; money is fake.

2. Your collateral is the FDIC. This is the most common response to my question. The FDIC is not collateral; the Federal Deposit Insurance Corporation is just that, an insurance company. The FDIC collects premiums from the banks to insure up to $100,000 of each depositor's money in one account at any one bank. "Regulators are bracing for one hundred to two hundred bank failures over the next twelve to twenty-four months," says Jaret Seiberg, an analyst with financial services firm The Stanford Group. If you are in tune with what's happening in our country right now, you understand what the failed sub-prime market is doing to the banking industry. Although it is very unlikely, the FDIC can run out of money and go belly up right along with those banks. It happened in this country once in 1980.

In the 1980s, during the savings and loan crisis, the Federal Savings and Loans Insurance Company (FSLIC) became insolvent. It was recapitalized with taxpayer money several times, including with $15 billion in 1986 and $10.75 billion in 1987. However, by 1989 it was deemed too insolvent to save and was abolished along with the FHLBB; savings and loan deposit insurance responsibility was transferred to the FDIC.

The reason that people like their money sitting in a bank is to protect their principal from losses. That sounds like rational thinking to me but I have already shown you the effects that inflation has on your deposits. You are losing principal daily in the form of lost purchasing power. So much for protecting your principal! By the time you get around to using the money in your CD, it may have half the purchasing power you originally started with.

That said, it is easy to see why you don't want to loan your money to a bank. After all, how does the bank make its money? The bank will simply pay you an interest rate on your money then turn around and lend it to a borrower at a higher rate. I am going to call this arbitrage (spread of money).

You will find as you progress through this book that "arbitrage" will become your new favorite word.

If the bank is paying you 4% and turns around and loans it to another borrower (the scary part is that sometimes they loan the money right back to you—something is wrong with this picture!) at 8%, then the banker has created a 4% spread on the money (arbitrage). This is essentially free money and why banks get richer.

On top of that, banks can loan out up to twenty times the amount of money they have on reserves and can borrow from the Federal Reserve Bank. Unfortunately, I will not be able to pull that magic off for you but, hey, you live in the system.

So my question to you is: Why do you insist on having a middleman involved in the transaction? If people are willing to pay 8% to borrow money, why wouldn't you borrow money below 8%, say 6%, and loan it out to people at 8% and collateralize their assets?

I already know your responses. First of all, how can you borrow at 6% and, secondly, how the heck can you find these borrowers who are willing to let you collateralize their assets and borrow at 8%? Well, that is exactly why you have this book in your hands. As you read and digest these pages, I am not only going to make it clear about how to pull this off, but I will show you how I'll help you do it as well.

I will go a step further and show you how to borrow at 4% and receive 12-25% interest from borrowers who will allow you to collateralize their assets. I am essentially going to show you how to create your very own banking system.

As we progress, I will show you how you can borrow money on an average of 6% and still be credited interest on that money on an average of 9%. You are earning a 3% return on your money even when it is sitting in your front pocket.

Wealthy people don't let it stay in their front pocket. They would then loan it out at 12% or more, which gives them a total return of 15% on their money. Then I will show you how some, if not all, of this money will be in a tax-free zone!

Moving at the Speed of Wealth™ has two primary goals for Middle America: First and foremost, I want to educate you today regarding personal finances. I do not preach the same old buy and hold strategies that have been preached by financial planners for years. I want to show you strategies that create massive wealth quickly—though not overnight.

I believe in the safety of your money. After all, we are talking about people's life savings, the money that needs to be there to provide them with a comfortable lifestyle in retirement.

Unlike Wall Street and many product pushers, I want to get rich with you, not in spite of you. As a member of The Speed of Wealth Gold Club™, you will be introduced to unique, alternative investment opportunities that are only available to our members. All of our investments are collateralized by something real and tangible to protect your principal.

In this book, I will show you some techniques and strategies that are available to everyone—but nobody is learning them. You will discover:

- How to generate up to $2,000,000 (that's two million dollars) of additional retirement savings without changing your current investments and without one single extra dollar out of your pocket. Sounds "too good to be true"? Then put down this book now because you do not have the mental attitude to be wealthy.
- How to make infinite returns on your money;
- How to have one dollar of your investment money working in up to four places at the same time;
- How to create a tax-deferred qualified plan that allows you to invest anywhere you choose with no fees;
- How to create a banking system that you can utilize to hedge other investment opportunities;
- Why your qualified retirement plan may be the worst place to save and how to explode the plan and take control once and for all;
- A simple technique that will allow you to roll out your Individual Retirement Arrangement (IRA), eliminate the tax bill, and explode the growth all at the same time;
- How to convert your current traditional IRA to a Roth IRA and stretch out the taxes owed indefinitely, and take a tax deduction on the money you send to the IRS;
- The uses of arbitrage—how to create it easily and how to capitalize on the spread of money;

Introduction

- Why life insurance is a poor investment but perhaps the greatest investment tool available today;
- Why your primary residence is a very poor investment and how to use it to create massive wealth;
- How to pay off your home loan early with absolutely no additional money out of your pocket;
- How to easily receive up to 25% returns on your money annually in an investment that I believe to be safer than a bank CD;
- How to start a self-directed IRA or 401(k) plan and blow away your neighbors' retirement plans by a long shot;
- Why you should never pay cash for a car again;
- How to properly fund a college education;
- How to earn 14% return on your money when you purchase large-ticket, depreciating items such as business equipment, cars, boats, and more;
- Why you must start your own business yesterday and how to do it on a shoestring budget—I will also introduce you to some amazing business opportunities;
- And much, much more!

I will show you how to use simple techniques and strategies that will simply explode your wealth—in most cases, with no more money out of your pocket. As you read on, all that I ask is for you to let this sink in with an open mind. I am going to challenge your traditional beliefs about building wealth. I am going to be pointing out techniques and ideas that are 180 degrees from what you have been led to believe. I am asking for a paradigm shift in your thinking.

This will not be easy for you at first. Most people do not like change and want instant gratification. Americans are the worst when it comes to seeing results. You must be patient and stick to a plan with proven strategies that build wealth.

Of course, if you have not started saving for retirement then it's about time you got started. I lecture at many colleges across the country to try to give these young kids a head start. There is absolutely no reason kids in college cannot retire soon and retire wealthy; they have time on their side. What I teach them only makes retiring wealthy sooner more of a reality.

Most of you must eliminate your fears. Professional planners, the media, the government and Wall Street have been secretly planting these fears in your mind systematically for years. The reason should be obvious: In order for them to survive, they need you to think that you need them. They try to convince you that they can show you the way to wealth but they do this in spite of you.

Don't even get me started on these fee-based managers. Unless they offer alternative investments to mutual funds, exchange traded funds, and bonds and stocks, you just do not need them. In fact, I believe anyone giving you advice had better be investing in the same investments they recommend to you and they should only make money if your money grows (call me old-fashioned, but I think we should be paid for production).

Continue reading…and my hope is, at the very least, that your mind starts to question conventional wisdom when it comes to retirement planning. Many of the so-called experts will tell you the exact same thing: Save more money and invest it in mutual funds, bonds and stocks for the long run. Folks, this conventional wisdom is not working and it's time for you to discover how the other 5% of Americans invest—the wealthy people in America. Open your mind to my unconventional methods and the light will shine in.

Wealthy people have figured this out long ago. If you can't beat them, join them. Wealthy people are making the rules so you must take advantage of the rules they make and, best of all, you do not have to be wealthy to participate.

This is just the beginning of your "new financial education." One thing I have learned over the years is that investment environments change often and they change on a dime. You need to always be abreast of new techniques, strategies and investments.

I want to be here to mentor you and teach you ways of exploding your wealth. If you have not already done so, I want you to become a member of The Speed of Wealth Gold Club™ today. This is an educational forum and membership; the rewards are mind-boggling. Let me quickly explain what The Speed of Wealth Club™ is:

- ✓ An educational forum to show members how to build tremendous wealth
- ✓ Members must be truly motivated to build wealth and be open-minded and explore their fears about investing. These fears have been programmed into you and you must overcome them.
- ✓ Members must be willing to act immediately. When you are educated properly, making decisions quickly should come easily. This is why you must continue the education process.

Introduction

✓ Members are notified of REAL opportunities that provide REAL returns. You will not be introduced to "hot stock picks" or any options, commodities, FOREX (foreign currency exchange), software programs and ETF strategies. There are countless newsletters for that and the money being made is only going to the publishers of these letters. You may enjoy the stock market and do very well but we are here to show you how to use your "gift" and explode your portfolio.

✓ Members can bring deals that are scrutinized and put into action if they make sense. We primarily focus on real estate and members are encouraged to always be looking for big deals. One big deal that you bring and introduce to our members can set you up for life.

✓ Members share common goals and interests. This is very important. We must all be like-minded individuals. You must understand that we are more powerful as a group than as individuals. By bringing our resources together, we are able to open more doors than you would ever imagine. As you read on, you will come to understand this.

✓ Successful wealthy people mentor you and are working with you side by side. You will be introduced to many specialists in many different areas. No one person can specialize in everything and succeed. I can show you what I specialize in but my goal is to open your eyes across the board and to do this, I must introduce you to successful people. This could be particular investment opportunities, business opportunities, strategies, self-help, college planning…the list goes on and on.

✓ Play with the BIG BOYS, quit playing around with real estate. If you want to go it alone, that's fine. I will introduce you to people who specialize in helping individuals. But let me say right here and now that fix-n-flipping properties one at a time is a full-time job, not an investment, and you are not going to build great wealth. Buying rental properties and holding is a great strategy and can offer you a comfortable retirement, but nowhere near what having equity in large development projects can provide. We will show you how to benefit by investing with the true moneymakers.

✓ Truly build an empire using real estate as your preferred tool. You may occasionally hear about opportunities other than real estate but real estate has made more self-made millionaires than any other investment vehicle. We focus 80% of our energy on real estate-related opportunities.

✓ We provide monthly teleconferences, workshops, seminars, opportunities and newsletters. You cannot benefit as a member unless you pour yourself in one hundred percent. You will be invited to participate in many educational forums, including many webinars. You must participate to truly build wealth.

The following are some of the goals of The Speed of Wealth Club™:

✓ To help our members create their own personal banking system that puts them in control of all of their investing decisions. Once you have created a personal banking system, the world is your oyster and you can protect all of your investments. Like this introduction suggests, banks are very wealthy because they are in control of the money and create free money. You know the golden rule: "He who has the gold makes the rules!" When you have a personal banking system, you will be making your very own rules and controlling your destiny.

✓ To provide our clients with alternative means of investing in a more stable environment. I don't know who said "high risk equals high returns and low risk equals low returns," but this simply is not true if you know what you are doing. Robert Kiyosaki makes this point in his *Rich Dad* books. I will say my version now: "Strong education and knowledge equal high returns; the absence of education and knowledge equals low returns!"

✓ To enable our clients to expand their portfolios into real estate-related investments passively. If it is true that more self-made multi-millionaires are created from real estate then why don't more people invest in real estate? Because

Introduction

they lack knowledge and time. Real estate investing is very time-consuming. We will teach you how to invest in real estate passively and make huge returns. We want you drinking Mai Tais in Bermuda as your money swells to gigantic proportions.

✓ To ensure future growth as our clients move into retirement. Growing your money does not stop in retirement. I do not want to make light of it but money is the score of life. Some people have more money than they will ever need yet they continue to grow their money. It is not greed; it is not ego. It becomes a game that you want to win. You will soon find how giving you truly are when you have excess money.

✓ To accelerate the growth of our clients' portfolios by borrowing from an insurance contract and generating arbitrage. I will show you how to use insurance as an investment tool that can explode the growth of your money. Not all members take advantage of this and that's okay with us. We just want you to know about the technique and it is our job to uncover and explain all wealth-building strategies to you. You decide which strategies work with your personality and goals.

✓ To shelter a portion of our clients' portfolios from taxes. Let's face it…if we do our job right—and we will—you will be in a higher tax bracket in retirement than you are now. If you are in a higher tax bracket, then you are obviously making more money. Not to mention the chances are very strong that taxes will be higher in the future than they are today. Our goal is to help you shelter as much money from taxes as possible using simple strategies, not the complicated off-shore type of plans. Our government gives you plenty of tools to reduce your tax burden but you must be educated to take advantage of them.

✓ To build tremendous wealth by utilizing leverage and/or by creating arbitrage between investments.

I want to make it very clear that membership is not free but you need to join today. However, do not join if you will not participate. You may be asking

Moving at the Speed of Wealth

why anyone would offer all of this education for such a low membership fee and the answer is simple: Like anyone, I like to share my opinions and ideas with others and this forum gives me the opportunity to achieve the feeling of doing something to help Middle America.

And, yes, I do make money. This is what I do for a living. Although I will never ask you for a dime for a portion of the education or a penny to help you personalize a plan, I do make money on the investment opportunities. Do you really mind if I make money if I am showing you ways to explode your wealth and introducing you to opportunities that make 12% returns or much more annually? I would hope not. If so, don't bother to join. Keep in mind that I am trying to get wealthy with you, not in spite of you. We are all in this together and, as a group of like-minded individuals, there is nothing we cannot accomplish.

I do not profess to have all the answers. In fact, I just question all the conventional wisdom that has been handed down and come to my own conclusions. You may disagree with me on some of the topics I present and that is fine. At least I got you thinking about it and you are seeing another viewpoint.

If you never invest a dime in the opportunities we present to you then I will still be happy knowing that I have shown you strategies that will help you grow wealthier using your own investment criteria. You will learn techniques that will put you in charge. "Moving at the Speed of Wealth"™ is a trademark and branding phrase used by my company, Retirement TRACS, LLC. TRACS stands for "Total Retirement Asset Control System." We want you to be in control of your future and it starts with education.

STEP ONE: This is where you start. Reading this entire book is the very first step. Read this book in its entirety; hopefully, you won't want to put it down. If the book does not satisfy you for any reason, simply request a refund. I will refund your money with no questions asked and you can keep the book. All I ask in return is that you give the book to someone you know in exchange for the refund. Of course, I will have no way of knowing if you did this so we are going on good faith.

STEP TWO: If you have already joined The Speed of Wealth Gold Club™, congratulations! You are well on your way. If you have not joined, then join today by visiting our website at *www.SpeedofWealth.com* and clicking on "The Speed of Wealth Club"™ button to learn more. If it appeals to you and you think membership is affordable, then join instantly.

Once you are a member, there are many webinars, videos, free publications and other educational material included in this website.

Introduction   xxix

Keep in mind that many of the strategies I introduce to you take some time to sink in and the book gives you more details and the ability to go back and review.

Don't forget to review our testimonial page and blog page.

STEP THREE: Get actively involved and dip your toe. Attend seminars, workshops, teleconferences, and webinars, and read the emails you will receive. Supercharge your education and learn about our current investment opportunities. I suggest you take a portion of your portfolio and invest in the opportunities that feel good to you. Test us out and see how we perform. We are very transparent on all of our opportunities and you will have the opportunity to do your own due diligence.

STEP FOUR: Remember that we are more powerful as a group than as individuals. The more members we have, the better the opportunities we can introduce to you. Spread the word to your friends, neighbors, co-workers and relatives. Encourage them to become members and to order the book. You will get a lot of resistance but, hey, at least you tried.

STEP FIVE: Ignore people who tell you that what I teach is b.s. I am talking about financial planners, bankers, brokers, insurance agents, lawyers, etc. Keep in mind that they want to build their own wealth in spite of you. It's all about assets under management and if you move your money, they lose their commissions and/or fees. Of course they are going to try to debunk everything I teach you. They stand to lose a great deal if you leave them. And if they say, "I can do that for you," you need to ask them why they haven't—then pack up and leave. Once you show them my strategies and techniques, they will tell you they're all wrong, then they will wait about six months and start preaching what I have taught you because I have now taught *them*. Make no mistake, you will get resistance from these people. People hate to see others succeed more than they do. Get started today—you can complete all five steps in a matter of minutes. You can view all six videos of my introductory seminar online without becoming a member. Each video is between thirty and sixty minutes, and well worth your time.

You can reach us by calling 303-690-2002 or emailing support@speed-ofwealth.com. I am looking forward to personally talking to you and helping you down the road to riches.

Chapter One

The Big Lie—Conventional Wisdom Is Not Working

IMPORTANT WARNING: *Before you proceed, I want you to be aware of a few things. First of all, there are a lot of numbers in this book. Many people struggle with numbers and it can make the head spin. The numbers themselves are not that important, but the points and strategies I am using the numbers to justify are. Do not get lost in the numbers—just take them at what they are. I only use them to back up my statements. A second warning is that there are some redundancies in this book. You will see me make the same point, sometimes from different angles, in more than one chapter. I did this purposefully. I really need these wealth strategies to sink into your subconscious so that you understand them so well that you could easily explain them to a friend. One last thing: I need you to read this book in its entirety and with a wide-open mind. I am going to try to change your core foundation and the beliefs you have been taught over time. Just because the government, financial planners, so-called "gurus," your parents, your grandparents and so on have taught you about finance, that does not mean it is correct. In fact, you just might find that most of this advice was dead wrong all along. Sit back, dig in, open your mind, challenge me and come to your own conclusions.*

I'm tired! Tired of all the propaganda, half-truths, myths and out-and-out lies that are being preached out there. I do not profess to be the smartest man around, just a man with a lot of opinions and some sense to make what's up and down seem horizontal.

This book is not about statistics. Heck, you have heard all about the statistics. I will tell you this: Depending on what you want to convey to the public, you can manipulate statistics to earn your own respect. I do need to mention a few in this book but, and this is a big but, these will be my own statistics, averages, medians, etc., based on my *own* experience.

Just to keep the record straight, I am not a financial planner, I am not licensed to sell securities, real estate, home mortgages, health care, skin care, dentistry, pharmaceuticals…well, you get the idea. The only license I own is that of an insurance producer, which I am glad to get rid of if the "powers that be" deem fit to take the "privilege" from me. I have had a whole bunch of these privileged licenses but I have a different agenda for the American public…LET US BE! If you care, and I presume you do, otherwise you would not be reading this book by a novice writer, then let me make my own damn decisions. You see, our government thinks that you are stupid but we will talk more about this later.

I do not have any fancy designations behind my name. I think the public is too smart for that. I have, however, created my own special designation called CRLE: Certified Real Life Experience (clever, you think?). Basically, if you have experienced it, there is a good chance that I have as well. I've been broke, almost bankrupt, have had tax liens, been rich, broke again, more tax liens, rich again, never broke again but close and so on. I have been foreclosed on (a story you will hear when you get to know me), I have been pissed on, I have been beaten up and I have beaten others up.

I once asked my dad, "Why does every American think that they are the center of the universe?" My dad is the smartest man I have ever known and his answer was very simple. He said, "Because, you knucklehead, look where you are. From your perspective, you *are* the center of the universe." Guess what? He was right. As much as I would like people to change, or the government to change, yada, yada, yada, all I can control is myself. Keep in mind that this includes my fifteen-year-old twin daughters. I can do the best parenting money can buy (that's a joke) but ultimately peers have more of an impact on my kids—and you are an idiot if you pick their peers because it will backfire every time. I digress, but that may be a subject for my next book.

So what does all this ranting and raving have to do with personal financial goals? Here it is in a nutshell: I have read more books on the subject than I would wish upon my worst enemy. I will not name authors but out of

The Big Lie—Conventional Wisdom Is Not Working 3

possibly one hundred books, only two have any merit whatsoever. The rest break down into five simple categories:

Category One: The Bach, Orman, Babylon, Ljlafjdl, Jdfljf, etc., bull*&#% strategy.

I love these books because they are bestsellers and it just goes to show you that we, as Americans, are morons. You could read 20,000 pages from these guys and I can sum it up in a short paragraph.

Pay yourself first, at least 10% of your salary, then put it into a well-balanced portfolio (primarily consisting of mutual funds, gag me with a spoon). Wait for a while and you will be just fine in retirement. I wish Penn and Teller would tackle this on their Showtime original show, *Bull Shit*. There are some very fundamental problems with all this crap that they are telling us.

Let's assume for one minute that you *can* put 10% of your money away each and every month. You and I both know this is impossible for most Americans. We are Americans and, damn it, if whatever is left after those knuckleheads in Washington get at it is reasonable, then we are going to spend it. By the way, those knuckleheads in Washington want their cake and to eat it, too. They tell you to save money and spend money in the same breath. You need to spend money to keep our economy flourishing. You need to save money so their sorry asses don't have to take care of you when you decide to sit back and retire.

Okay, so you have saved 10% of your money and you decide to put it in a nice mutual fund. Which mutual fund or stock do you buy: the funds that will go up or the ones that will go down? Therein lies the problem. Most mutual funds will go up over time but which ones? Global, utilities, large cap, small cap…oh, hell, just balance yourself—get a little bit of money in all of them, right? This strategy does nothing at all for you. By the time you are done *balancing* your money, and paying the commission to do it, you cannot even beat inflation. Man, you are not Warren Buffet and you never will be. Why? Because times have changed. You are not going to make it in the stock market, period. The market is for institutions and insiders now, not for you and me. The market was up over 12% in 2006 as a whole and how much did you get?

Oracle, the largest business software maker in the world, acquired over forty companies. The increase in the market in 2006 was due mostly to mergers and acquisitions. You are not an insider if you are reading this book and you never will be.

There was a very small article in the *Denver Rocky Mountain News* last

4 *Moving at the Speed of Wealth*

month that I found very interesting. To paraphrase, this short article said that the S&P 500 Index® was at the exact same place, on that very date, nine years earlier. In a nutshell, this article proves my point. If you would have invested your money in an index fund tied to the S&P 500 Index®, you would have had zero growth on your money in the last nine years. In fact, you would have lost money because of fees, commissions and, my favorite, financial planners' fee-based concepts. Keep in mind that many sources will tell you that 80% of all mutual fund managers cannot even match or beat the S&P 500 Index®.

Sure, you think you did better because you watch your portfolio and are smarter than these professionals. Give me a break. Go back to your starting point and subtract every contribution that you and/or your employer has made to your account and see how well you did to date. You will be in shock. I had an interested party sit down with me just last week who stated, very confidently, that he had been averaging about 20% returns on his investments. After he told me how much was in his account and how much money he and his employer contributed over time, I simply did the math and showed him he had averaged 9.1%. The truth is, he did better than most Americans. Most investors are delusional when it comes to their returns. People actually believe their returns are much higher than they truly are.

I believe in the stock market but not for your growth money. Seven out of ten millionaires in the great old U.S. of A. made it with real estate. That's a fact. Now for my opinion on the other thirty percent: I would venture to guess that two or more of the remaining millionaires did it because they are either CEOs of large corporations or entrepreneurs. That only leaves one person out of ten who did it in the stock market and I have news for you—it ain't you! It's insiders, brokers, CEOs, and brokerage house chiefs.

You could put every dime you have in the market and be delusional about the returns and still not have enough for retirement. What I mean by delusional is that you may think you are getting good returns today, but take off your blinders. In fact, a study done by J.P. Morgan found that most investors believed they averaged 13.1% on their money. Folks, if this were true you wouldn't be reading this book because you would be set.

It's amazing to me that when I sit with a lot of people to help them come up with a strategy (notice I didn't say "plan") and to truly set a number they need to reach, it never fails. When I ask what they believe they are averaging as far as returns in their portfolios, the people that tell me 13% or more have absolutely no money. The realistic folks actually have accumulated something. There are better ways to make money.

The largest 401(k) plan I have seen to date is just over one million dollars. I have bad news: That is not enough money to retire on for most of us. Being a millionaire just isn't what it used to be. If you were truly averaging 13.1% on your money and were consistently contributing $500 per month, and your employer was matching this with another $500, you would accumulate over $3.8 million in thirty years…and I haven't seen that yet.

For that matter, if you were only contributing a total of $500 per month, it would grow to over $1.9 million in thirty years and I haven't seen that, either.

Let's make this clear: The chances that you are averaging 13.1% on your portfolio are slim to none—and if you are, let's write a book together.

Putting aside 10% of your income, my rear end! How are you going to pull that off? Between the girls' cheerleading costs and horseback riding, the boys' hockey, the high price of gas to drive these kids to and fro, not to mention the car payment, where the heck did your budget go?

And don't get me started on budgets. It is not going to happen. You see, there are only four types of people in America when it comes to money:

1. Savers who live like paupers
2. Savers who don't save enough
3. People who want to save but have no clue how
4. And people who will never save

Oh, there is a fifth:

5. Savers who have a blast!

That's what this book is about. Imagine that every time you make a payment on something, you actually smile. Keep reading to find out how.

Now, let's get back to the b.s. of most financial books.

Category Two: Financial planners who insist they can get you to the Promised Land by purchasing stocks and/or mutual funds.

Invest in a well-balanced portfolio for the long term. Rebalance your portfolio as you go along and don't forget that it's okay if the market drops because then, when you buy more stocks or mutual funds, you are buying for a lower price. This is called dollar cost averaging. This makes sense in theory, but I would prefer that my portfolio not decrease in value at all.

Of course, portfolios do decrease in value. In a free market, stock prices go up and they go down. The idea is that these prices will trend up over time and if you are balanced, you will offset the stocks that go down in value.

So here is my question to you: Do you want a predictable future? If you want your retirement to be as predictable as possible, then why do you invest in an environment that resembles a rollercoaster ride? Up and down, up and down, then you throw in the fact that you and I are emotional human beings and we start losing focus.

I am not saying to disregard these planners altogether, but don't you get tired of the same old rhetoric? Today they are swinging their opinions and telling you to focus on exchange traded funds (ETFs). I have to admit, I agree one hundred percent with this— get out of those expensive mutual funds and invest in ETFs. ETFs do not charge nearly as much as mutual funds and you can focus on any segment you want. You can even get into ETFs that focus on a declining market.

I am not an expert on the market. I have never directly invested in the stock market myself. I never saw the need to when I was earning between 12% and 48% returns on my money safely and securely.

There are those people who always know of somebody or know somebody directly who is making a killing using options. Folks, options are a zero sum game. For every winner, there is a loser. I would venture that you know of someone who has never lost money in Vegas before. They always win. I meet people all the time who tell me they never lose in poker. Then why are they not rich?

If you have a 50/50 chance at the roulette wheel, how does the casino make money? Because of the two green pegs, you no longer have a 50/50 chance. With options, guess what those green pegs are? Broker commissions.

Yes there are a few people out there who have made good money in the stock market, mostly the people who are selling you a newsletter or some high-tech software system. I recently saw an ad for a class at one of those free universities here in Denver. The ad promoted how to double your money in the stock market every six months. Now, I ask you, if this guy could do that, why the hell is he teaching this $35 class? Give me a break! Wealth comes with a plan, solid strategies and better returns. Wealth does not happen overnight unless you inherit the money, in which case you will probably blow through it soon anyway.

Do you think rich people have mutual funds? Doubtful! Do you think they ever did? Doubtful! So why do you? Probably because you have not learned of any other way.

The Big Lie—Conventional Wisdom Is Not Working   7

If you are a stock market guy or gal, this book isn't for you because I do not know enough about making money in the stock market to be your guide. Trust me, there are plenty of books out there that promise you the Holy Land. Remember that I am teaching you strategies in this book and if you are tuned in to the equities market, then these strategies will work for you as well, so read on.

Category Three: The "preying mantis" that focuses on your fears by preaching doom and gloom.

I have subscribed to over one hundred newsletters over my life regarding investing, mostly because I am curious, but no newsletters pique my curiosity more than those written by the "doom and gloomers." I will admit right here and now that I do not like the way America is heading. We have some serious issues we will have to contend with in the very near future (more on this later), but it is what it is.

Every time we hear of some looming crisis, it never materializes. Remember Y2K? Many were predicting that our whole infrastructure was going to shut down on January 1, 2000. Many "preying mantises" made a fortune fixing your problems—for a problem that never existed.

Today we have global warming. I am not convinced of this but that's my opinion. Did you know that in the mid-'70s, there was a cover story in *Newsweek* about global cooling? In the '80s we had the savings and loans crash. Today it's the sub-prime meltdown and the declining dollar. It is always something and, to be sure, these are problems. But we are resilient and always seem to come out of them okay.

The one thing about these "doom and gloomers" is that they always have the answer for you. First they make you aware of your fears and then they pound on you to buy their solution.

You need to step back and smell the roses.

A thousand things could go wrong at any given moment; the key is to see that while things go wrong, new opportunities materialize. Today there is a foreclosure crisis and the sub-prime meltdown. Do you think there might be opportunities for you as an investor? The declining dollar also provides great opportunities to you as an investor. You need to buck the trends.

A declining dollar means more foreigners are bringing their money to America and they are looking to purchase our land…can you say "opportunity"! A declining dollar means more exports for our country. Yes, a declining dollar is bad but some good can come of it.

8 *Moving at the Speed of Wealth*

I will share a little doom and gloom in one chapter of this book but there is hope for everyone who is educated. You need to quit walking around with blinders on, hoping everything will just work out, and get more proactive.

Category Four: "Preying mantises" who focus on your belief that you can get stinking rich with real estate with bad credit, no money, and no character.

All I have to do is advertise a get-rich-with-foreclosures-even-with-no-money-and-bad-credit seminar in the local paper, and I will fill the room every time. These vultures really get under my skin. I know of individuals perceived to be "experts" who will charge you over $50,000 for their course. What a rip-off! You can buy books at the local bookstore that will share these formulas with you for thirty dollars or less.

The last I heard, one of these folks selling a "Make it Big in Real Estate" system has made over fifty million dollars (I shall not tell you his name but you have probably heard of him). His fortune did not come from real estate but rather from unsuspecting folks like you paying for these overpriced courses. That's *millions* that had nothing to do with his real estate ventures. I like this guy. I think he is genius but I also think that he, like so many others, preys on unsuspecting minds. I once attended his Commercial Real Estate Bootcamp and paid $6,000. All he was doing was trying to charge people to bring him good deals that he could partner with them on. He was essentially charging people to be "bird dogs" for him (a "bird dog" is someone who goes out and finds deals).

You will not build wealth in real estate by purchasing course after course on how to get rich in real estate. You get rich in real estate by taking action. You will learn plenty as you go along. Sure, you need a basic foundation as to where to start and what glaring pitfalls to avoid, so read and study. Work with people who have done or are doing it.

I cannot tell you how many times seminars roll through my hometown of Denver, trying to pull money out of people's pockets to teach them how to work foreclosures and/or fix-n-flips. They preach how easy it is to build wealth using these techniques, not once mentioning how many people have lost their shirts applying these models. I can tell you from experience that for every one person I meet who has succeeded on at least one deal, I meet two or three who have lost a lot of money.

There are better ways. My advice is to quit pissing away your money on outdated and unrealistic programs that claim anyone can get rich in real estate.

The testimonials do not tell the whole story: "I have made over $5 million in real estate since I took Xyz's course." What they don't tell you is that they also have $5 million in loans against that property, hundreds of properties to manage, negative monthly cash flow and all the other wonderful pitfalls of this type of investing.

The big pitch is to buy real estate to create positive monthly cash flow. Great, but the real world does not always work that way. In fact, you should never buy real estate based solely on positive monthly cash flow—you should always buy real estate based on your projections for internal rate of return when you sell the property. Positive cash flow is nice, but negative cash flow is not bad if you understand it. I go into great detail regarding this in my "Boot-camp Course" (no, you are not ready to purchase that course yet).

These real estate cheerleaders rant and rave about all of the tax benefits of owning real estate. Folks, you can take tax deductions on expenses of owning real estate. But to take deductions, you have to spend money. Call me old-fashioned, but I would rather pay twenty-five cents in taxes for every dollar I earn than to save twenty-five cents on taxes on every dollar I spend.

Sure, depreciation is a phantom tax benefit and one that I really appreciate. However, if and when you liquidate your property, the government will collect a "recapture of depreciation" on you as well as capital gain taxes (if you hold the property over one year). I meet people every day who have large real estate portfolios that they would love to liquidate (they are sick of being a landlord), yet they do not want to deal with the huge tax bill so they continue to 1031 exchange their properties until they die.

Lucky for these folks that with my advanced strategies and techniques, I can show them how to liquidate their entire portfolio, pay no taxes, receive better cash flow and receive a huge tax deduction to boot. I can also show them how to consolidate all their properties without a tax burden and have no managerial duties any longer. Again, these topics are not covered in this book but are available to you as a Speed of Wealth Gold Club™ member.

If you are looking for inexpensive, real advice on investing in real estate, check out John Reed's books. You can order them at www.JohnReed.com. I do not make any money off of John Reed, but I really like this guy. He is a straight shooter and very experienced. While on his website, click on the link to the right titled "Real estate guru ratings." This section is cool. He gives his experienced opinion on all of these so-called "gurus" and his findings and insights may be very helpful to you. The findings on Russ Whitney and Robert Kiyosaki are very interesting, to say the least. Please let me point out that just because these are Mr. Reed's opinions, that does not necessarily make them true. I enjoy reading them for fun. In fact, I know several of the people he bashes on his site and I totally disagree with his assessments.

I do not profess to be the world's greatest real estate investor. In fact, I have never owned real estate rentals nor have I ever done a fix-n-flip (*almost never...*I fixed up a house I lived in and sold it for a very handsome profit. In fact, it was the greatest deal I have ever done because I never owned the property and, two years later, I walked away with $50,000 after all the rent payments I had made. I will reveal this technique in my next book, *Moving at the Speed of Wealth for College Kids*). If you are truly looking for what I believe to be the best source for a real estate education, check out John Reed. John does not even know me but I have read several of his books and his no-nonsense approach is refreshing.

Category Five: "Preying mantises" that focus on your lack of self-esteem and motivation.

Look, I am all for motivation and looking deep within yourself to figure out who you really are, but at what expense? Think of the millions and millions of dollars spent on these "self-help" programs and you can easily see why there is a huge transfer of wealth from the middle class to the rich. Just how rich is Anthony Robbins? Well, he is a multi-millionaire because he wants to release the tiger (or lion or whatever) within you.

Once again, I have never ordered his package nor have I ever ordered any other self-help program. I simply do not need to. I have, however, met hundreds of people who years ago have ordered these programs and are no better off today than they were then. Can these guys help you? Sure, but only a very small percentage of you out there. In fact, people who claim that these programs took them places were probably going to get to those places anyway.

How many times do you have to be told to set goals, write them down and dream? How many different ways can it be told to you? First of all, I have never set goals and written them down. I have written business and marketing plans and set objectives. The funny thing is that I have never met one of my objectives because my objectives change as I get closer to meeting them. This book is a great example. Originally I was going to write it and only provide it to my clients and seminar attendees. Obviously, that has changed. As I began writing this book, I planned on self-publishing. This could change as well. But since you have this book in your hands, you know I have met the objective of writing it—and it has also changed the entire course of my core business.

Let me provide you with all the self-help you will ever need. Go to a mirror

The Big Lie—Conventional Wisdom Is Not Working

right now, stare into your own eyes for five minutes and tell yourself who you are and what you like and don't like about yourself. Build on the things you like and try to change the things you do not like.

I used to be a heavy drinker and I did not like that about myself. My wife and kids hated it, my parents hated it, I lost friends over it. Drinking held me back from the life I wanted. It didn't matter what any of these people said to me and, mind you, these are people I love. Nothing changed until I looked in the mirror and decided what I liked about me and what I could achieve, and addressed the fact that I hated being a drinker.

Don't get me wrong...I still have a few drinks, but not to the point of destruction. Man, did I do some stupid things when I was a drinker! I never drank nightly; I was a binge drinker and it was destructive. This may be a story for another book but you will not change until you're ready internally. I don't care what any self-help guru tells you. You will be motivated for about two days and it all goes bye-bye until you spend money on the next program to be motivated for a couple of days.

To understand these self-help gurus better, all you have to do is refer back to my previous category. I am not saying that Anthony Robbins or others couldn't care less about you. In fact, I think people like Tony Robbins really want to help you. I believe he gets a lot of joy out of the success stories. All I am saying is that we are all capable of what we are capable of and that is it. The fact that you are reading this book tells me that you are willing to let others mentor you. To be really successful, you need a successful mentor.

Understand that you don't know what you don't know and that the more you read (and I mean both sides of every issue), the more you will develop.

This book is not designed to help you become a better person or rich over night. This book is presented to you only to open your eyes to other strategies and my opinions. What you take from it is entirely up to you but it will be educational in one way or another.

By the time you are finished, you will either buy into what I preach, somewhat buy into what I preach or think I am the biggest flake on the planet. I assure you, the majority of financial planners who read this book will think I am a flake but, hey, everything they have offered you isn't working out so well, is it?

I just got off a three-way call with a wealthy client of mine who is working with an estate planning attorney. I was structuring a life insurance policy and banking system for the client, who was approved for life insurance with one caveat. It was a second to die policy and if both my client and his wife died within the next three years, the death benefit proceeds would be taxable.

It was a million-dollar policy that would leave about $600,000 after taxes

12   *Moving at the Speed of Wealth*

to their heirs if they both died within the next three years. The policy was approved and ready to be issued but would expire in three days. I recommended signing off on it immediately.

The attorney on this three-way call said, "I'm glad you're not managing my money." How unprofessional! (I could write a hundred-page essay on why I don't like 95% of all lawyers. Did you know that lawyers are the only group of people that go to school to learn how to kill deals? The rest of us go to learn how to *strike* deals.).

But, you see, this lawyer did not know the entire story. He made assumptions and in the end the client apologized for the lawyer's remarks and signed off on the policy. I knew the entire story and gave my advice in the best interest of the client.

Oh, how egos get in the way of sound decisions. Everyone wants to be right, the most knowledgeable and the most respected. In reality, things change and circumstances differ for everyone. Here is one circumstance that remains for all of us: If you want to build great wealth, you need to look at unconventional ways of doing it.

Conventional Wisdom Is Not Working

Generations ago, people would work for the same company for thirty years, live in the same house for thirty years, do the same day-to-day tasks for thirty years and retire with a pension and Social Security. More often than not, this would be sufficient to allow them to retire comfortably.

Well, it's no mystery, but things have changed dramatically. Today we move frequently, we change jobs frequently, we even begin new careers at middle age to try to advance more quickly. We can no longer rely on pensions and Social Security to get us through retirement. And if that were not enough, Americans are living longer. In fact, it is estimated that children born today could live to be 120 years old. Now, if this child wants to retire at sixty-five, he better have a LOT of money. This longevity is forcing Americans, young and old, to worry about outliving their money. The truth is that most of us *will* unless we take corrective action sooner than later.

Pension Plans

Pension plans are going bust. IBM, United, Delta, and General Motors are among the large companies now saying that it is no longer their burden to take care of you in retirement, despite your lifelong loyalty and contributions. These pensions have been replaced with 401(k) savings plans and these plans will provide you

The Big Lie—Conventional Wisdom Is Not Working 13

with the same effect as the vicious villain tying you up on the railroad track. You are strapped, helplessly hoping someone will come to save you. The problem is that you do not realize that you need saving until you can hear the whistle blowing from the approaching train.

Your other qualified retirement accounts are having the exact same effect but you still cannot hear the whistle. The Pension Guarantee Benefit Corporation, the government agency that insures these pensions, recently announced that its $11-billion surplus has been replaced with a $14 billion-deficit and this is only the beginning. If the PGBC does come through, you can bet it will only be for a fraction of the benefits you were expecting.

Social Security and Medicare

Top this off with the fact that Social Security and Medicare are going bust and you are in a world of hurt. Where do you think the government dips its hands into to pay for the seemingly endless war on terrorism? If you answered Social Security, then give yourself a hand. Use common sense: If there are only two workers supporting one retiree, how can this plan survive? And we are only a few years away from this ratio. Medicare is already paying out more than it is taking in. If you want to maintain your same standard of living in retirement, then planning on Social Security was a waste of time anyway. In fact, the average Social Security check issued each month is a meager $995. Good luck surviving on that.

Qualified Retirement Plans

It's time to accept the fact that you've been sold a bill of goods with regard to qualified retirement plans (QRP). Does the following statement from your financial advisor sound familiar? "You should contribute the maximum amount to your 401(k) or IRA and take the tax deductions; your marginal tax bracket will be much lower in retirement." What a great way to convince you to buy their "outstanding, unbelievably performing investment product." The truth is that you are not only likely to be taxed at the same rate in retirement as you are now, but you are probably going to be in a higher tax bracket. Unsure of this? Answer the following question:

In the future, you believe tax rates will be...

- Lower than they are today
- About the same as they are today
- Higher than they are today

14   *Moving at the Speed of Wealth*

The truth is that we do not know, but considering that the cost of long-term health care, Social Security, Medicare, the war on terrorism and a record national deficit that is increasing daily, I would bet that the chances of tax rates going higher are pretty good—and not just a little higher, but a great deal higher! Also consider that in retirement you have typically lost three of your largest tax deductions: your home mortgage, your dependents and you are no longer making contributions to your retirement plan. I work with seniors all the time who have $100,000 or more income at retirement, spend every dime enjoying retirement and have absolutely no tax deductions. (There is a proven way to fix this problem safely.)

If you wish to maintain the same standard of living in retirement that you enjoy now, then you need to take a long hard look at your QRP. The chances are very high that you will wipe out all of the deductions you took while contributing to your qualified plan during your earning years in the first three years of retirement—your fixed income years. That does not strike me as sound planning.

QRPs leave you handcuffed. You are typically investing in what I call the "money current." This would include mutual funds, stocks, bonds, money market funds, etc. You may think you are diversified, but are you really? You are strictly invested in the stock market. You need to be investing where the rich and elite invest. You need to be in what I call "undertow investments"—that's where all the strength is. Imagine getting 10-150% rates of return consistently and safely. Can it be done? You bet, and I am bringing this knowledge to Middle America.

The Stock Market Will Get You Where You Want to Be

Ponder this next question carefully. Are you planning for a predictable retirement? My guess is that you said yes. Then why in the world would you put the majority of your retirement savings in an environment that is highly volatile and unpredictable? The answer is that most people have not been shown a better alternative. Were you one of the millions of Americans who lost trillions of dollars in the first part of this decade? In reality, you didn't lose anything. Your earnings were only on paper anyway and I guarantee you that for every dollar you lost, a savvier investor took it from you. I'm sure that doesn't sit well with you, but it's true. The moral of that story is: Don't swim with the sharks unless you fancy yourself one of them.

Why would you want to invest money in something that is totally out of your control? You are not involved in the day-to-day management of these

The Big Lie—Conventional Wisdom Is Not Working   15

companies. Remember, the "TRACS" in Retirement TRACS, LLC (my parent company) stands for "Total Retirement Asset *Control* System." You need to get up off the couch and get active if you want to retain the same (or better) standard of living in retirement that you enjoy today.

Would you plop down $30,000 for a $1,000 annual income stream? Of course not. That is only a 3% rate of return and you can get that all day long without any risk. Every time you buy a stock with a price to earnings ratio of 30/1, that is exactly what you are doing, right? Blue chips! Give me a break! Their pensions alone will cost them billions of dollars that they cannot make up.

There are many factors that will hurt Wall Street, but one glaring and imminent issue is the fact that baby boomers hitting age 70½ will be forced to take money out of the stock market by way of required minimum distributions. It's inevitable. And when money leaves the market, especially with this kind of magnitude, prices go down. Don't believe me? Japan's baby boomer market was ahead of ours and there is a direct correlation to the fall of their stock market to their baby boomer curve historically. Some books will tell you this is just fabrication. In truth it may be, but it may be true as well. Truth be told, I have people coming to me daily who have money in the stock market and are just sick and tired of it and are looking for a better way. I know of at least $20 million that came out of the market just last year with my clients. I know that this is just a very small fraction but it is happening nationwide. Make your own conclusion.

Now, you may be the darling of the market, realizing returns of 12% per year for thirty years (which is highly unlikely), and my strategies will still blow yours out of the water, without fail. The truth is that the average investor received a rate of return of 5.5% from 1988 to 1999 (according to a study done by Dalbar Research)—this during the greatest bull market in history! Please correct me if I am wrong, but isn't this paltry return barely beating the unreliably low inflation rate the government publishes? The reason most fail is because they chase returns and try to "beat" the market rather than match it. An overwhelming majority of mutual funds don't even match the returns of the S&P 500 Index.

As you continue your path of education with Moving at the Speed of Wealth™ and become a member of The Speed of Wealth Gold Club™, you will learn about more powerful investments that provide you with 10 - 150% rates of return (that's not a misprint) and these returns are *never* affected by the stock market or interest rate environment. Yes, it's true, whether you choose to believe it or not, and the wealthy have been doing it for centuries. The key is to create your own *banking system.*

Chasing Market Returns Will Make You Wealthy

As I said above, you can be the darling of the market, reaping 12% returns year after year after year, and I will still beat you to the finish line even if I am only getting a mere 6% rate of return in the proper vehicle. "Why?" you may ask. Because while you sit in front of your computer watching your investments' performance, a large majority of your wealth is quietly sneaking out your back door. Consider that the average American will spend well over a million dollars in his or her lifetime on debt and taxes alone. This is typically 65% of every dollar you make. I find this to be criminal. What's even more criminal is the fact that most people can learn how to slam this back door shut forever, yet refuse to educate themselves. The good news is that you are not one of them and this book will show you the light.

Home Equity Management is Failing

Millions of Americans are doing the exact opposite of what they should be doing. They fall into one of two categories.

CATEGORY ONE: Americans are trying to pay off their home mortgage as soon as possible by going into a fifteen-year loan or making extra principal payments annually. This is a costly mistake. Home equity is a "dead" asset with absolutely no rate of return. Your home will appreciate the same whether you are mortgaged to the hilt or your home is paid off. The equity in your home is a source of great wealth when put to work. For a case in point, take a look at this example illustrated by Figure 2.

What is your "return on investment"? Most people answer 4.5%. They do this because they are using the $100,000 figure. However, you are not out of pocket one red cent. The earnings from your $100,000 paid the mortgage payment and you are left with $4,500 pure profit. The truth is that you achieved an infinite rate of return. That is the power of arbitrage and using "OPM" or other people's money and leverage. Rich people build empires by only receiving a 2-3% return on their money. You may ask how this is possible. The answer is that, in reality, they are receiving an infinite rate of return and are using other people's money. The key is to find an investment with a consistent return of more than the borrowed money (I can show you where).

Let's take this a little further: If you reinvest your net profits annually in the same investment, by year five your return on investment is a

The Big Lie—Conventional Wisdom Is Not Working

You Are in 25% Tax Bracket		$100,000 in Equity		
	Refinance at 6% Interest Only to Put This Money to Work		You Reinvest in a Safe Undertow Investment Yielding 12% Annually	
Payment: $6,000	Effective Payment after Tax Deductions: $4,500		Interest Earned: $12,000	Net Interest Earned after Taxes: $9,000
		Net Profit after Mortgage Payments: $4,500		

Figure 2

whopping 150.1% after taxes. I might point out that your original $100,000 has not disappeared; it was only repositioned and left highly liquid. You have the ability to pay off that loan at any time. If you put this money in the stock market, you are taking a risk. Your $100,000 could lose value and this obviously defeats our purpose. If you are approached by someone preaching the merits of pulling equity out and investing it in the stock market, run...fast!

CATEGORY TWO: This is a shame. This is the typical Middle American homeowner. They refinance their home to pay off credit card debt and other loans such as cars. The slick mortgage guy convinces them to do so because the homeowner's monthly cash flow will increase and that extra portion on their loan is tax deductible. The loan officer never once mentions that the homeowner has just turned unsecured debt into secured debt and amortized that car over the life of the new loan. So, when Joe Homeowner is ready to go out and buy a new car in five years and takes out new financing, Joe is still paying for the old car. It is a vicious and financially disastrous cycle. And it is costing Americans dearly in terms of their financial future.

On top of that, many loan officers are selling the new Option ARM product, which has very small monthly payments but forces negative amortization. For most Middle Americans, this is a very bad idea because they will consume the monthly savings and be between a rock and a hard spot down the road. My clients understand how powerful this loan is IF they "conserve" the monthly savings and put that money in a tax-deferred compounding account.

Imagine: By using this Option ARM and placing the monthly savings into the proper place (I will show you where), you can explode your wealth. Let's assume that Joe Homeowner has an average monthly savings of $500 and "conserves" that savings by putting it into a tax-deferred (or free) compounding account paying an average rate of return of 7%. By year twenty, this savings has grown to $260,463. By the end of year thirty, it has grown to $609,986.

I can show you how to explode that savings by an additional $250,000 or more just by becoming your own banker. You have to see this to believe it. You receive the same rate of return and make the same monthly contributions, but you create much more wealth.

I will uncover many reasons to pull your equity out and explode your wealth without increasing your monthly budget one dime. Here is a hint: Your equity is not safe and it is not as liquid as you may think.

A Total Disregard for Taxes: The Conventional Wisdom that Taxes Will Not Be an Issue in Retirement

Tell that to the millions of seniors who are presently paying taxes on their Social Security benefits. My goodness, when they paid into the plan, it was with after-tax dollars. Isn't this double taxation? Franklin Roosevelt, in all his wisdom, firmly stood and said while introducing the New Deal that Social Security will never be taxed. My, how times change. Not only will you lose some of your benefits, the government will probably tax what you do earn at an even higher rate (don't worry, though...if you end up poor in retirement, they won't tax you).

I've already made a strong case above when I was speaking out against your qualified retirement accounts, but it goes even further. You need to create a tax shelter for your money. A good start is a Roth IRA but these plans still have too many rules and regulations for my liking.

The Big Lie—Conventional Wisdom Is Not Working 19

Most Middle American families look at the rich and complain that they do not pay their fair share of taxes. Wanna bet? The rich get richer because they take the time to learn what is available to them to lower their tax bills. The truth is that those same benefits are available to you and all of Middle America. You probably just didn't take the time or thought it necessary to reduce your tax bill because you felt it would be too much effort. You may think that you need offshore accounts and all of the other glamorous vehicles floating on the Internet, when all along you could have created a tax shelter with a stroke of your pen—a shelter that will allow you to contribute money before taxes, grow your money tax-deferred, take tax-free distributions, and transfer your money to your heirs tax-free. Didn't you just erase the IRS's involvement in your retirement plan? To top it off, we can teach you how to reduce your taxes from the get-go. And all of it is very legal and safe.

There is one other tax you must be aware of. This one we cannot control but you must be aware of it. This tax is inflation and it taxes the rich and the poor equally. Most people in their earning years know inflation exists but it really doesn't affect them. This is because your income tends to keep pace and your home appreciates on track with inflation. You will not truly understand the effects of inflation until you are living on a fixed income. Ask any retired person you know if they feel the pain of inflation. Keep in mind that when you see an inflation rate of 3.5% on average, this does not include energy costs or food. What is really inflating today? You guessed it: energy costs—and they are only going to continue to increase.

It is very important to understand that it is not what you accumulate over the years—it's *what you keep* at the end of the day. Your IRA or 401(k) may grow into a massive nest egg over the years but when it is time to live on this money, you will be taxed and you will be taxed on every last penny.

So ask yourself: Are you saving pennies to pay dollars? If you are currently saving in an IRA, 401(K) or other qualified account, you bet you are. My advice is quit living for today and plan for your future or you will live to regret it.

Here is my favorite line from so-called financial planners: "Don't worry, you will be in a lower tax bracket at retirement!" There couldn't be anything further from the truth. Consider these facts:

1. If you want to maintain the same (or better) standard of living in retirement that you enjoy today, you will still need to have the same amount of cash flow. The only thing that really changes at retirement is that you no longer make retirement contributions. This

money is easily eaten up by the traveling and basic enjoyment of retirement. If you take out the same amount of money in retirement as you do today, doesn't your tax bracket remain the same? If you missed this one, the answer is YES!

2. If you subscribe to conventional wisdom, you will lose your two biggest tax deductions in retirement: your home interest deductions and your children.
3. Taxes could possibly be higher in the future (see above).
4. The cost of living will most certainly be higher in the future (think inflation).
5. Retirement is not cheap. If you want to enjoy your retirement, you are more than likely going to spend more money than during your working years. What are you going to do with the newfound ten hours each day, sit around and play cards?

You may have less debt but, to be certain, every time you pay off debt you could be losing thousands of dollars in retirement income (it all depends on the type of debt and interest rate). You will understand this better as you read on.

Chapter Two

Secret of the Super-Rich #2:

Super-Rich People Create a Personal Banking System to Accelerate the Growth on Their Money Using a Properly Designed Life Insurance Contract

Make no mistake, life insurance is a very poor investment (although I would put it up against most mutual funds any day). But when using the right product and design, life insurance becomes a very powerful investment tool.

This chapter will, without a doubt, be the most boring but I still need you to wade through it and absorb it all. To be sure, life insurance has a stigma tied to it by people who don't understand just how it can be used as a great investment tool that accelerates the growth of your money and hedges against risks in other investments.

Imagine using a life insurance policy as a banking system. You find a rental property that you consider to be a great deal. Anyone who has ever invested in real estate knows that you always leverage real estate (borrow against it). The problem with this is that you have to deal with a traditional bank. You now have a monthly payment that must be made come hell or high water.

You go out and find a renter, and if you haven't had experience with tenants, let me tell you something: They can be very unreliable. You have read all the books, bought a single-family residence, rented it out and created positive cashflow. Herein lies the problem: You never buy rentals based solely on cash flow. In fact, it should be the last consideration. You always buy real estate for its internal rate of return.

The fact is that if you have a loan on the property, these experts are telling you that the renter will make your payment. Folks, there is a reason most renters rent: They do not have a track record that banks are comfortable enough with to loan them the money to buy their own home (this does not apply to all renters so, please, if you are currently renting, don't take offense unless you should).

The fact of the matter is that there is a strong possibility that sooner or later your renter won't make their payment and/or you will have a vacancy in your home. If you have no renter, who is going to make the payment? You are, of course, and this is negative cash flow. To be a successful real estate investor whose primary goal is to build a portfolio of rental properties, you must have adequate reserves to handle these situations. YOU WILL HAVE NEGATIVE CASH FLOW OCCASSIONALLY.

Here is your first lesson: It is okay to have negative cash flow when you understand the truth. When you put money into your qualified retirement plan [401(k), 403(b), etc.] or Individual Retirement Arrangement (IRA), this, too, is negative cash flow. My point is that if you need to dip into your pocket and make the payment with no renter, consider this a contribution to your retirement plan. As you read through this book, you may decide to abandon your work-sponsored qualified plan anyway. For some reason, people who invest in real estate just don't understand this simple concept. It makes the idea of negative cash flow more bearable.

But there is a better way: Create your own Family Insured Banking System™, otherwise known as a properly designed life insurance contract.

Imagine now that you have built up your Family Insured Banking System™ and you borrow $100,000 from your life insurance contract to buy a rental property. Even though you borrowed your own money, you will be charged an interest rate. This interest rate is tied to current AAA bond rates and averages about 6% recently. Even though you have the money in your front pocket, it will continue to be credited with the upside gains of the S&P 500 Index® with no downside risk. In other words, you get the upside of the market but no downside. This has historically averaged about 9%.

You borrow at 6%, the same money is being credited on average 9%, and you are earning 3% on money that is in your front pocket. You take this money and pay cash for the $100,000 rental property. Now, let this sink in: You do not have scheduled payments to make back to the insurance company. You pay back the loan when you are good and ready. When you have a renter who makes a payment, instead of sending it to a bank, you send it back to your insurance company, and it eventually ends up back in your retirement account.

No payment from a renter, make no payment to the insurance company—how is that for a hedge against the risk of rental properties?

You could easily make a fortune even if you do not have a renter. Buy a property for $100,000 and hold it for five years with no renter. Let's assume the property appreciates 5% per year. The property will appreciate to $127,628. If history holds, the $100,000 is making a spread of 3% (before costs and expenses within the policy), so you have another $15,927 of tax-deferred growth within the policy. You make no payments at all and you have a total aggregate gain of $43,555. That's a total return of 43.56% on your money with an internal rate of return of 8.7% annually in a relatively risk-free environment.

Now, imagine doing the above but that you do have a renter making payments to you that you forward to your life insurance contract…and don't forget the tax benefits associated with purchasing real estate investments.

Now that I have your mind open just a tad, let's explore this banking system a little more. Here we go with the boring, educational part.

Important Note: *For some readers, it will not matter what I teach. You will just be averse to life insurance. That is no reason to put down this book and not read this chapter. Please understand it, but in no way, shape or form do you have to use an insurance contract in order for me to show you how to explode your wealth using several other strategies.*

What is the "Speed of Wealth" System?

It is no secret that more and more Americans are getting frustrated with the stock market, financial advisors, company-sponsored retirement plans, so-called media experts and so on. Unfortunately, one big problem many Americans have is that they tend to put blinders on when it comes to their retirement accounts. A good analogy would be to compare it to the way men view doctor visits. Men are notorious for avoiding the doctor at all costs. They figure that "no news is good news," and that is how many people handle their retirement accounts.

It's a good bet that if any of you sat down and really studied your 401(k) accounts, for example, and added up all the contributions you have made as well as those made by your employer, you would be shocked to realize the lack of growth you have really achieved. The majority of the money in these accounts, in many cases, consists largely of your combined contributions.

The fact of the matter is that people need to treat their retirement plan like a business. They must put more effort into managing these accounts if they are to achieve their retirement goals. They need to *take control of their future* and get

24   *Moving at the Speed of Wealth*

it out of the control of mutual fund managers and those who do not genuinely have their best interests at heart. Keep in mind that "TRACS" stands for "Total Retirement Asset *Control* System." We want to encourage and teach people how to get involved and participate in the most important business they will manage during the course of their lifetime: their retirement planning.

So we propose to prospective clients that they incorporate the right type of cash-value life insurance as an alternative or complement to their current plan, and that they actively and aggressively manage this policy, enabling the vehicle to make a single dollar grow in two places at one time by utilizing a side account consisting of what we call "undertow investments."

The Argument for Change
First, let's look at the specific advantages of life insurance as an alternative retirement planning vehicle and/or supplemental retirement plan.

- **Unique tax advantages**—Premiums can be paid with before-tax money (once you set up a business) that grows tax-deferred (not tax-free); the money can be withdrawn tax-free via policy loans that are never repaid, and the money transfers tax-free to heirs. In essence, you can beat the taxman in all four stages of retirement planning.
- **Protection for family**—In the event of premature death, the insured's family is protected and the client's estate value increases the minute the policy is placed in force. Very few people can honestly say they have no need for life insurance. Life insurance is the ultimate wealth-transfer vehicle. Case in point: Malcolm Forbes had $55 million in life insurance at his death.
- **Self-fulfilling plan**—By adding a disability rider, the plan's premiums will be paid in the event of a disability. A disabled policy owner will continue to see his cash value grow as if he were putting money in the plan himself.
- **The banking system**—By taking out policy loans and making purchases that would ordinarily require a monthly payment, policyholders have the ability to recapture the entire purchase price plus all interest, and create arbitrage in the process. A typical car purchase goes from an account depreciation move to a move that will instead turn a 12-14% return, just from buying a car. A more

powerful strategy is to borrow from the policy, create arbitrage (spread of money) within the policy and reinvest the money in an appreciating investment.

- **Mortgage acceleration plan**—Most Americans are unaware that pulling equity out of a home and reinvesting that money in a tax-deferred account will actually accelerate a mortgage payoff and, in many cases, with no more money out of pocket.

- **Two columns of growth**—By taking out policy loans that have the ability to create arbitrage and reinvesting in other outside investments, the policyholder can actually have money growing in two columns at the same time. For example, let's say you have $100,000 you can borrow inside your policy. Historically, the policy has returned 9% on average. The policyholder borrows the $100,000; the money will still be credited 9% over the year or $9,000. Borrowing implies an interest rate. This rate is tied to bonds and we will assume you can borrow at 6%. You borrow the $100,000 at 6% or $6,000 per year; you turn around and invest in deeds of trusts (undertow investment) paying 12%. You earn $12,000 in the second column (this column is typically taxable while the insurance side is not). The policyholder has just accelerated the speed at which his money grows.

- **Three columns of growth**—After reading the chapter regarding home equity arbitrage, you understand that your home will appreciate at the same rate regardless of the underlying home loan. You borrow your equity from your home, you reinvest the money in an "undertow investment" that pays 12%, you take the after-tax returns on the money and put it into a life insurance contract, you borrow from the life insurance contract to reinvest in another "undertow investment" that has a 20% IRR. What a mouthful!

Let's break that down. Let's assume you borrow $100,000 from home equity with an interest-only loan at 6% and your annual payment is $6,000 (forget about tax deductions for now and taxes owed). We will also assume your home will appreciate at 5% per year. Even though you pulled out $100,000, your home will still increase 5%

over its entire fair market value (that's one column of growth on your money).

I then show you where you can receive a 12% return consistently and safely and your $100,000 generates $12,000, of which you take $6,000 and make the increase in your monthly house payment (you are zero dollars out of pocket). You take the remaining $6,000 and place it into a life insurance contract (the 12% investment is the second column of growth).

The cash value inside your policy begins to grow on an average rate of 9% annually (disregard cost of insurance and expenses for now). Basically, interest from another investment is building your banking system (this is your third column of growth).

Like for any well-run business or real bank, it takes time to build up your cash value. In about three to five years, you begin to borrow from your plan at an average of 6% and reinvest it in another investment (see real estate) that earns you 20%+ on your money annually (this is your fourth column of growth).

All of this money acceleration happens because you started with your home equity and this cost you no extra money out of your pocket. You will see the power of this as we continue through the book.

Many circles of financial advisors will stoutly tell their prospects and/or clients, "Life insurance is a poor place to build wealth and a poor place to invest." I have to agree with the second part. If I can show you how to receive 12% or more returns on your money safely and consistently, why would you want to put money in a place that averages less than 9% after cost of insurance and expenses? Because by using the right type of policy, you can create a banking system that allows you to create arbitrage within the policy over time by borrowing from the policy and reinvesting. Life insurance is a place to put money to build wealth when managed correctly.

Many say to always buy term and invest the difference. The truth is that *all* life insurance is term insurance. What's the difference? Term is temporary; it expires after a certain period of time at which point it becomes too expensive to purchase again.

Additionally, what differentiates term from permanent insurance is what the insurance company does with the extra money placed in the policy. With term insurance, you are strictly paying for the cost of insurance and small expenses for a specific period of time. There is no extra money going into the policy. This means there is no opportunity to build cash value that you can borrow from; you are strictly paying for life insurance.

Less than 1% of all term policies ever pay out, making it a great cash cow for the insurance company. Once your term ends, that's it! Your money is gone. Permanent policies, on the other hand, are designed so that if you follow the "Target Premium" schedule, you will not only have life insurance, but your cash value will exceed the money placed into the policy around year twenty. Cost of insurance is the same whether it is a whole life policy, term policy or universal life policy.

Again, with a term policy, no extra premium goes in so there will be no growth. Whole life policies will typically pay dividends (essentially a return of premium) based on bond market returns. Whole life policies amortize the cost of insurance over the expected life expectancy of the insured and level the premiums over that span of time. Whole life has very little flexibility and can catch clients off guard if anything in their life should change (and things do change).

Universal life was created with the idea of "buy term and invest the rest." Much like with a whole life policy, the insurance company will amortize the cost of insurance and expenses over the life expectancy of the insured. *(Note: With term, the costs are amortized over a much shorter period, the term of the policy, making the costs of insurance and expenses less in a term policy)*. This makes universal life a "permanent" policy. The excess premium is then reinvested on your behalf by the insurance company and the policyholder is relying on the insurance company's expertise to manage this money (much like an owner of a mutual fund relies on the fund manager).

Until the mid 1990s, this money was typically invested in bonds, keeping the insured's excess money safe, but limiting the growth. *(Note: Some insurance companies and policyholders went broke in the 1980s because some aggressive insurance companies were investing in junk bonds—remember Michael Milken? Since this time, the government has placed restrictions on the percentage of an insurance company's assets that can be placed in various investments. Insurance companies must now invest in AA bonds or better, and in government bonds.)*

For a very conservative investor, whole or universal life policies offered a very good place to store cash if they had a need for life insurance (which most people do). However, most people, conservative or not, were not excited about the costs of a permanent life insurance policy and receiving returns tied to the bond market. In addition, historically, life insurance agents and the life insurance companies themselves would present plans that would keep premiums as low as possible.

28   *Moving at the Speed of Wealth*

A question often asked at our workshop is this: "If life insurance were free, how many of you would have it?" We ask this question because of the stigma associated with life insurance. With all the "not-so-smart" financial advisors advising against life insurance, and the mentality of "what good does it do me while I am living," people are very averse to life insurance and so turn to term insurance to fill the need. This question is designed to help us overcome this stigma because in every instance, every single hand in the room is raised, confirming the fact that it is not the life insurance that they are opposed to, but rather the premiums (costs) they have to pay. They perceive it to be a waste of money. Having this mentality, the logical choice in their minds was to keep the premiums as low as possible.

So life insurance agents were selling "life insurance" and *not* an alternative or supplemental retirement account. Remember that cost of insurance and expenses equates to just that: costs. Anything above and beyond these costs would be invested by the life insurance company on behalf of the policyholder. By keeping premiums low, however, there was little "excess" money to place in the side fund and, thus, the growth, in most cases, was rarely anything of consequence, much less impressive. This is part of the stigma you must overcome as an investor looking to create a banking system.

Figure 3 shows an example of minimum funding a policy. Pay particular attention to the growth of the surrender cash value column. This stunt of growth is the same regardless of the type of policy used because there is not enough excess money to provide for growth (Figure 3 shows Indexed Universal Life).

Important Note: *The illustrations provided throughout this chapter are for just that, illustration. Although life insurance companies offer guarantees, I will be showing you the non-guaranteed assumed value of these policies based on historical data. Of course, past performance is no guarantee of future performance but these policies are tied to the S&P 500 Index® and the stock market has been pretty steady in this performance over the last twenty years. I will be illustrating based on a 9% average return and we all know that nothing works on averages. These policies offer you most of the upside of the index with no downside risk. If the market is down 10%, your account value is simply credited with 0%; of course, you must still pay the cost of insurance and expenses. I will also be showing an illustrated rate of 6.5% to borrow from the plan. This rate can and will fluctuate as well because it is tied to the average AAA bond rate available at the time of the loan. At the time of this writing, you could borrow from your plan at around 5.5%. If you are looking for guarantees in investments then make sure you continue reading this book as I discuss* *this very important fear factor. I will also be illustrating based on a male non-smoker, age fifty-five, with a death benefit of $500,000.*

End of Year	Age	Model Premium	Times Per Year	Annual Premium	Cash From Policy	Annual Outlay	Non-Guaranteed Assumed			
							Surr Cash Value	Surr Charge	Account Value	Death Benefit
1	56	6,417	1	6,417	0	6,417	0	23,090	1,875	500,000
2	57	6,417	1	6,417	0	6,417	0	21,551	3,725	500,000
3	58	6,417	1	6,417	0	6,417	0	20,011	5,302	500,000
4	59	6,417	1	6,417	0	6,417	0	18,472	6,876	500,000
5	60	6,417	1	6,417	0	6,417	0	16,993	8,133	500,000
6	61	6,417	1	6,417	0	6,417	0	15,393	9,396	500,000
7	62	6,417	1	6,417	0	6,417	0	13,854	10,285	500,000
8	63	6,417	1	6,417	0	6,417	0	12,315	11,173	500,000
9	64	6,417	1	6,417	0	6,417	842	10,775	11,617	500,000
10	65	0	1	0	0	0	0	9,236	0	0
				57,753.00	0	57,753.00				

Figure 3

You can see in Figure 3 that this policy lapses in year ten. Why would any life insurance agent sell this product? The answer is obvious: Commissions are based on the death benefit so the agent wants to maximize this amount. Agents are also keenly aware that you do not like to pay for life insurance so they try to minimize the premiums.

The agent responsible for this made a handsome commission and is probably long gone out of the business. Meanwhile, this policyholder, if he is still alive, has put over $57,753 into this policy and will see no benefit. Term would have been a much better alternative. However, the policyholder got what he wished for, over half-a-million-dollar death benefit for a very low cost.

The solution to this problem is to over-fund a policy to the maximum extent allowed by law. During the 1980s, bond returns were extremely high, ranging anywhere between 12-18%. Many people were liquidating their brokerage and bank accounts and moving the money into life insurance in lump sums. At the time, life insurance was loosely defined. To be entitled to the tax advantages of life insurance, it had to actually be life insurance; in other words, there had to be a death benefit attached.

At the time, if you put $100,000 into the policy, you would typically be required to have $100,000 of death benefit. This low amount of death benefit would keep the costs down and the policyholder could still net 10-16% returns after expenses, in a tax-deferred environment. It should be easy to see why so many people were moving money into these policies. To no one's surprise, the banking and brokerage industry was outraged and insisted on changes.

More specifically, they wanted Congress to define life insurance. So,

Congress came back with a corridor rule. Loosely explained, Congress said that based on age, gender and health, there had to be a corridor between the total premiums that were expected to be placed in a policy and the death benefit. This corridor, or gap, between the minimum face-amount of insurance required, which was based on total premiums to be spent on the contract, is larger the younger the insured is. At age 100, these two amounts match and you are essentially self-insured, but are still receiving the tax benefits of life insurance.

This minimum amount of life insurance can vary from insurance companies but it is very close and based on other internal factors. As an example, if you were a non-smoking, fifty-five-year-old male, the minimum amount of death benefit you could carry, if you plan on making premium payments of $40,000 per year for only five years, would be about $545,000. Contrast that with a non-smoking, forty-year-old male who, when making the exact same $40,000 per year for five years, would need at least $992,000.

This is important to understand because it shows you that this banking system is right for you at any age. The costs associated with life insurance are based on the death benefit. You must understand that as you age, the costs go up because you are closing in on the end of your journey. However, our fifty-five-year-old is buying much less life insurance. Essentially, the cost associated with both of these men will be about the same. This said, it does **not** make sense to insure a prospect's child or someone much younger to make our plan work. Any age works just as well.

In the end, educated investors had no problem with these stipulations and so continued to move money from brokerage accounts and bank accounts at a record pace. Why not! The costs might have increased, but you were still getting unbelievable net returns in a tax-deferred environment (with few rules); you could still take money out tax-free and your estate value (protection for your family) would increase dramatically overnight—again, not much to dissuade the wise investor from making use of such an effective wealth-building vehicle.

As a result, Congress was forced to come up with a few other provisions, i.e., if the policyholder places money into a policy in one lump sum, paying no other premiums, the contract is to be considered a modified endowment contract or an MEC. Basically, an MEC still provides for tax-deferred growth and tax-free transfer, but the tax-free benefit of policy loans is removed. Essentially, when you take money out, it is treated as a withdrawal and taxed like an annuity (LIFO, or "last in, first out"). The policyholder is taking out interest first, which is taxed as ordinary income. Once you get to principal, it is not taxed because it is assumed that premiums were paid for with after-tax dollars.

When making withdrawals from a non-MEC life insurance contract, you are taxed as FIFO ("first in, first out"), which means the first money you take out is tax-free because it is return of principal. Of course, making withdraws from a policy is a dumb way to access your money; as you will learn, the smart way is to take out policy loans that you never repay.

In order for policyholders to benefit from policy loans, the contract had to meet the "7-pay test." Instead of one lump sum, premiums would have to be placed in the contract for a minimum of seven years in equally divided installments. One misunderstanding is that this plan can be funded in less than seven years and the same results would be achieved. This is not true. The plan can be funded for less than seven years (we typically plan for a five-year contribution plan), but there is still room for more money/premium.

As an example, a forty-year-old male in standard health who wants to put $40,000/year into the plan, based on the seven-year plan, will receive $992,864 in death benefit. This policy owner can put $40,000 in for one year and it would still not be considered a MEC. He can also fund this $40,000/year for up to five years, not seven, and the death benefit would remain the same—and he could fund it for any number of years in between. Obviously, the more money in the plan, based on minimizing costs, the larger the cash value will grow.

Although Congress calls this the "7-pay test," referring to putting premium in for seven years, you fully fund in five years or four years and one day. If he were to fund this plan at $40,000 per year for seven years, his minimum death benefit would have been $1,392,927. This plan would cost much more money and not receive the same growth.

Putting It All Together: Over-Funding a Life Insurance Policy
As noted previously, costs of insurance and expenses remain the same regardless of the amount of money placed in the plan. Knowing that the insurance company "peels" off the excess cash (over and above the costs) and reinvests the money on your behalf, it only stands to reason that we fund the plan to the maximum extent allowed by law, the seven-pay plan.

Let's go back and take a look at our forty-year-old client in Figure 3. The illustration below shows us four important items that need to be considered when building a plan.

Using the same forty-year-old male example, this illustration shows the costs of insurance and expenses for the first year (an explanation as to why the cost of insurance decreases with age will be provided later).

When an agent runs an illustration, he will be able to determine the first-year cost of insurance (COI) and expenses. Using our same example, I can determine that these costs equal $4,078.47. This is the total cost of that policy in year one. Based on maximum funding this plan, the insurance company will accept your $40,000 premium and "peel" off $4,078.37, placing this money into an account that is linked to bond returns.

Remember that insurance companies think like insurance companies and will divide this $4,078.37 into twelve monthly payments of $339.86. Although we are maximum funding this policy at $40,000, the insurance company is pulling out $339.86 from the $4,078.37 monthly. The remaining balance continues to earn returns based on prevailing bond rates.

The magic is what happens to the remainder of the $40,000, less the expenses of $4,078.37—or $35,921.63. This is the amount placed into a side account (for old policies, a bond account) and credited annually with interest earnings. This is the money that will grow the cash value account.

Important Planning Note: Based on the above example, is it safe to say that this policy will stay in force for another seven years providing no credited interest to the side account? The answer is yes, which provides you with planning options. If no other money is placed in this policy, the insurance company will simply go to the side fund the next year and withdraw the costs. This $35,921.63 will sustain the policy another seven years. However, keep in mind that because there is no cash value being built, the cost of insurance will not go down over time. This provides us with an idea as to the flexibility within this policy.

In our example, it is clear that we are basically buying term and investing the difference. But the astute person will see that providing a $992,864 death benefit for a forty-year-old male at a cost of $4,078.37/year is much more expensive than buying a straight term policy.

A twenty-year term policy will cost about $1,164/year with this same company (cheaper with most others). So why is the universal life policy so much more expensive? Because the universal life policy is *permanent* life insurance and the premiums are amortized over the insured's life expectancy. At the end of the term, when our client is sixty years old, if he wanted to renew this same death benefit for another twenty years, it would cost him $5,918 annually. Do you see how this averages out?

Building Life Insurance the Traditional Way May Be a Very Poor Investment Decision

Financial planners may be right when convincing clients that life insurance is a poor investment vehicle, but only if it is built based on minimizing premiums, i.e., the traditional approach. The figure below shows three different approaches for our forty-year-old male: minimum premium, target premium and over-funding a policy.

Secret of the Super-Rich #2   33

Contract Premiums   Target Premium $14,079.00
                         Minimum $6,327.26
                         7 Pay/MEC $44,270.58

The following three examples represent the three very distinct ways to fund the plan. Remember that you can fund the plan in a various number of ways but I am keeping it simple. As a member of The Speed of Gold Club™, you will be shown more advanced strategies to fund your plan, which involve a combination of the three.

End of Year	Age	Model Premium	Times Per Year	Annual Premium	Cash From Policy	Annual Outlay	Non-Guaranteed Assumed Surr Cash Value	Surr Charge	Account Value	Death Benefit
1	41	6,327	1	6,327	0	6,327	0	27,273	2,021	992,864
2	42	6,327	1	6,327	0	6,327	0	25,455	4,228	992,864
3	43	6,327	1	6,327	0	6,327	0	23,637	6,374	992,864
4	44	6,327	1	6,327	0	6,327	0	21,818	8,768	992,864
5	45	6,327	1	6,327	0	6,327	0	20,000	11,097	992,864
6	46	6,327	1	6,327	0	6,327	0	18,182	13,726	992,864
7	47	6,327	1	6,327	0	6,327	0	16,364	16,288	992,864
8	48	6,327	1	6,327	0	6,327	4,661	14,546	19,207	992,864
9	49	6,327	1	6,327	0	6,327	9,328	12,727	22,056	992,864
10	50	6,327	1	6,327	0	6,327	14,603	10,909	25,512	992,864
				63,273	0	63,273				
11	51	6,327	1	6,327	0	6,327	21,384	9,091	30,475	992,864
12	52	6,327	1	6,327	0	6,327	29,100	7,273	36,373	992,864
13	53	6,327	1	6,327	0	6,327	36,762	5,455	42,217	992,864
14	54	6,327	1	6,327	0	6,327	45,509	3,636	49,145	992,864
15	55	6,327	1	6,327	0	6,327	54,248	1,818	56,066	992,864
16	56	6,327	1	6,327	0	6,327	64,250	0	64,250	992,864
17	57	6,327	1	6,327	0	6,327	72,314	0	72,314	992,864
18	58	6,327	1	6,327	0	6,327	81,622	0	81,622	992,864
19	59	6,327	1	6,327	0	6,327	90,815	0	90,815	992,864
20	60	6,327	1	6,327	0	6,327	101,465	0	101,465	992,864
				126,545	0	126,545				
21	61	6,327	1	6,327	0	6,327	111,925	0	111,925	992,864
22	62	6,327	1	6,327	0	6,327	124,022	0	124,022	992,864
23	63	6,327	1	6,327	0	6,327	135,698	0	135,698	992,864
24	64	6,327	1	6,327	0	6,327	149,169	0	149,169	992,864
25	65	6,327	1	6,327	0	6,327	162,060	0	162,060	992,864

Figure 4

1. **Minimum Funding:** By minimum funding the plan, because our agent wanted to minimize the premium, our client has paid $6,327.26 per year until age sixty-five and has only accumulated a surrender cash value of $162,060. The total premiums paid in

34   *Moving at the Speed of Wealth*

this period were $158,175. By minimum funding this plan, this policyholder only has a gain of $3,885 and could not start banking with the system until the eighth year. He would have been better off buying term and investing the difference.

2. **Target Premium:** By funding based on a target premium of $14,079, the surrender cash value would have grown to $947,188 by age sixty-five with a total outlay of premiums of $351,975. Not only was the policyholder insured for twenty-five years, he could receive all premiums paid in *plus* an extra $595,213 in growth. For the curious, intelligent investor out there, that is an internal rate of return on investment of 6.76%. This is pretty bad but consider the safety and the fact that this client had insurance and a banking system (we will get into this later). This is certainly a better approach than buying term. They receive all their money back plus some tax advantage gain.

End of Year	Age	Model Premium	Times Per Year	Annual Premium	Cash From Policy	Annual Outlay	Non-Guaranteed Assumed Surr Cash Value	Surr Charge	Account Value	Death Benefit
1	41	14,079	1	14,079	0	14,079	0	27,273	9,436	992,864
2	42	14,079	1	14,079	0	14,079	0	25,455	20,388	992,864
3	43	14,079	1	14,079	0	14,079	7,766	23,637	31,402	992,864
4	44	14,079	1	14,079	0	14,079	22,419	21,818	44,237	992,864
5	45	14,079	1	14,079	0	14,079	37,214	20,000	57,214	992,864
6	46	14,079	1	14,079	0	14,079	54,138	18,182	72,320	992,864
7	47	14,079	1	14,079	0	14,079	71,319	16,364	87,683	992,864
8	48	14,079	1	14,079	0	14,079	90,979	14,546	105,525	992,864
9	49	14,079	1	14,079	0	14,079	111,043	12,727	123,771	992,864
10	50	14,079	1	14,079 / 140,790	0	14,079 / 140,790	134,974	10,909	145,883	992,864
11	51	14,079	1	14,079	0	14,079	161,285	9,091	170,376	992,864
12	52	14,079	1	14,079	0	14,079	191,673	7,273	198,946	992,864
13	53	14,079	1	14,079	0	14,079	223,159	5,455	228,614	992,864
14	54	14,079	1	14,079	0	14,079	259,443	3,636	263,080	992,864
15	55	14,079	1	14,079	0	14,079	297,244	1,818	299,063	992,864
16	56	14,079	1	14,079	0	14,079	340,736	0	340,736	992,864
17	57	14,079	1	14,079	0	14,079	384,314	0	384,314	992,864
18	58	14,079	1	14,079	0	14,079	434,519	0	434,519	992,864
19	59	14,079	1	14,079	0	14,079	487,293	0	487,293	992,864
20	60	14,079	1	14,079 / 281,580	0	14,079 / 281,580	547,954	0	547,954	992,864
21	61	14,079	1	14,079	0	14,079	611,960	0	611,960	992,864
22	62	14,079	1	14,079	0	14,079	685,455	0	685,455	992,864
23	63	14,079	1	14,079	0	14,079	763,395	0	763,395	992,864
24	64	14,079	1	14,079	0	14,079	852,711	0	852,711	1,040,307
25	65	14,079	1	14,079	0	14,0797	947,188	0	947,188	1,136,626

Figure 5

3. **Maximum Funding:** When you maximum fund the plan at $40,000 for the five years, you have placed a total of $200,000 in the policy, received life insurance protection for your family and grown your surrender cash value to $1,209,593 by age sixty-five! Not only can you receive your premiums back (if you decide you don't need life insurance any longer), but you receive the gain of $1,009,593 as well. This is an internal rate of return of 20%. That is the time value of money and compounding your money tax-deferred (covered in the next chapter). If you are someone looking for guarantees and the safest possible investment, life insurance may be a great place for you to put your money. In most cases, it can outperform annuities, certificate of deposits (CDs), money market and government bonds. This is as good as other cash equivalent accounts plus you have life insurance and at some point down the line, let's say at age sixty-five, you are going to want to create income for yourself from your investments and will need to make one of these decisions regarding your policy:

End of Year	Age	Model Premium	Times Per Year	Annual Premium	Cash From Policy	Annual Outlay	Non-Guaranteed Assumed Surr Cash Value	Surr Charge	Account Value	Death Benefit
1	41	40,000	1	40,000	0	40,000	6,841	27,273	9,436	992,864
2	42	40,000	1	40,000	0	40,000	48,929	25,455	20,388	992,864
3	43	40,000	1	40,000	0	40,000	91,436	23,637	31,402	992,864
4	44	40,000	1	40,000	0	40,000	141,067	21,818	44,237	992,864
5	45	40,000	1	40,000	0	40,000	191,534	20,000	57,214	992,864
6	46	0	1	0	0	0	212,712	18,182	72,320	992,864
7	47	0	1	0	0	0	227,426	16,364	87,683	992,864
8	48	0	1	0	0	0	252,145	14,546	105,525	992,864
9	49	0	1	0	0	0	269,468	12,727	123,771	992,864
10	50	0	1	0	0	0	300,527	10,909	145,883	992,864
				200,000	0	200,000				
11	51	0	1	0	0	0	325,114	9,091	170,376	992,864
12	52	0	1	0	0	0	364,136	7,273	198,946	992,864
13	53	0	1	0	0	0	393,688	5,455	228,614	992,864
14	54	0	1	0	0	0	440,565	3,636	263,080	992,864
15	55	0	1	0	0	0	476,204	1,818	299,063	992,864
16	56	0	1	0	0	0	532,688	0	340,736	992,864
17	57	0	1	0	0	0	573,874	0	384,314	992,864
18	58	0	1	0	0	0	640,097	0	434,519	992,864
19	59	0	1	0	0	0	690,271	0	487,293	992,864
20	60	0	1	0	0	0	770,716	0	547,954	1,001,931
				200,000	0	200,000				
21	61	0	1	0	0	0	831,828	0	611,960	1,064,739
22	62	0	1	0	0	0	929,157	0	685,455	1,170,738
23	63	0	1	0	0	0	1,002,969	0	763,395	1,243,680
24	64	0	1	0	0	0	1,129,447	0	852,711	1,366,945
25	65	0	1	0	0	0	1,309,593	0	947,188	1,453,511

Figure 6

a. You no longer feel you need life insurance and you decide to withdraw the money, at which point you will owe taxes on the gain of $1,009,593. This, of course, is the wrong decision. You have collapsed your banking system and are paying taxes, two things we are trying to avoid.

b. Take out policy loans to supplement your retirement income *(recommended)*. Based on this illustration, and if everything goes as is illustrated, which it won't, you can take out tax-free policy loans of $159,562 starting at age sixty-six into perpetuity. Your break-even point, the amount of premiums paid into the policy vs. the amount taken out, is in less than 1.5 years. If you take these loans until age ninety, you will have a total tax-free supplemental income of $159,562 annually. This totals $3,989,040 of tax-free income by age ninety, and you still have $2,752,249 of death benefit to pass along to the next generation (in most cases, tax-free).

							Non-Guaranteed Assumed			
End of Year	Age	Model Premium	Times Per Year	Annual Premium	Cash From Policy	Annual Outlay	Surr Cash Value	Surr Charge	Account Value	Death Benefit
26	66	0	1	0	159,562	-159,562	1,180,697	0	1,351,351	1,437,454
27	67	0	1	0	159,562	-159,562	1,105,709	0	1,458,881	1,368,307
28	68	0	1	0	159,562	-159,562	1,081,524	0	1,629,902	1,358,607
29	69	0	1	0	159,562	-159,562	1,002,504	0	1,759,659	1,284,049
30	70	0	1	0	159,562	-159,562	985,577	0	1,966,022	1,280,480
				200,000	797,808	-597,808				
31	71	0	1	0	159,562	-159,562	903,346	0	2,122,605	1,179,285
32	72	0	1	0	159,562	-159,562	897,245	0	2,371,919	1,158,156
33	73	0	1	0	159,562	-159,562	813,788	0	2,561,633	1,044,335
34	74	0	1	0	159,562	-159,562	823,579	0	2,863,587	1,024,031
35	75	0	1	0	159,562	-159,562	741,677	0	3,094,158	896,385
36	76	0	1	0	159,562	-159,562	774,364	0	3,461,040	947,416
37	77	0	1	0	159,562	-159,562	696,610	0	3,740,715	883,646
38	78	0	1	0	159,562	-159,562	757,144	0	4,183,525	966,321
39	79	0	1	0	159,562	-159,562	685,346	0	4,520,578	911,375
40	80	0	1	0	159,562	-159,562	781,822	0	5,054,329	1,034,538
				200,000	2,393,424	-2,193,424				
41	81	0	1	0	159,562	-159,562	719,630	0	5,459,810	992,620
42	82	0	1	0	159,562	-159,562	861,873	0	6,102,239	1,166,985
43	83	0	1	0	159,562	-159,562	813,809	0	6,589,132	1,143,265
44	84	0	1	0	159,562	-159,562	1,013,780	0	7,361,250	1,381,842
45	85	0	1	0	159,562	-159,562	985,386	0	7,944,788	1,382,625
46	86	0	1	0	159,562	-159,562	1,257,091	0	8,870,946	1,700,638
47	87	0	1	0	159,562	-159,562	1,254,506	0	9,568,321	1,732,923
48	88	0	1	0	159,562	-159,562	1,614,111	0	10,676,545	2,147,938
49	89	0	1	0	159,562	-159,562	1,644,315	0	11,507,412	2,219,685
50	90	0	1	0	159,562	-159,562	2,110,741	0	12,830,162	2,752,249
				200,000	3,989,040	-3,789,040				

Figure 7

Secret of the Super-Rich #2

If you look closely at Figure 7, you will see that your surrender cash value and your death benefit are reduced as you start taking out policy loans, which you never repay. But look very closely at your account value; this is the account that is credited with returns tied to the stock market. Notice that this account continues to grow as you take out loans.

Your account is truly only worth the surrender cash value because the insurance company is collateralizing your account value when making loans. However, the account is still credited with returns because the insurance company is not loaning you money from your account but rather from the company's general account. This is how the arbitrage is created within the policy.

Look again at your surrender cash value column at age eighty-eight. Notice that the surrender cash value begins to grow again along with the death benefit. Again, this is due to internal arbitrage as you borrow at an average of 6.5% and the account value continues to earn on average 9%. How sweet it is!

As nice as this picture looks, remember that you did all of this with a vehicle that I said was a poor investment. I stand by my words but you can see that it just might blow away what you are currently doing, especially if you maximum fund the plan.

What is not shown is how powerful the plan is when you use it as a banking system and borrow from the plan to reinvest. You are allowed to borrow from your plan with a simple phone call when you have built up your surrender cash value. Going back to the illustration next to "maximum funding," you can see that there is cash value you can borrow from at the end of year one. Take a look at year five. You can borrow from the $191,534 surrender cash value and invest in real estate, just like I described at the beginning of this chapter. Of course, you could borrow sooner.

Using our above examples, it may become clear that life insurance might not be the greatest place to store cash. After all, you could have bought term insurance at $1,164 a year until age sixty, or a total outlay of $23,280, and placed the entire $200,000 in a side fund earning 8% to grow to $1,369,695 by age sixty-five in this side account. (Of course, if it is in a taxable environment, it will be quite a bit less, and if it is in a qualified account and/or IRA, this *entire amount* is taxable). But this does not take into account that you had life insurance protection during the entire time and, more importantly, *a banking system.*

It may not be clear yet as to why Speed of Wealth recommends these policies. Using our above examples, we see that there is a time and place for properly structured life insurance, but perhaps the planners are correct in that it is not a good place to invest your money.

A strong alternative, then, to the above planning is to maximum fund a *variable* life insurance contract. Everything mentioned above would remain constant with one distinct difference: The "side fund" is now under the client's control and the policy provides a variety of mutual funds to invest your money in. It is our opinion that a variable life insurance contract would be the second choice for holding money because of all the tax advantages once again. That said, if the only choice was a whole life policy or a policy crediting the side fund based on the bond market, then Retirement TRACS and the Speed of Wealth, as we know it today, would not exist.

The Speed of Wealth Alternative

Indexed Life Insurance was developed in the mid-1990s to provide policy-holders with an opportunity to combine the benefits of insurance with an investment vehicle. Unlike a variable life policy, however, Indexed Universal Life is a fixed product.

This means that all of a client's money is actually invested in nice, safe bonds yet they are credited with the gains of the stock market with *no* downside risk.

> **(Note:** *Please read all literature provided by an agent before moving forward.)*

The premise was really quite ingenious: create a life insurance product with all the advantages of life insurance, credit the side account with almost all the upside of a popular market index (S&P 500®, Dow, NASDAQ, etc.) and lock in all gains annually so that, once credited, the policy owner cannot lose money.

Getting Stock Market Returns with No Downside Risk

Although this strategy can be used by you, and has been available for years, nobody seems to know it exists. If you want upside market gain, and no chance of losing principal, it is easy—determine what government bonds are paying and work backward.

> **Example:** You have $100,000 to invest and don't want to lose the money, but you want market index returns. If government bonds are paying 5%, you simply determine how much of your $100,000 is needed to grow back to $100,000 at the end of the year. In this example, you would buy $95,133 worth of one-year treasury bonds. Now, take the remaining $4,867 and buy one-year index call options, at which point you are betting a particular market index will go up in value. (Options provide

you with tremendous leverage.) If the market goes down, you lose your entire $4,867, but your bonds grew back to $100,000— you lost no principal! If the market goes up (call options), you get the market returns plus your $100,000 bond money.

You will never get the entire upside of the market because you have to pay commissions and premiums on options, and returns are very small for average investors using this strategy on their own. To make it really worthwhile, millions of dollars are needed to invest. This is an overly simple example so don't rush out and try to create it on your own; there are better ways of going about it and it takes some expertise.

This strategy is used on Wall Street and the product is called a MITT (Market Index Target Term Security). Speed of Wealth also has a wealth fund in which we employ similar strategies but with more targeted growth.

This is the philosophy behind an indexed product, but it doesn't work quite that way within the policy. Rather, the insurance company does not use any of the client's money to buy options. It comes from the insurance company's general account. The "downside" is that the client will never get all of the upside of the market due to costs of options. Based on experience, it is a safe bet that clients will get credited about 1.5 to three points less than how the index actually performs, but does this really matter if there is no risk of losing money? The answer is a resounding NO, depending on your indexing strategy.

So, to reiterate: Once the side account has been credited with index returns (once annually), the money in that account is locked and you cannot lose the money (principal) to a downward movement in the index.

If the market is down, can your account value decrease if the policy stipulates that it cannot lose money in a down market? Yes. The cost of insurance and expenses still has to be paid. If you are no longer funding the plan, the costs of the policy are deducted from the account's value (surrender cash value). If our forty-year-old male has cash value of $100,000 and the market tanks, the account is credited with 0%, and the costs must still be deducted, reducing the account by $4,630.

Put in layman's terms, do mutual funds have fees? Even no-load funds have some fees, but our average client is buying loaded funds that also include management fees. A typical management fee in a mutual fund is between .5%-2.5%. So let's use 1% for our example. If our client had his $100,000 in a mutual fund and the market stayed flat, it would still reduce the account by $1,000. If the market loses 10%, then his mutual fund would lose 11%. With the indexed insurance policy, on the other hand, the market could drop 30% and our policyholder would only have the expected $4,630 in expenses to contend with.

Also, keep in mind that our costs remain the same regardless of the growth in the policy. If our male funds $100,000, the costs are $4,630. With the mutual fund, the cost is $1,000. If our cash value grows to $300,000, our costs remain steady once again at $4,630 (and, in reality, it actually goes down). A $300,000 mutual fund, on the other hand, would bear a cost of $3,000.

Knowing this, I want to point out that life insurance is the second most expensive place to put your money in the early years but, when properly structured, becomes the least expensive in the later years.

Financial "experts" can argue all they want, but the merits of the indexed life insurance contract stand on their own. If a planner argues against or dismisses this product to you, they are arguing the issue only because they are so conditioned to believe in their view of the world that they cannot get out of the proverbial box themselves. Our colleagues still sell variable life insurance. But it begs the question: why? We can get most of the upside of the market with no downside risk in an indexed product.

Their response is that you cannot get all of the upside (many products have caps on how much they will credit your account; many have no caps at all or caps so high that they are unlikely to ever be triggered). Your response should simply be, "It's the losses that kill you!" and if they are worth their salt, they will acknowledge and agree to this very important reality. Also, you cannot create internal arbitrage on policy loans within a whole life and variable life policy. This, of course, is the biggest reason we recommend using life insurance as an investment tool…THE BANKING SYSTEM!

So back to our average 401(k) holder who lost 40% of his account back during the bust of the early 2000s. It is important to note that this investor will need 67% returns to get back to even, not just the 40% that was lost. He is now working from a lower dollar amount. And what happens if his plan was to begin taking money out the year of the crash? Uh-oh! He'd have to wait until he could get his money back. What happens if he is already pulling money out of his retirement account (typically interest-only) and the market crashes? This affects his cash flow dramatically. This is why many retirees will move their money into low interest-bearing money-market accounts, CDs or bonds during retirement. Most cannot withstand the hit. With the indexed life product, there is no hit because their principal is always protected.

The Speed of Wealth plan is better for another major reason: We have *no rules* governing how, when and what we use our money for. We can take out policy loans at will and create arbitrage.

Historically, our policy performs at 9%. When you take out a policy loan, the IRS demands that the insurance company charge a reasonable interest rate on

Secret of the Super-Rich #2

that loan. The rate that the insurance company charges is the average Moody's AAA bond rate two months prior. Looking back twenty years, we have an average rate of 6.5%. If the money borrowed is being charged 6.5% on average and you are earning 9% on average, you have created 2.5% arbitrage. You are being charged bond rates and credited with stock market returns on the borrowed money. Historically, the stock market (equities) will outperform the bond market (debt), and when we create arbitrage over time, we can amass a small fortune.

Let's put this in perspective. By looking at Figure 8, you will see that If you were to borrow $100,000 from your life insurance policy, take it to Vegas and plunk it all down on the color red at the roulette table and lose it because black was called, you would still earn 2.5% *on lost money* over time (not a strategy we encourage). But this illustrates the power of arbitrage borrowing.

Take a look at the following example:

Borrow $100,000 from Surrender Cash Value (true equity in our plan). Typically, it is the third year before we can benefit from this strategy.		
Historically the plan continues to pay 9% even on this borrowed money. $9,000 tax-free growth	Borrow $100,000 at bond rates—in this example, 6.5% (cannot exceed 9.5% or be less than 3.5%). -$6,000	Reinvest! As long as we can create arbitrage over and beyond the 6% divided by one (client's tax bracket), you win. Example: 13% deeds of trust. $100,000 @13% =$13,000 gain, less taxes
$9,000	Minus $6,000	Plus after-tax gain, i.e., $10,000
Total return of $13,000 or 13% on our money (3% arbitrage)		

Figure 8

Finally, it's important to understand that you may experience negative arbitrage in some years. If the market loses money or you are credited with less than 6.5%, you have created negative arbitrage. On the other hand, if the market is way up you are credited 20%, you have created 13.5% arbitrage. Over time, your client will win the arbitrage game as long as the market follows past trends, which is very likely. (The government will not allow our market to tank for very long. Corrections are always needed.)

> **Important Note:** *When we build illustrations, we are always using an average and any sane person knows that there is no such thing as an average. The numbers you are shown will never be exact. You can manipulate the software to reflect more accurate examples by looking to the past and entering numbers accordingly.*

The reality is that in our new scenario (Figure 9), as long as we can get better returns than you are paying for the policy loans, taking taxes into account, you will never lose money. The example below assumes that the market tanks and your policy is credited with zero.

Borrow $100,000 from Surrender Cash Value (true equity in our plan). Typically, it is the third year before we can benefit from this strategy.		
Market tanks; your money is credited with 0% even on this borrowed money.	Borrow $100,000 at bond rates—in this example, 6.5% (cannot exceed 9.5% or be less than 3.5%). -$6,000	-$6,000 Reinvest! As long as we can create arbitrage over and beyond the 6% divided by one (client's tax bracket), your client wins. Example: 13% deeds of trust. $100,000 @13% =$13,000 gain, less taxes
$0	Minus $6,000	Plus after-tax gain, i.e., $10,000
Total return of $3,000 or 3% on our money in a down market		

Figure 9

The Bigger Picture, Advantages

There are some distinct advantages to using cash value life insurance policies as an alternative to traditional retirement planning vehicles (Figure 10). Most Americans will use employee-sponsored savings plans (qualified plans) and/or Individual Retirement Arrangements (IRAs) to save for their future. Others will turn to real estate. All of these "traditional" methods have their merits, but let's compare by looking at Figure 10.

By now, it should be easy to get your arms around this concept and develop some passion for what I am preaching. People can save for retirement and build fortunes *without* the worries and rollercoaster ride that "just go with the territory" when investing directly in the market—not to mention that you can feel comfortable knowing that your money is safe and that their family is protected with life insurance all in one, a complete and highly effective approach to retirement goals.

As we progress through this book, I will show you examples of how the insurance policy can enhance just about any investment you participate in. To benefit, you must be willing to manage the plan and start borrowing to reinvest as soon as you can.

	Cash Value Insurance Policy (Specific policies)	Real Estate	Qualified Accounts and/or IRAs
Tax-Deductible Contributions	Yes, when using business insurance	Yes, when using home equity	Yes
Tax-Deferred Growth	Yes	Yes	Yes
Tax-Free Withdrawals	Yes	No	Yes
Tax-Deductible Expenses	No	Yes (only on losses and depreciation; losses are never good. Depreciation is recaptured by the IRS at 25%.)	No
Tax-Free Transfer to Heirs	Yes	Yes	No
Stock Market Gains	Yes	No	Yes
Stock Market Losses	No	No	Yes
Minimum Guarantees	Yes	No	No
Ability to Borrow Against	Yes	Yes	No
Ability to Use Leverage to Build	Yes	Yes	No
Ability to Create Arbitrage on Loans	Yes	Yes	No
Ability to Withdraw Cash at Any Time	Yes	Yes	Yes
Penalty on Early Withdrawals	No	No	Yes
Forced to Withdraw Money at Certain Age	No	No	Yes
Banking System	Yes	Yes	No
Create a "Dead Asset"	No	Yes	No

Figure 10 (continues)

	Cash Value Insurance Policy (Specific policies)	Real Estate	Qualified Accounts and/or IRAs
Expenses	Yes (COI and expenses)	Yes (closing costs, taxes, insurance and the big one: maintenance)	Yes (management and hidden fees)
Advantages to Expenses	Survivor benefit: family protection from death	Tax deductions (but losses are losses)	None, only depletes total return
Self-Fulfilling Plan in Case of Disability	Yes, disability rider can be added	No	No
Surrender Charges	Yes, decreasing	Yes, closing fees	Penalty for early withdrawal

Figure 10 (continued)

I hope this chapter has opened your eyes to the power of life insurance when used correctly. There are many other advantages to life insurance but, for our purposes, we are looking to it as a tax shelter, a banking system and, of course, for survivor benefits as well.

Now that we have established why you may want to look at life insurance as an investment tool, let's begin to dig into strategies, techniques and concepts.

In the next part of the book, I am going to reveal some interesting Finance 101 concepts that, for some reason, have escaped the minds of most Americans. This is probably because these basic rules of finance have never been taught to us. I will then go into a few specific wealth-building strategies and, finally, we will take a look at some alternative investment ideas.

Concepts, strategies and techniques will be intermingled throughout most chapters so be on the lookout for them. You will not miss the important points I am making, I assure you. Brace yourself for a fun ride and remember to keep an open mind.

This is where your education begins but it most certainly will not stop here. If you are anything like me, you are always learning new ideas and concepts.

Chapter Three

Secret of the Super-Rich #3:

Super-Rich People Understand the Power of Compounding Returns and How to Use Them Coupled with Simple Interest

I believe that Albert Einstein called compound interest the eighth wonder of the world. Now, this is a brilliant man we are talking about so you might want to listen. Wealthy people understand that given the choice between investing in a tax-deferred compounding environment and a taxed as earned simple interest environment, you go for deferral and compounding every time.

Let's take a quick look at the magic of compounding. If I were to offer you one penny that I would double every day for thirty days or $100,000 today, which would you choose? To explain, this means that my one penny (.01) will double to two pennies on day two (.02). On day three, my two pennies will double to four pennies (.04). You get the picture and I am sure by now you know the answer: Always take the penny. Let's just make sure we made the right choice.

In the chart on the next page you can see that by day twenty, our penny has grown to $5,242.88. Are you sure you don't want to change your mind and take the $100,000? Of course not, because you can already see the final results. Our penny doubling every day for thirty days grows to an amazing $5,368,709.12. That's over five million dollars.

Of course, our penny was compounding tax-deferred or free. By compounding, I mean you earned interest on the principal, interest on the interest earned and interest on money you would have ordinarily paid Uncle Sam (the money you must pay Uncle Sam stays in the account until a later date if it is tax-deferred). In a tax-deferred

DAY	GROWTH
1	$0.01
2	$0.02
3	$0.04
4	$0.08
5	$0.16
6	$0.32
7	$0.64
8	$1.28
9	$2.56
10	$5.12
11	$10.24
12	$20.48
13	$40.96
14	$81.92
15	$163.84
16	$327.68
17	$655.36
18	$1,310.72
19	$2,621.44
20	$5,242.88
21	$10,485.76
22	$20,971.52
23	$41,943.04
24	$83,886.08
25	$167,772.16
26	$335,544.32
27	$671,088.64
28	$1,342,177.28
29	$2,684,354.56
30	**$5,368,709.12**

Figure 11

environment, all of this five million would be taxable except for our original principal amount of one penny. In a tax-free compounding environment, you would owe no taxes but you might have paid taxes on the original penny.

Now, for a couple of bad news scenarios. First of all, I am pretty darn good at investments but I do not know of any that pay a 100% return daily (which is what I have just illustrated). A second bit of bad news is that you are limited on where you can achieve this tax-deferred/free compounding magic.

Tax Bracket:	30%
DAY	GROWTH
1	$0.0100
2	$0.0170
3	$0.0289
4	$0.0491
5	$0.0835
6	$0.1420
7	$0.2414
8	$0.4103
9	$0.6976
10	$1.1859
11	$2.0160
12	$3.4272
13	$5.8262
14	$9.9046
15	$16.8378
16	$28.6242
17	$48.6612
18	$82.7240
19	$140.6308
20	$239.0724
21	$406.4231
22	$690.9193
23	$1,174.5629
24	$1,996.7569
25	$3,394.4867
26	$5,770.6274
27	$9,810.0666
28	$16,677.1132
29	$28,351.0925
30	**$56,702.18**

Figure 12

The reason for the illustration is just to make a point but now I want to drive that point home.

Let's take our penny and put it into an investment that pays 100% daily for thirty days, but is not a tax-deferred account. Now you will have to pay taxes on the interest you earn as you go. You are still starting out with the same principal, one penny, and you are in the same investment. You are in the 30% federal marginal tax bracket.

The chart on the right reveals a very

surprising and gloomy outcome. When you are taxed on the interest you earn, even though it is still compounding, you come up with extremely different results.

At the end of the thirty days our penny has been doubling—and being taxed each day—it has only grown to $56,702.18. So if I posed the question one more time and offered you the penny doubling in a taxable environment or $100,000, you might still have chosen the penny, only to find out you made a huge mistake.

This is how destructive taxes can be to your investments. Compounding is very important but tax-deferral is more important. If you can achieve compounding within a tax-free environment, then you are that much better off.

Yes, you do have *tax-free* options but you would have to pay taxes on the penny up front in most cases.

Look at the chart to the right. In this example, instead of starting out with one penny, the government taxed it and left us with seven-tenths of a penny. Now I put this seven-tenths in a tax-free environment [such as life insurance, a Roth IRA or, better yet, a self-directed Roth 401(k) plan, available to business owners]. These are examples of shells or environments. You then chose your investments within these shells.

Now my taxed penny has grown to over $3.7 million. That's not quite as much as $5.3 million in the original tax-deferred illustration, but this $3.7 million can now come to me 100% tax-free and will not affect my income, which in turns affects taxes on all of my other income (this is the same with life insurance policy loans).

When you pull money out of a tax-deferred investment, it goes right on the top of your other income and falls within your marginal tax bracket. However, the biggest disadvantage is that it will affect taxes owed on other income and especially Social Security.

Tax Bracket:	30%
DAY	GROWTH
1	$0.0070
2	$0.0140
3	$0.0280
4	$0.0560
5	$0.1120
6	$0.2240
7	$0.4480
8	$0.8960
9	$1.7920
10	$3.5840
11	$7.1680
12	$14.3360
13	$28.6720
14	$57.3440
15	$114.6880
16	$229.3760
17	$458.7520
18	$917.5040
19	$1,835.0080
20	$3,670.0160
21	$7,340.0320
22	$14,680.0640
23	$29,360.1280
24	$58,720.2560
25	$117,440.5120
26	$234,881.0240
27	$469,762.0480
28	$939,524.0960
29	$1,879,048.1920
30	**$3,758,096.38**

Figure 13

Yes, if you make a certain amount of income, your Social Security benefit will be taxed. In fact, there are two tiers. However, like our entire tax code, this is complicated and I cannot fully cover the details here. If you are interested in learning more about taxes on your Social Security benefits, read IRS Publication 915—that is, if you want more bad news today.

If you want to eliminate taxes on your benefits, make sure your money is growing in a *tax-free* environment such as a life insurance policy, Roth IRA or self-directed Roth 401(k). It really is that simple to avoid.

Now, let's look at a phenomenon known as "The Rule of 72." This rule states that if your money is compounding in a tax-deferred or tax-free environment, you can accurately predict how long it will take to double your original principal. If you are averaging 8% returns, you simple divide seventy-two by eight and you can conclude that your money will double in nine years. Here is an exercise for you. If you are averaging 24% returns on your money,

The Rule of 72 vs. The Rule of 108

Rule of 72: to determine how fast money will double, divide 72 by your rate of return
[assumes tax-deferred {free} compounding environment]

Rule of 108: the same but in a tax-as-earned environment
[assumes 33% combined marginal tax bracket]

Rule of 72:	**8%**	**9 years**
Rule of 108:	**8%**	**13.5 years**
CD (taxable)	**5%**	**21.6 years**

Figure 14

how long will it take to double if it is compounding tax-deferred or free? Three years. Pretty simple, wouldn't you agree? These are the types of returns we want you to shoot for.

If you start out with $100,000 and can average a 24% return you can do wonders. Imagine that you have a twelve year window to build wealth. You know your money doubles every three years and if you divide twelve years by three you come up with four doubling periods.

The first doubling period is not that exciting but then it really takes off:

First doubling period (third year):	**$200,000**
Second doubling period (sixth year):	**$400,000**
Third doubling period (ninth year):	**$800,000**
Final doubling period (twelfth year):	**$1,600,000**

Now, that's "Moving at the Speed of Wealth"™! This is our goal and I assure you that it is possible. You will come to believe this as your education continues.

How many of you have ever heard of "The Rule of 108"? This parallels "The Rule of 72" but now it is assumed that you are in an environment where your interest is taxed as earned. Unfortunately, this is the majority of your private savings plans (providing you have a private savings plan outside of work).

When using "The Rule of 108," it is assumed that you are in the 33% federal marginal tax bracket so it does not apply to everyone and it will be different for all of you, but you will get the general idea.

Take your returns and divide this number into 108 to find out how long it will take for your money to double. If you are receiving an 8% return, it will take you 13.5 years to double your money, as opposed to nine years. Which is better? How much better? A whole lot better!

So, you are convinced to put your savings in a money market fund paying 5% because you want to keep your money safe. If you are in the 33% federal marginal tax bracket, it will only take you 21.6 years to double your money. Good luck on that wealth-building plan of yours! If you remember the point I made in the introduction, then you understand that you are losing purchasing power daily. You are actually seeing your principal disappear before your very eyes without even realizing it.

Knowing what you now know, is it safe to assume that you understand that you should be putting as much emphasis on investing in a tax-deferred environment as you do on where you invest your money? Sadly, there are only a few places you can put your money to allow it to grow tax-deferred or free.

- **Qualified retirement plan**—work-sponsored savings plan such as a 401(k), 403(b), etc.
- **Individual Retirement Arrangement—IRA,** but as we go on you will discover that you are limited with these plans and you must make it self-directed.
- **Roth IRA**—Again, there are many limitations to most

investors but I will show you how to create a self-directed Roth 401(k) plan and this will blow your socks off.

- **Tax-exempt bonds**—Yes, these are safe and tax-free, but the returns don't keep up with inflation. In reality, all they do is reduce your taxes. Your income tax, after all, is what is paying the interest on these bonds.
- **Life Insurance Contract**—You know my stance on this.
- Annuities—You don't know my stance on these, but suffice it to say...YUCK!
- **Real Estate**—My favorite of all. Once I show you how to use your self-directed Roth 401(k), you will never have to worry about 1031 exchanges again. I really love teaching what I know, and hopefully you will take advantage of my forty-five years of knowledge.

That's it; there is the list of the environments and/or investments that grow tax-deferred or free. You will notice that life insurance contracts (variable life insurance), qualified retirement accounts, IRAs and Roth IRAs are shells; you then pick your investments within the shell. Real estate, tax-exempt bonds and annuities are the investments and they offer tax-deferral or tax-free benefits.

What the Wealthy Know about Teaming up Compounding Returns with Simple Interest Loans

Now that you have a clear understanding of tax-deferral and compounding, let's put this knowledge to good work. Everything you are learning will come together as you read this entire book...you will have one of those "Ah-ha" moments!

Wealthy people understand that, typically, when you borrow money, you are paying simple interest back to the lender. If you borrowed $100,000 on an interest-only loan at 6%, you will pay $6,000 the first year. You will also pay $6,000 the following year and so on. The payment does not compound. Even when you take out an amortized loan, you are paying simple interest (although there is a slight bell curve that indicates compounding, but for our purpose you are paying simple interest. This is providing you did not finance your home with one of those ugly "pick a payment" loans. If you are only making the small minimum payment, then you are creating negative amortization, which, of course, compounds your payments back to the lender. Why do you think lenders invented the darn things...greed, maybe?).

So, here is what wealthy people do. They will borrow money at simple interest then turn around and invest it in a tax-deferred or free compounding environment. They will create free money for themselves.

Imagine that you have the ability to borrow $100,000 (it can be less or more. I use round numbers for illustration purposes only)—and most of you have the ability to borrow money, at 6% interest only. Again, your payment will be $6,000 each year without fail. You turn around and place this payment in a tax-deferred environment and in an investment that pays only 6%.

Notice I borrowed at 6% simple interest and reinvested the money at the very same rate of 6% (compounding annually), but in a tax-deferred or free compounding shell or investment. A strange thing is about to happen.

My $100,000 has grown to $574,349 in thirty years. My $6,000 annual payments have totaled $180,000 in that same thirty years. I still owe $100,000 on my loan. After paying back the loan and paying yourself back the $180,000 (now back in your pocket), you still have $294,349 left over. Was that magic or simple math?

You see, all you have to do is change your mindset. Instead of thinking of that $6,000 as a payment back to a lender, think of it as payments into your retirement plan. You will learn more about this in another chapter.

Wealthy people understand the power of tax-deferral and compounding, they understand simple interest, and they are able to combine the two and grow richer. Remember, in this example, you borrowed at 6% and received only a 6% return on your money.

Let's continue with this discussion a little further in the next chapter.

Chapter Four

Secret of the Super-Rich #4

Super-Rich People Understand the Power of Arbitrage and Get Stinking, Filthy Rich on Small Returns

While you are out there chasing the bigger, better deal and looking for the investment that can provide you with double-digit returns and **guarantees** (laugh out load), wealthy people are quietly getting richer on very small returns.

Let's continue with our discussion from the previous chapter. Wealthy people will borrow money at simple interest and reinvest it in a tax-deferred or free compounding environment. In the last chapter, I showed you an example of borrowing at 6% simple interest, reinvesting and only receiving the same 6% in a tax-deferred or free compounding environment.

Let's add a little spice to this scenario. After all, if you can only receive 6% returns on your investments, then you are doing a whole lot of things wrong. I will assume that you are a little bit better than the average American and you can receive an 8% return on your investment in this compounding environment.

Your annual payment is the same $6,000 but now your tax-deferred/free compounding annual growth on your $100,000 is $1,006,266 in year thirty. Yep, that's right: over one million dollars. The first part of the scenario has not changed. You paid a total of $180,000 in payments over that thirty-year period; you still owe $100,000 on the loan, for a total of $280,000. Subtract this $280,000 from your growth of $1,006,266 and you still have $726,266. This does not include the $180,000 that you paid yourself back for all the payments but you need to understand that money is in your pocket as well.

Our Speed of Wealth thinker created over three quarters of a million dollars with only a 2% arbitrage in thirty years. Just a lousy 2% spread between what he was paying and what he was receiving. Folks, when I am done with you, this 2% will seem like a rip-off.

You may not have thirty years to wait but principles are principles, and strategies work. If it works in thirty years, it works in ten and twenty years, too. In your very first year, you paid $6,000 but you had $8,000 in growth on your $100,000. How many of you would trade me $6,000 for $8,000 today? And the rest, as they say, is history.

Pretty simple Finance 101 stuff, wouldn't you say? Yet I wonder how many of you readers have ever heard of this. Probably not many, which is a shame because you would be well ahead of the game if you had. In an upcoming chapter, I will show you how to pull off remarkable ways to build wealth using these strategies with no money out of your pocket. Yep, that's right—keep your $6,000. I don't want it.

I want to take a look at what can happen using a nice, safe life insurance contract like we discussed earlier. You will still borrow $100,000 and have a monthly payment of $500. Instead of paying $500 in premiums each month, let's guide the $100,000 into the policy over five years (I will compare the outcome using both scenarios, funding it over five years with your lump sum of money and funding with the same outflow of cash that you would pay on the loan, $500 per month).

Let's say you are thirty-five years old and will retire at sixty-five. You are a non-smoker and in good health.

The following illustration demonstrates saving $500 per month and redirecting the money into a properly designed life insurance contract that you will use as a banking system. On day one, this thirty-five-year-old man has life insurance protection in the amount of $433,045.

Looking ahead in Figure 15 to a retirement age of sixty-five, this man has deposited $180,000 into this supplemental retirement plan at $500 per month (life insurance contract) and has accumulated $700,326 of surrender cash value. He can then start to take out policy loans that he will never repay, in the amount of $92,772 tax-free (of course, this is not guaranteed and this illustration is working on averages; nothing works on averages in the real world but you'll understand the point I am trying to make). This is a pretty good plan considering he created a banking system for thirty years, which allowed him to borrow from the policy and pay for things such as:

Secret of the Super-Rich #4

End of Year	Age	Model Premium	Times Per Year	Annual Premium	Cash From Policy	Annual Outlay	Non-Guaranteed Assumed			
							Surr Cash Value	Surr Charge	Account Value	Death Benefit
26	61	500	12	6,000	0	6,000	464,522	0	464,522	594,588
27	62	500	12	6,000	0	6,000	514,536	0	514,536	648,316
28	63	500	12	6,000	0	6,000	571,276	0	571,276	708,383
29	64	500	12	6,000	0	6,000	631,788	0	631,788	770,781
30	65	500	12	6,000	0	6,000	700,326	0	700,326	840,392
				180,000	0	180,000				
31	66	0	1	0	92,772	-92,772	669,906	0	769,128	816,040
32	67	0	1	0	92,772	-92,772	640,101	0	845,443	792,281
33	68	0	1	0	92,772	-92,772	609,637	0	928,475	767,478
34	69	0	1	0	92,772	-92,772	580,360	0	1,020,585	743,653
35	70	0	1	0	92,772	-92,772	550,762	0	1,120,813	718,884
36	71	0	1	0	92,772	-92,772	523,089	0	1,231,990	683,248
37	72	0	1	0	92,772	-92,772	495,743	0	1,353,147	644,248
38	73	0	1	0	92,772	-92,772	471,544	0	1,487,785	605,454
39	74	0	1	0	92,772	-92,772	448,557	0	1,634,658	562,983
40	75	0	1	0	92,772	-92,772	430,364	0	1,798,143	520,271
				180,000	927,723	-747,723				
41	76	0	1	0	92,772	-92,772	414,745	0	1,976,831	513,586
42	77	0	1	0	92,772	-92,772	405,162	0	2,175,065	513,915
43	78	0	1	0	92,772	-92,772	398,570	0	2,390,735	518,107
44	79	0	1	0	92,772	-92,772	399,958	0	2,629,838	531,450
45	80	0	1	0	92,772	-92,772	405,641	0	2,889,761	550,129
46	81	0	1	0	92,772	-92,772	421,677	0	3,177,711	580,563
47	82	0	1	0	92,772	-92,772	443,610	0	3,490,462	618,133
48	83	0	1	0	92,772	-92,772	478,783	0	3,836,670	670,616
49	84	0	1	0	92,772	-92,772	521,850	0	4,212,395	732,470
50	85	0	1	0	92,772	-92,772	581,602	0	4,627,930	812,998
				180,000	1,855,445	-1,675,445				

Figure 15

- Car purchases
- Business equipment
- College education
- Investments
- Much more

However, it will take him until the end of the fourteenth year before he has accumulated over $100,000 to borrow from. Although he can borrow beginning in the second year, he can only borrow about $4,000. When funding a plan this way, it takes longer for the banking system to kick in.

If, however, this thirty-five-year-old man could take a $100,000 loan at simple interest and feed it into the policy at $20,000 a year for only five years, the results are quite different. Remember that his monthly payment on this $100,000 home loan at 6% interest only is $500 per month. In essence, the illustration below will show that it costs this man the exact same money out of pocket but with very different results. Placing $20,000 a year in for five years

56   *Moving at the Speed of Wealth*

(a total of $100,000—we have to play by the rules) will maximize your policy. Let's take a look at what happens in Figure 16.

							Non-Guaranteed Assumed			
End of Year	Age	Model Premium	Times Per Year	Annual Premium	Cash From Policy	Annual Outlay	Surr Cash Value	Surr Charge	Account Value	Death Benefit
26	61	0	1	0	0	0	676,383	0	676,383	865,771
27	62	0	1	0	0	0	730,372	0	730,372	920,269
28	63	0	1	0	0	0	816,177	0	816,177	1,012,059
29	64	0	1	0	0	0	881,350	0	881,350	1,075,248
30	65	0	1	0	0	0	984,938	0	984,938	1,181,926
				100,000	0	100,000				
31	66	0	1	0	128,195	-128,195	926,566	0	1,063,673	1,128,664
32	67	0	1	0	128,195	-128,195	904,978	0	1,188,723	1,118,948
33	68	0	1	0	128,195	-128,195	843,131	0	1,283,709	1,061,362
34	69	0	1	0	128,195	-128,195	826,288	0	1,434,600	1,055,824
35	70	0	1	0	128,195	-128,195	761,513	0	1,549,221	993,896
36	71	0	1	0	128,195	-128,195	751,724	0	1,731,299	976,793
37	72	0	1	0	128,195	-128,195	685,072	0	1,869,853	890,755
38	73	0	1	0	128,195	-128,195	685,941	0	2,090,193	874,058
39	74	0	1	0	128,195	-128,195	619,256	0	2,258,237	777,332
40	75	0	1	0	128,195	-128,195	635,487	0	2,525,514	761,763
				100,000	1,281,948	-1,181,948				
41	76	0	1	0	128,195	-128,195	571,653	0	2,730,179	708,162
42	77	0	1	0	128,195	-128,195	608,359	0	3,054,050	761,062
43	78	0	1	0	128,195	-128,195	548,059	0	3,300,888	713,113
44	79	0	1	0	128,195	-128,195	610,264	0	3,691,562	794,842
45	80	0	1	0	128,195	-128,195	556,147	0	3,988,761	755,585
46	81	0	1	0	128,195	-128,195	651,005	0	4,459,356	873,973
47	82	0	1	0	128,195	-128,195	606,329	0	4,816,538	847,156
48	83	0	1	0	128,195	-128,195	742,541	0	5,382,546	1,011,669
49	84	0	1	0	128,195	-128,195	711,398	0	5,811,076	1,001,952
50	85	0	1	0	128,195	-128,195	899,447	0	6,490,755	1,223,985
				100,000	2,563,896	-2,463,896				

Figure 16

By maximum funding the plan, this man has only placed $100,000 into the policy but has accumulated $984,938 by age sixty-five. He is out of pocket the same $180,000 over the course of thirty years because he had to make payments on the home loan. Of course, he still has an outstanding loan of $100,000 but who cares? He can now take out $128,195 tax-free annually into perpetuity (forever). If he doesn't repay the loan, and he shouldn't, he still has a $6,000 annual payment. After making the payment on the loan, he is still left with $122,195. That is in increase over the previous plan of $29,423, even after making the payment on his underlying loan of $6,000 per year.

More importantly, by maximum funding the plan, he built up his surrender cash value much more quickly and can turn to the most powerful part of the insurance policy, the banking system, much earlier. In fact, looking at the illustration below (Figure 17), you will see that this young man has enough in his surrender cash value after the second year ($24,887) to buy an inexpensive car. He has built up over $100,000 by the end of the sixth year; he is capitalizing his banking system sooner. Keep in mind that both of these examples reflect this man contributing $500 each month to his retirement plan but with huge differences in the end results.

End of Year	Age	Model Premium	Times Per Year	Annual Premium	Cash From Policy	Annual Outlay	Non-Guaranteed Assumed Surr Cash Value	Surr Charge	Account Value	Death Benefit
1	36	20,000	1	20,000	0	20,000	3,890	13,142	17,032	625,516
2	37	20,000	1	20,000	0	20,000	24,887	12,266	37,153	625,516
3	38	20,000	1	20,000	0	20,000	46,107	11,390	57,496	625,516
4	39	20,000	1	20,000	0	20,000	70,896	10,514	81,410	625,516
5	40	20,000	1	20,000	0	20,000	96,111	9,367	105,748	625,516
6	41	0	1	0	0	0	106,693	8,761	115,455	625,516
7	42	0	1	0	0	0	114,056	7,885	121,941	625,516
8	43	0	1	0	0	0	126,435	7,009	133,444	625,516
9	44	0	1	0	0	0	135,126	6,133	141,259	625,516
10	45	0	1	0	0	0	150,703	5,257	155,960	625,516
				100,000	0	100,000				
11	46	0	1	0	0	0	163,005	4,381	167,386	625,516
12	47	0	1	0	0	0	182,539	3,505	186,044	625,516
13	48	0	1	0	0	0	197,328	2,628	199,957	625,516
14	49	0	1	0	0	0	220,793	1,752	222,545	625,516
15	50	0	1	0	0	0	238,618	876	239,494	625,516

Figure 17

Why is the Banking System so Powerful?

I have said all along that life insurance is a poor investment. Why settle for these returns when you can do much better with my "undertow investments"? One reason you may use a life insurance contract as a supplement or replacement retirement vehicle is that you are very conservative and feel like you need as much safety as possible. Life insurance contracts are very safe. The most important reason to take a hard look at funding a life insurance contract is to create the banking system I have been talking about.

Let me explain how this works. In our example above (Figure 17), I am showing how this thirty-five-year-old man is maximum funding his life insurance contract at $20,000 a year for five years—then he is done putting premiums into the plan. In a previous chapter, I told you that you could only borrow from the balance in your surrender cash value. By looking at the illustration above, you can see that he can start borrowing as early as the end of the first year. However, there is not a lot there so he may want to wait until the end of the second or third year.

Like any business, it takes time to capitalize the plan. Remember that you are creating a banking system that you will use the rest of your life, so be

58   *Moving at the Speed of Wealth*

patient. Understand that using the banking side of this component will take a few years.

Now, let's jump ahead. Although this man can borrow from the plan in year two, let's take a look at why this banking system is so valuable. To make sure I do not skew the numbers, let's look at this young man borrowing $98,600 in year seven to place in an investment that will double in value in five years (once again, this is very easy to do).

Important Note: *The reason I am jumping to year seven is to show you the results without skewing the picture by making premium deposits. Again, you can borrow much sooner but I am illustrating the power of the banking system.*

End of Year	Age	Model Premium	Times Per Year	Annual Premium	Cash From Policy	Annual Outlay	Non-Guaranteed Assumed Surr Cash Value	Surr Charge	Account Value	Death Benefit
1	36	20,000	1	20,000	0	20,000	3,890	13,142	17,032	625,516
2	37	20,000	1	20,000	0	20,000	24,887	12,266	37,153	625,516
3	38	20,000	1	20,000	0	20,000	46,107	11,390	57,496	625,516
4	39	20,000	1	20,000	0	20,000	70,896	10,514	81,410	625,516
5	40	20,000	1	20,000	0	20,000	96,111	9,367	105,748	625,516
6	41	0	1	0	0	0	106,693	8,761	115,455	625,516
7	42	0	1	0	98,600	98,600	8,601	7,885	121,941	520,061
8	43	0	1	0	0	0	13,650	7,009	133,444	512,061
9	44	0	1	0	0	0	14,499	6,133	141,259	504,889
10	45	0	1	0	0	0	21,691	5,257	155,960	496,504
				100,000	98,600	1,400				
11	46	0	1	0	0	0	25,024	4,381	167,386	487,535
12	47	0	1	0	-137,981	137,981	182,539	3,505	186,044	625,516
13	48	0	1	0	0	0	197,328	2,628	199,957	625,516
14	49	0	1	0	0	0	220,793	1,752	222,545	625,516
15	50	0	1	0	0	0	238,618	876	239,494	625,516

Figure 18

If a typical investor used $98,600 to invest in this investment that will double in five years, he would receive $197,200 at the end of year five. That is a 20% internal rate of return. He would also owe taxes on his profit of $98,600. Not a bad investment, taxes or not.

Our Speed of Wealth investor borrowed $98,600 from his plan in year seven and put the money in the exact same investment. Five years later, he collected $197,200, just like our typical investor above. Now our Speed of Wealth investor pays the loan back to the insurance company in the amount of $137,981 (although he does not have to, we recommend it). On the surface, this would seem like he only had a profit of $59,219. Again, on the surface, it seems like our typical investor did better because he had a profit of $98,600. How deceiving the surface can be.

While our Speed of Wealth investor only netted $59,219, after paying back the loan to the insurance company, take a close look at the column labeled "Account Value." Although our Speed of Wealth investor borrowed $98,600 from his policy, you will notice that no reduction was taken from the "Account Value" column when this money was borrowed; it shows a balance of $121,941. If you follow along that column for the next five years, you will notice it growing even though the money is not in the plan. By the end of the fifth year, this "Account Value" has grown to $186,044.

Herein lies the magic. You see, when you borrowed from the policy, the insurance company loaned you the money out of the company's general account at current corporate bond rates (in my example, I am using 6%). The insurance company then collateralizes your account and that is why you see a reduction in the column labeled "Surr Cash Value." This column reflects the true equity left in your plan.

This "phantom" money continues to grow even though it's in your hand and ultimately in another investment. Your "Account Value" grew from $121,941 to $186,044 in five years, or $64,103. This money grew tax-deferred inside the policy. On the outside you gained $59,219 before taxes. Add them both together and you have a total growth of $123,322, most of which was tax-deferred.

Important Note: *If you are wondering if the interest paid to the insurance company is tax-deductible, my answer is check with your accountant. I have my own ideas but they may be aggressive. For now, assume it is not tax-deductible. However, remember that we at Speed of Wealth believe you should own your own business…enough said.*

The typical investor gained $98,600, all taxable, from this investment. Our Speed of Wealth investor, putting his money in the exact same investment, gained $123,322. Our SOW investor is ahead by $24,722 using the same investment but with a different angle…he used the banking system.

By the way, let's not forget that a portion of the SOW investor's growth was tax-deferred and he had life insurance to protect his family over that same five-year period.

This book is not about life insurance. This book is about unconventional ways to build wealth and how you can build more wealth using the same investments by looking at them differently. As I said, life insurance is a poor investment but an awesome investment tool. This is what I tried to illustrate above, and I hope you are starting to see life insurance in a different light.

I do want to point out again that this is simply an illustration. The interest rate I used in the illustration to borrow money will change. The rate charged can be higher or lower. The returns inside the "Account Value" are illustrated at 9.1%, which is an historical average. Some years it could be 0% and other years it could be much higher than 9.1% because your returns are based on a stock market index (in this case, the S&P 500 Index®). Again, you must understand the principles of building wealth. Once you understand, you won't be able to help but grow richer.

Because this chapter is about how wealthy people get richer on small returns by using arbitrage to their advantage, I have included this banking side of the insurance piece. What you just witnessed was a small amount of arbitrage, within the insurance policy, working in your favor.

In our illustration, the SOW investor borrowed from the policy at 6% but the money continued to grow as if it were never taken out at 9.1%. He has created a 3.1% arbitrage while the money was placed in another investment. This will always create more growth. While our traditional investor saw an internal rate of return of 20%, the SOW investor's IRR was 24.66%. Remember that wealthy people get richer on small returns by creating arbitrage scenarios.

Chapter Five

Secret of the Super-Rich #5

Super-Rich People Know About the Best-Kept Secrets in the Investing Community

It's no secret that bankers are wealthy. I am not talking about the presidents of banks or the tellers or worker bees; I am talking about the owners of banks. Bankers set all the rules and because you have been conditioned your entire life, you simply follow the rules and block out the idea that they are creating a ton of wealth from your money...it's just part of life in America.

If bankers make all the wealth, and if banks are on every major street corner across America, then why are you *not* creating your very own banking system without all of the licensing requirements and scrutiny? The answer to this question is very simple: You just have not been shown how. Well, this chapter will give you some quick and easy answers to building tremendous wealth by becoming your own banker and guide you to the next steps you should be taking to continue your education process.

Introduction to Your Own Banking System

It doesn't take a genius to understand why banks make huge profits. It is a very simple and logical strategy that has been going on for centuries. If you can find some sucker who will loan you his money at a very low interest rate (that would be most of America), then turn around and loan that sucker's money out to some other proactive entrepreneur type (who understands that it takes money to make money) at a higher rate than you are borrowing from the sucker, then, well...you stand to make a whole heck of a lot of free money. Banks earn the majority of their money from arbitrage. This is a word that must now become ingrained in your mind. This one little word, when understood and put to work, will make you wealthy.

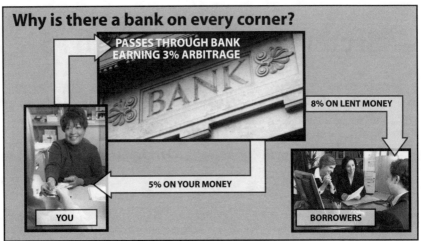

Figure 19

Figure 19 shows a slide that I use at my free introductory seminar that I conduct across the nation. When you deposit money into a certificate of deposit, money market fund, checking account or any other account that is considered a "cash equivalent account," you are essentially loaning money to the bank at a predetermined interest rate. This rate is usually lower than the "true" inflation rate, meaning you are losing money every day. Then the bank turns around and invests, or loans, your money to someone else at a higher interest rate and creates arbitrage in doing so.

In this example, you are depositing money in a certificate of deposit (a CD that is FDIC insured, but more on this later) with no guarantees—although you may think there are. The bank contracts to pay you 5% and on a $100,000 deposit, you will earn $5,000 annually that is usually taxable. If this money is not coming from a qualified retirement account or an individual retirement arrangement (IRA), then the interest is taxed as earned. Depending on your tax bracket, your true rate of return will decline. For example, if you are earning 5% on your money and you are in a 33% marginal state and federal tax bracket, your true return is only 3.30%, which, of course, is much lower than the true rate of inflation (discussed in a later chapter). In our example, the banker turns around and loans your money out at 8%. The spread between what they are paying you, 5%, and what they are receiving, 8%, is 3%, and this is pure arbitrage and pure gross profits or FREE money!

Just to make you feel worse, many times the bank just turns around and loans you your own money back at a higher rate (these guys have it figured out). Think of it: You deposit money in XYZ Bank and use XYZ Bank to finance a car. Boy, have you been taken to the cleaners!

Important Note: Always finance car purchases. Never pay cash; you are costing yourself hundreds of thousands of dollars in additional retirement savings when you pay cash for a car. You will learn more about this important topic in a later chapter.

So that you do not feel completely had, I want to point out that banks are allowed to borrow money from the federal government at a very low interest rate as well. This federal fund rate helps banks create arbitrage. The bank can borrow up to ten times the deposits they have on hand. It must be wonderful to be in the banking business. Unfortunately, you cannot borrow from the federal government at these rates; you are on your own.

Let's assume the bank has ten million dollars on deposit and is paying on average 5% to the depositors. The bank is paying out $500,000 to depositors each year. The bank loans it out at 8% and is collecting $800,000 each year, leaving them with gross profits of $300,000 each and every year. Obviously, the bank will borrow another $100,000,000 from the fed and loan that out and make more than $3,000,000 in gross profits each year. Not bad for a small bank in some small town. Imagine what the big boys do each and every year.

Now why would the federal government loan the bank this money at such a low rate when they, like you, know that the bank is just going to turn around and loan it to someone else at a much higher rate? The fed will do this for the same reason that you are doing it. You, like the fed, do not have the resources, knowledge, time or experience to find these folks to loan to at a higher rate.

It only stands to reason that if you could find people to loan your money to safely and bypass the middleman (bank) altogether, you probably would. If not, you should stop reading this book and pass it along to someone who is ready to invest to win and not to lose.

Obviously, if you were to loan your money to someone, you would like your money to be secured and have a reasonable interest rate paid back to you.

This money could easily come from your IRA, your 401(k) or any other asset you have, including your home equity. The trouble is, where do you go to find these folks and how do you structure it for safety?

This is where Speed of Wealth can step in and help you. We have people approaching us daily to borrow money who are willing to pay up to 25% for the privilege. You are the benefactor of these returns and your money is safe and secure in what I believe to be a safer place than in the bank.

If you are looking for a safe environment for your principal that provides predictable, consistent and long-term returns, look no further than deeds of trust or loans backed by real estate as collateral.

Deeds of Trust
One of the primary investments that I have participated in for over a decade has been deeds of trust, also known as a "mortgage" east of the Mississippi. Many of you may be familiar with them by the use of the term **hard money loans**, but the stigma tied to these is often false.

Most people believe that hard money loans are loans with a high interest rate made to people in desperate need of money: people facing foreclosure, in bankruptcy, without a job or facing any number of scenarios that would make a borrower look very weak to 'A' lenders (traditional banks).

While this is true with some hard money lenders, it's not the case when I make loans. I usually will make hard money loans to developers and real estate investors. These are people with excellent incomes, strong assets (many times, multiple millions of dollars) and great collateral (real estate holdings).

An Overview
Perhaps one of the best-kept secrets in the investment world today is how many people, of all ages and incomes, are earning very competitive returns and earning passive real estate income through high-interest private money loans (hard money loans) secured by trust deeds. As we say, as you go through the Speed of Wealth process, being the banker is much safer and more rewarding than being a direct investor in real estate.

What is a deed of trust? When an entity wants to borrow money, especially large amounts, banks will require collateral. If you have ever borrowed money to purchase a home, then you are very familiar with deeds of trust (mortgages). Here, you are on the **wrong** side of the fence. In other words, you have collateralized your home to borrow money to buy the home. More than likely, you are what is considered an 'A' borrower. You will get the most favorable interest rates, get the highest loan-to-value ratios (discussed later) and pay the lowest fees. You will also have a smorgasbord to choose from when it comes to different types of loans.

Many of you may be tired of hassling with tenants, contractors, leasing agents, real estate agents, brokers and attorneys. Trust deeds offer a way for investors to benefit from other people's efforts, stay in touch with real estate, and provide much better returns than they would typically receive in CDs, money market accounts, bonds and other low-risk, low-interest-paying options.

Simply put, trust deeds are the instruments that allow you to foreclose on the borrower if he does not follow the terms of the promissory note. Hard money loans are no more than private mortgages. These are short-term loans to real estate investors and/or homeowners secured by the value of the real property as collateral. These types of investors typically make between 12% and 18% annualized return, with monthly payments made to the lender, with relatively low risk. You can enhance your lifestyle dramatically, with little risk to your principal, in a short period of time.

When making these types of private loans, secured by trust deeds, you can anticipate a spread between prime rate of about 4% or more. What I mean by that is if the prime rate is 7%, you can generally add 4% to arrive at what interest rate you will charge the borrower—in this case, 11%. Because corporate bond rates and prime rates tend to move in the same direction, this ensures you will always create arbitrage when borrowing from your equity or insurance policy, creating the three-column wealth-building strategy (learn even more at *www.SpeedofWealth.com*).

Depending on the market, we will typically loan no more than 75% loan to value. Loan to value (LTV) is a percentage of the appraised value of the home (very conservative appraisals modified for market conditions). For example, if we are in a soft market, we might only loan to 65% LTV. If the home were conservatively appraised at $100,000, we would loan $65,000 and collateralize the $100,000 property.

Typically, but not always, we will loan to investors on income-producing properties and to developers, securing the land at an even lower loan-to-value ratio. The interest rate we can charge is sometimes predicated by the state in which we are loaning. Because of this, we prefer to loan to a commercial entity since laws governing commercial loans are much more lenient. When you start loaning to consumers that are having difficulty making payments on a lower interest rate loan, you will be accused of being a "predatory lender" and you will lose in a courtroom. We want to do business where it is a win-win for all parties.

We will examine the property and perform due diligence to ensure the appraised value is indeed the "fair market value" (fair market value being what

66 *Moving at the Speed of Wealth*

a prudent buyer would really pay for the property). Appraisals are not approached scientifically and can vary dramatically from one appraiser to the next. We use only selected appraisers who are aware of our conservative tendencies. We are not so concerned with the borrower. The property value and equity are our primary concerns. The number one question to consider in any loan is: If all goes bad for the borrower, do we want the property?

In the majority of cases, we will be looking for a first position or first lien. Occasionally, we will take a second position but the combined loan to value must still meet our requirements. Seconds are a bit riskier but offer higher returns. We will look at seconds on a case-by-case basis.

A typical loan may look like the following:

- Interest-only loan for six to twelve months with an extension option. Points will be required to extend the loan. The points charged to extend a loan will go to the investor.
- Ten percent or higher—this is what the investor receives and is determined by prevailing market conditions.
- Up to five points that may be financed into the loan. Points go to the originating loan company and to service the loans.
- Seventy-five percent or lower loan to value determined by market conditions where the property lies and by state laws.
- Typically, first lien position (seconds will be considered on a case-by-case basis).

Your money is very secure and backed by real estate. If you are at 75% LTV in a one-year note, the market would have to drop 25% in one year to put you in jeopardy. Remember, you still have the property to sell to get your principal back. If real estate markets drop this much in one year, where you put your money will be of little consequence because the entire U.S. economy would be in shambles.

Trust deeds pay out monthly to investors except in the case of foreclosure. If we have to foreclose on a property, the interest continues to accrue but it could take up to eighteen months or longer to finalize the procedure. During this time, the investor receives no monthly payments. This is one big factor in using trust deeds to diversify your portfolio. If you own ten trust deeds and one has to be foreclosed on, you continue to receive an income stream on the other nine. This is only important if you rely on the income stream. If not, then foreclosure proceedings just tie your money up longer but you typically will receive a higher return because each note has a higher default interest rate. As I said, interest continues to accrue and all costs involved to foreclose are added to the final payoff.

Once the foreclosure process is complete, the investor owns the property and can proceed in any fashion deemed fit to recover principal and interest:

1. You could hold on to the property and convert it to a rental.
2. You could improve the property and sell it traditionally.
3. You could sell or lease with option to buy (which is never the option I recommend).
4. You could sell the property at a discount to another investor (this is usually the option we choose). Remember that you are bankers now, not real estate investors.

We always recommend selling at a discount that actually improves your rate of return. The following is an example:

You loan $100,000 at 65% loan to value, twelve months at 12% interest plus four points. The points go to the originating company. The borrower's payment is $1,000 per month. The borrower makes six payments and defaults (we automatically initiate foreclosure thirty days after default). In a rare case, it could take twelve months to foreclose and the borrower owes us $112,000 (plus fees to initiate foreclosure, attorney fees, etc). The property was originally appraised at $154,000. We do a quick-fire sale (typically to another investor) at 80% of value or $123,200. We've added an additional profit of $11,200. Our total return over this eighteen-month period is $29,200. This profit, divided by the original investment of $100,000, equals a return of 29.2%, divided by eighteen months times twelve months, giving us an annualized return of 19.46%.

In these examples, what do you believe is the worst thing that could happen with this type of investment? Most people say foreclosure. Given the fact that we were patient and foreclosed—and increased our annualized rate of return to 19.46%—I'll tell you that the worst that can happen is that the borrower makes his or her payments.

You see, the borrower did all of the legwork to find and negotiate on this property. The borrower took all of the selling risk and probably sank some of his or her money into rehabilitating the property. We have very little risk. We want the property. Unfortunately, we very rarely get a property back by foreclosure. Most of these borrowers, when the loan is structured correctly, make the payments.

Rather than foreclose on the individual in the example above, more often than not we would probably offer to buy him or her out at the first sign of trouble. If we were to give the borrower $10,000 to walk away from the property and quit their claim to it (give us the title with a signature, which they are almost always happy to do when they are out of money), we could immediately flip the property to another willing investor. These kinds of investors are never hard to find.

Let's assume the borrower made four payments and found himself in money trouble. This borrower undoubtedly did some repairs on the property inside of this time period. The original loan to the borrower was $100,000 and the property is worth $154,000. You have collected $4,000 but we gave the borrower $10,000. We are now into this deal approximately $106,000, but we have no costs to foreclose. We now flip it to another borrower at 80% LTV for a purchase price of $123,200, giving us a profit of $17,200 (a sale price of $123,200, and money into the deal worth $106,000). Our return is 16% (a profit of $17,200, divided by the $106,000). Let's assume we could flip this to another borrower in one month. Our annualized rate of return is now 38% (16% return divided by five months times twelve months). Now that's a good, safe rate of return.

Many times if the borrower does not have enough equity in the property he is trying to borrow against, we can do a cross collateralization. For example, I had a borrower approach me in Denver who wanted to borrow one million dollars against his commercial building. The property only appraised at $1,500,000, which would have been a 67% loan to value. This is pushing it for me since he also asked me to finance the annual payments and closing costs, which brought the LTV even higher. I was leery and told him that there was not enough equity for me to make the loan.

During our discussions, I found out he also owned two other commercial properties with equity in them. I told him I would make the loan if he allowed me to put a deed of trust on the other two properties as well, tied to the one promissory note. I knew I was in second position on the other two properties but felt good with my new loan to value of 37%. I loaned him the money at 13% plus four points and all the payments for the year were collected up front. The total loan amount was $1.1 million or an annual payment of $143,000. Because I collected the payment up front, I was able to turn around and loan out this $143,000 to another investor at 13%. Essentially I was earning 15% on this commercial loan because I was able to reinvest the pre-collected payments.

The point is that you can get very creative about how to drive up your returns. We always have a late payment clause and a pre-payment penalty clause in our promissory notes. If the borrower is ten days late on a payment (which they almost always are), you charge 5% of the payment as a late fee. Assume that he makes every payment late for twelve consecutive months on a $100,000 loan with a payment of $1,000 per month. We would collect an additional $600 on top of the $12,000. Our new return is 12.6% annually.

Many clients ask us who would be crazy enough to borrow money at 12% or higher and pay these points. The answer is thousands of people—and, surprisingly, many very wealthy individuals. The trade-off is good for these types of borrowers because they can secure the money quickly (within forty-eight hours) and they do not have to provide financial history to a banker. Remember, all we care about is the property. Another question I am asked all the time is how we can make so many demands from the borrower. This comes down to the golden rule: **"He who has the gold makes the rules!"**

As you can see, investing in deeds of trust can be a very lucrative, safe place to earn better-than-average returns without all the hassles of being a real estate investor. Keep in mind that we reinvest every payment coming our way; this immediately drives up our returns even higher.

Combining a Properly Structured Insurance Policy as an Investment Tool with Safe Investments Like Deeds of Trust

Important Note: The following section is taken from our "Three-Day Intensive Investment Survival Bootcamp." You can learn more about attending a bootcamp at www.SOWBootcamp.com. Although you may feel a bit confused while reading this next section, lights should go on, suggesting that you should learn more. I highly recommend that you continue to read and don't miss any section of this book.

Let's assume, for this section, that you have listened to my advice and created your life insurance policy or "banking system," and you borrowed funds from your surrender cash value account in the policy to invest in trust deeds. By borrowing from your insurance policy at 6% (remember that the interest rate you can borrow at fluctuates and is tied to the prevailing AAA corporate bond rates), you can reinvest the funds at 12%. This rate will fluctuate over time but for this illustration I will assume an average interest rate to borrow from the policy of 6%, an average trust deed rate of 12%, and an average return within the policy of 9%, excluding cost of insurance and expenses.

Important Note: *Deeds of trust offer us an excellent way to always create arbitrage when we borrow from our policy. They provide us with the two columns of growth that we desire. Remember that as bond rates rise, so does the interest rate we can charge on these trust deeds—meaning that if the bond rates rise, the insurance company will charge a higher interest rate to borrow from your plan but the interest rate you can charge a borrower moves the exact same amount, always creating arbitrage.*

BORROW $100,000 FROM POLICY			
9%	6%	12%	
$ 9,000	$ (6,000)	$12,000	Gross Return
		$ (6,000)	Less Policy Loan
		$ (1,800)	Less Taxes
		$ 4,200	Net Return
		$ 9,000	1st Column Growth
		$13,200	Total Return

Figure 20

When looking at Figure 20, you can see that by borrowing from the policy, you have generated a 13.2% after-tax return on your money, assuming you are in the 30% federal and state marginal tax bracket. If you were to receive a 12% return on your money outside of the policy and outside of a qualified plan or IRA, your effective return would have been 8.4%. This is a big swing and will make a big difference. The chart below shows the difference in growth of $100,000 at an after-tax rate of return of 13.2% and 8.4%.

You can plainly see in Figure 21 that utilizing the insurance policy "banking system" and then investing in trust deeds makes a huge difference. By year ten, you have over $96,000 in additional growth and by year twenty, you have over $672,025 of additional growth.

Using IRA Money

No one said you can't invest in trust deeds with your IRA. In fact, we encourage this. You can simply roll over a portion or all of your IRA into a "self-directed IRA." I encourage every reader to start a self-directed IRA with at least a portion of your IRA. You can split your IRA as often as you like. We work with several

Secret of the Super-Rich #5

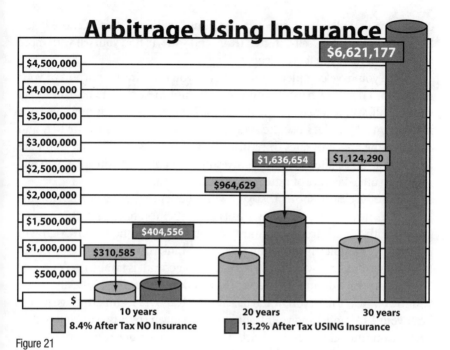

Figure 21

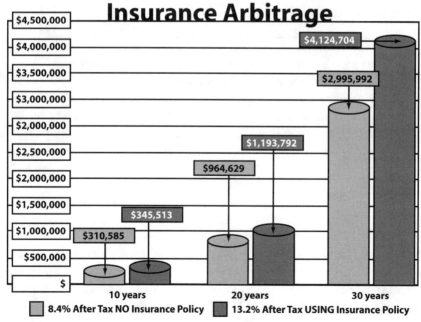

Figure 22

72   *Moving at the Speed of Wealth*

custodians that allow self-directed plans but I will cover this in more detail later. Simply Google® "self-directed IRAs" and you will find yourself with more information than you'll ever need.

Once you have completed this roll over, you can direct a portion of your money into deeds of trust. If you use us to find these private borrowers on your behalf, you will need to use the custodian that has already approved our investments. Now, let's use the same $100k but use funds in your IRA and compare the after-tax rates of returns. Using your insurance policy, you are receiving a 13.2% after-tax return. Investing straight from your IRA, you will receive an after-tax rate of return of 12%. Let's compare:

Figure 22 clearly shows that you will experience more growth with just 1.2% of arbitrage. By year thirty, this is dramatic. You have $1,128,712 more growth with the arbitrage. You must keep in mind that the 12% IRA growth columns are completely misleading. You may think you have good growth but every single dime you withdraw from your IRA account is taxable. Let's use our 30% tax bracket example. If you were to withdraw the entire $2,995,992 from your IRA in year thirty, you would be left with $2,097,194. Our arbitrage model beats your IRA model and your traditional thinking by over two million dollars because our model is tax-free (learn how at: *www.speedofwealth.com*) and the taxes have already been withdrawn (remember that I am showing you an after-tax rate of return).

Important Note: *For you accountants and other people that would like to trash me out here, I am fully aware of the difference between marginal and effective tax brackets. I realize you will not pay 30% on every dime you withdraw but the point is still the point. Better is better and taxes are taxes. Thank you for your contribution, though, because I need to stay on my toes. For the reader trying to get something out of this, I will continue pretending throughout this book that you will pay marginal taxes on every dime.*

To take it one step further, assume that you withdraw 10% from each account each year starting in year thirty since, after all, retirement income is what this is all about. If you withdrew 10% from your $2,995,992 IRA account, your withdrawal would be $299,599. However, now you're in a higher tax bracket. Also, taxes are likely to be higher in the future. I'll be conservative and place your tax rate at only 33%. Your tax bill on this one withdrawal is $98,868, leaving you a net withdrawal of $200,731. Your 10% withdrawal from your insurance and side account of $4,124,704 is $412,470, which is all tax-free. This is a $211,739 positive swing in your net income.

Just look at what happens in only ten years. Again, using our example above, you pull out 10% of each account. Pulling money from your IRA account leaves you a net income of $21,740. Pulling 10% from your newly formed Speed of Wealth system brings your net income to $34,551. That's $12,811 more income to you every year by utilizing a life insurance contract and you had life insurance to protect your family the whole time.

Our passion about this program should be clear. We are strong believers in this insurance policy because it provides a perfect tax shelter and banking system that will not only explode your wealth but the cash flow you can enjoy at the end of the day.

The Power of Leverage

"People leverage"—I want to make one thing perfectly clear: **You are more powerful as a group than you are as an individual.** You may not have $150,000 sitting around to invest in private loans secured by deeds of trust. You may not know how to find the investors or developers looking to borrow money. You may not know how to structure the deal or service the deal or foreclose if necessary.

We do! At Speed of Wealth, we just want you to invest money and sit on the beach in Bermuda drinking Mai Tais and watching the sun rise with your loved ones. We are approached on a daily basis by investors who are willing to pay these interest rates on their real estate loans. We know how to structure them and we know how to service and foreclose on them. This is what we do.

Knowing this, we have created partnership arrangements either in the way of mortgage pools or investment clubs formed as limited liability companies (LLCs) to allow you to take part in these excellent opportunities. You can invest as little as $10,000. You see, we believe that all investors, regardless of their wealth, have the right to higher returns. After all, higher returns and more wealth mean less reliance on the government in the future.

Leveraging people's money allows us to fund deals on a consistent basis and offer these returns to the partners. Unless you are prepared to do this yourself, then I recommend that you join The Speed of Wealth Gold Club™. Membership has special perks, including belonging to a like-minded group of people with similar goals and ambitions. To learn more, visit *www.SOWGold-Club.com*. We have created specific real estate investment clubs to help you with education and to bring opportunities to you that would not present themselves to you on your own.

"**Money leverage**"—One of the most powerful strategies that we teach our members is how to earn infinite rates of returns on your money and how to create $35,000 of tax-free income in ten years with no money out of your pocket by using a "dead asset."

What is this "dead asset"? I am talking about that huge investment you may have that is earning a 0% rate of return: your home equity. Think about this: Your home will appreciate at the same rate whether it is paid off or mortgaged to the hilt. This means that you have no return on home equity. (The truth is that home equity does have a small rate of return, but more about that in another lecture.)

While many Americans are going around pulling out equity to consume (you know, buy a boat, pay off credit cards, and go on vacation), you should pull out your home equity for one reason: to reinvest. Now, I could write an entire book on this subject but I decided to add just one chapter to this book to explain. Suffice it to say that once you are a member of the The Speed of Wealth Gold Club™, you will get more than your share of my arguments on this point.

Summary Regarding Private Loans Secured by DOTs

In my opinion, investing in deeds of trust is safer than investing in CDs or money market accounts, which are quite a bit safer than other investments. I don't know who it was that said high returns equate to high risk, but apparently he never made private loans secured by trust deeds. Your money is collateralized by something tangibly "real," as in real estate, not paper, such as stocks, bonds, mutual funds and the like. Land is true gold and it will always have intrinsic value.

If you don't have at least a portion of your portfolio in deeds of trust, then you are missing the boat and need to reconsider. After all, if you currently have a home loan, you are already familiar with these deeds of trust because you have signed one along with your promissory note. You need to get on the other side of the fence and increase your wealth, starting today, by visiting *www.SpeedofWealth.com.*

Take a look at the following diagram and make your own decision. This shows the difference in how your money would grow if you could have received an average return of the S&P 500 Index® (not reinvesting dividends) or 17% trust deeds in the last ten years starting with $100,000.

Yes, I said earning 17% per year and I am about to show you how. Keep in mind that the following chart shows your 17% growing in a compounding environment and trust deeds pay out monthly, so the final number is off just

Volatility vs. Consistency: $100,000 for 10 years

S&P 500 Returns Jan. - Jan.*	Growth**	Steady 17% Returns	Growth#
24.69% - 1998	$123,190	17%	$117,000
30.54% - 1999	$158,964	17%	$136,890
8.85% - 2000	$170,648	17%	$160,161
-1.93% - 2001	$164,795	17%	$187,388
-17.26% - 2002	$133,879	17%	$219,245
-24.29% - 2003	$99,352	17%	$256,517
32.19% - 2004	$129,843	17%	$300,125
4.43% - 2005	$133,647	17%	$351,146
8.36% - 2006	$142,815	17%	$410,841
12.36% - 2007	$158,325	17%	$480,684

$322,359.00

* S&P 500 Index, not reinvesting dividends
** Less 1.5% management and hidden fees
\#Compounding Tax Deferred

Figure 23

a little bit. Once you understand why you want to put this into a life insurance contract that is created specifically for banking, you will understand why Speed of Wealth is now sweeping the nation at warp speed. Don't you think it is time to see if you want to get on the boat and visit new frontiers? If so, then visit us at *www.SpeedofWealth.com* and let's build wealth together.

If you look at Figure 23, you will see that you would have had a total growth of $58,325 over the last ten years if you had your money invested in a S&P 500® Index fund less a 1.5% management fee. When you divide this profit of $58,325 by your original investment of $100,000, you have total returns of 58.32%. To compute your internal rate of return, you must now divide your total returns by the number of years, which was ten, for an annual return of 5.832%. This is the reality, folks. You just never took the time to do the math.

On the other hand, if you would have put your $100,000 in nice, safe private money loans backed by deeds of trust paying 17%, your total profit would have been $380,684. That is a total return of 360% or an IRR of 36% annually. Of course, this would be the case only if you were investing in private money loans within a shell that provided tax-deferral, such as an IRA (which you can do).

It doesn't take a mathlete to figure out which option would have been better. I hope these refreshing ideas are the reason you are reading this book.

Chapter Six

Secret of the Super-Rich #6

Super-Rich People Use Home Equity to Build Empires

Discover How You Can Build Tremendous Wealth, with No Money Out of Your Pocket, Using the Powerful "Speed of Wealth Equity Arbitrage Strategy"™!

Perhaps one of the most powerful wealth-building strategies around has been underutilized by Middle America since the beginning of today's modern home loan. The strategy that I am talking about has been used by the wealthy for decades and it is time to unleash its power to you. I am talking about building massive wealth with The Speed of Wealth Equity Arbitrage Strategy.™

This strategy is very simple yet powerful and, as always, I face people every day who do not understand its strength or who want to poke holes in its foundation. Of course, they are wrong and I hope to prove that to you in this chapter.

What is "equity arbitrage"? I use the term "arbitrage" slightly out of context here, but I am referring to the spread of money. It is very simple; if you can borrow money at 6%, reinvest the same money and receive a higher after-tax return, then you have an infinite rate of return on your money.

Because most Americans learned their financial skills from their parents, who previously learned it from their parents, it is easy to assume that most Americans' ideas of a home loan are archaic, at best.

Let me talk a bit about the Great Depression for a moment. Back in the "Roaring Twenties," the stock market was just exploding. Business was booming for America and with the accessibility of the market, everyday people wanted a piece of the pie. In particular, Middle America wanted a piece of the pie and they could easily buy stocks. With stocks appreciating at an alarmingly accelerated level, and Wall Street's greed kicking into place, brokers were all too willing to allow investors to buy stocks on margin. That means borrowing money from the broker to buy stock and paying the broker back when that stock climbs in value. This seemed like a no-brainer with what was happening in the market, and people kept on buying stock on margin.

In the meantime, Americans were borrowing more and more money from local banks to "mortgage" their homes. Whether the case was a farmer looking to expand by borrowing to purchase more equipment or just the layman trying to buy a house to live in, this was the beginning of home loans. Americans also saved at a much greater rate than they are doing today.

These "home loans" were not the same as today's home loans. These were recourse home loans made with collateral: the borrower's real estate. A recourse loan simply meant that the bank could call the loan due at any moment and without any cause.

Well, the rest is history. The stock market crashed and brokers were calling in their margin (margin calls). In other words, people had to sell their stocks at a much lower price and come up with the difference to pay back the brokers. These savers rushed to the banks to withdraw their money to pay the margin owed and you know what happened next. The banks did not have the cash on hand to allow these withdrawals and they closed their doors.

The next logical step for the bankers was to call in the mortgages due in order to raise the money that the depositors were trying to withdraw. Notices went out and foreclosures began. It did not matter whether the borrower was making payments on time or was a solid borrower—these loans were called in and many Americans lost their homes because they could not come up with the cash to repay these loans.

This is a very simplistic view of what happened to trigger the Great Depression but it should give you some kind of idea as to how your grandparents think. After witnessing, if not experiencing, these massive home foreclosures, they came to the conclusion that you should never owe money on your home. Today, home loans are made as *non-recourse loans*. This means that as long as you are performing to the terms of your promissory note, the lender cannot call the loan due for any reason. If you keep your "promise to pay" as outlined in the note, you're covered.

Regardless of these new types of loans, our grandparents and great-grandparents instilled their ideals in their kids and it continues to be passed down from generation to generation, "Pay off your home loan as soon as possible and do not mortgage your home." Nothing could be further from sound advice today.

I understand the appeal to having your home "free and clear"! In fact, there are times when I think it's what my wife and I should do but it just does not make financial sense. My contention is that if you have a home loan (backed by a mortgage or deed of trust) on your home right now, then you might as well be mortgaged to the absolute maximum.

Here is the most important caveat to be aware of. I am recommending that you take out the equity in your home. In order to achieve this, you must refinance your home utilizing a "cash out" refinance. When you receive this "cash in hand," it is important that you do not follow the herd and consume the money. This "live for today" attitude is what has gotten a lot of Americans in deep financial straits.

I am advocating that you reposition your equity in a safe investment that will create a spread to help you enjoy more money at retirement. Keep in mind that if you take out a home loan using one of the two loans that we recommend, an interest-only long-term fixed rate or the "mortgage accelerator" loan, you are paying simple interest on your money. If you place that money in a tax-deferred or tax-free compounding environment earning the exact same interest rate as you are paying on the loan, you will still win the game (as witnessed in Chapter Three).

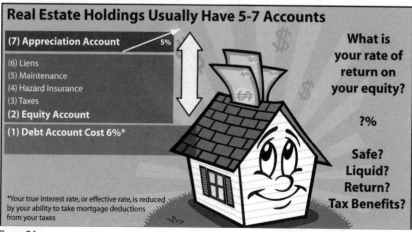

Figure 24

Moving at the Speed of Wealth

It's important to realize that your home has between five and seven accounts associated with it. Knowing this, you should be able to conclude that if you want to make the best of your investment, then you absolutely must *manage* your accounts in order to build wealth. Truth be told, your primary residence is typically a poor investment, as illustrated in my report, "The Banker vs. the Real Estate Investor," which can been viewed at *www.SpeedofWealth.com.*

Figure 24 illustrates these seven accounts that you may or may not have tied to your primary principal residence.

1. **Debt Account**—This is your underlying home loan. Some of you may have your home completely paid off, so you would not have this account—but for most Americans, this is reality. You can see that this "Debt Account" is costing you 6% per year. The question is: Are you really paying 6%? The answer for most of you is a big, fat NO! Most of us are entitled to home mortgage interest deductions from our taxes, one of the last true tax deductions left. This is a tax deduction right off the top of your income statement and it affects your marginal tax bracket. If you were in the 28% federal tax bracket, your "true effective" interest rate on this home loan is closer to 4.32%. Folks, that is very cheap money. If you have a $100,000 home loan and an interest-only rate of 6%, you paid $6,000 in interest during the year. You are going to save $1,680 in taxes at the end of the year so the true amount out of pocket to you is $4,320. When you divide your true out-of-pocket expense of $4,320 by the loan amount of $100,000, you have an interest rate of 4.32%. This is money you are not sending to Uncle Sam so it is real money to you. The problem is that you don't feel it monthly so you disregard it and continue to think your true interest rate is 6%. Now, I ask you: Do you think you may be able to borrow out some home equity at this true effective rate of 4.32% and reinvest it some place that provides a higher return? Remember that this is simple interest and you can actually reinvest this money in a compounding tax-deferred or free account and receive only 4.32% on your money, winning the game in the long run. This was explained thoroughly in Chapter Three.

2. **Equity Account**—Equity is what we are talking about in this chapter. Equity is the portion of the home that you own. Equity

is the difference between what you owe the lender and what the true fair market value of your home is. If you owe $50,000 and your home is worth $100,000, you have $50,000 of equity or the portion of the home you own is $50,000. Remember that the bank has a lien on the other $50,000 so, in essence, it belongs to the bank. Some of you may not currently have equity in your home. You may have just moved in, property values may have tumbled and you may actually owe more on the home than its true market value. Or you may have totally disregarded wealth-building strategies and have already taken out your equity and consumed it. Remember that paying off credit cards with home equity is the same as equity consumption. We are teaching you to reposition your equity and conserve it, but more on that later. If you currently do not have equity, give it time; you will build equity as time goes by if you leave it alone—and as you build equity, implement the strategy presented here and it will go a long way in helping you build wealth.

3. **Tax Account**—Most states in the union charge a property tax. This tax is usually set aside for the school district in which the property sits, but not always. Regardless of what the tax is used for, it is a tax and it costs you money. Taxes are a *liability* and if you do not pay your property tax bill, you will have a tax lien in first position. These tax liens represent the taxes owed plus fees and a state imposed annual interest rate. These tax liens are then auctioned off to, believe it or not, the lowest bidder—meaning that, in most states, the person who is willing to take the lowest annual interest rate can purchase the lien. The property owner has quite a bit of time to cure the lien plus fees and interest owed. Stay up late one night and dig into those infomercials. You are sure to find one claiming all the money you can earn with property tax liens and how you can own real estate for pennies on the dollar. Save your money. If you do purchase a property tax lien, the chances that you will ever take possession of that property for what you bought the lien for are slim to none unless the property is useless or condemned, and this is few and far between. On top of that, many purchasers of these liens are willing to take a mere 6% or less return on their money due to the safety of these liens. Make no mistake: These liens are probably one of the safest places

to put your money. You may have a first position lien for $5,000 and the property could be worth $100,000 or more—pretty darn safe. But 6% is not keeping up with inflation and you lose when the game is over. I am not here to go into tax liens (though there are many courses on the subject) because buying tax liens will not make you wealthy and that is what I am trying to teach you: how to build wealth. Remember that every state has different rules regarding tax liens so you must spend a great amount of time and energy not only learning the rules of each state but inspecting the properties you are interested in. Whether your home is totally free and clear of a mortgage or not, you will still owe property taxes.

4. **Homeowners (Hazard) Insurance Account**—If you borrow money to purchase a home, you are required to have hazard insurance on the property during the entire lifetime of the loan. Even if your home is free and clear, you would be a fool not to continue to carry hazard insurance. Hazard insurance is not that expensive but make sure you read the fine print. You need to be absolutely aware of what you are covered for. Hazard insurance typically will not cover you for floods; that would be flood insurance, which is very expensive. Be careful when making claims; you could be in for a shock when they adjust your premium. Once again, if you are wise, you will always carry hazard insurance on your home and this is an ongoing expense or liability.

5. **Maintenance Account**—This is perhaps the biggest expense of all next to the debt account. A home is very expensive to maintain. The improvement on the land (the actual structure sitting on the lot) is depreciable for a reason. Homes wear out over time and must be kept up. It's not only all that yard work, it's everything, from occasional painting to your hot water tank breaking down to concrete splitting and cracking, wood rot, masonry rot, the normal wear and tear on carpet (forget about it if you have a pet), appliances, wiring, plumbing, wall panels, etc. You get my point. Maintaining a home in good order is very expensive and is seldom factored in when people contemplate buying a home. You have the advantage with rental properties of taking tax deductions for these costs. By the way, you have to spend money to save taxes. I don't understand why you would want to spend $100 to

Secret of the Super-Rich #6

save \$28; that just doesn't make sense to me (however, the phantom depreciation deduction does make sense). Your friendly neighborhood IRS agent will not allow you to take tax deductions for the expenses incurred on your primary principal residence (although you could deduct a percentage of these costs if you owned a viable home-based business, covered in yet another chapter). Make no mistake, your maintenance account will cost you a whole lot of money over the years and it, too, is a liability.

6. **Lien Accounts**—I already mentioned that if you have a home loan, you have a lien on your home. If you owe back property taxes, you have a lien on your home. If you have a home equity line of credit (HELOC), you have a lien on your house. If you fail to pay someone that has done work on your home, you may have a mechanic's lien on your house. If you are sued and lose the case, chances are the winning party will sooner or later slap a lien on your house. And take it from someone who knows: If you owe the feds or state back taxes, you will have an ugly lien placed on your house. You cannot sell your home or refinance without satisfying all liens. It is very difficult to protect your primary principal residence from predators attaching liens. If you create a corporation and deed ownership of your home to the corporation, you have some protection. The problem is that when you go to sell the home, it will be treated more like an investment than a personal residence. You are foregoing your standard exemption (I will not go into this here; that is a tax course left to the professionals). Putting your home in a trust will not protect it, either (unless it is the right kind of trust) but, just in case, check with a competent trust attorney. When you become a member of The Speed of Wealth Gold Club™, you can log onto my website and I will show you how I made 24,000% annually by using liens. Anyone reading this book can do the same thing—and no, that was not a misprint: You can make 24,000% annually on your money. It is great to have a little bit of knowledge. I also spill the beans on this unique approach at my workshops. Anyway, by now I am sure you know what I am about to add: Liens are a liability.

7. **Appreciation Account**—This is the account that has everyone freaking out in today's market. It is very important to note that

homes will typically appreciate at the same rate as inflation. Houses do not grow new rooms; purchasing power drives up house prices. Purchasing power is directly affected by one or two independent economic conditions. First, your purchasing power will increase as your income increases and it will increase more as you eliminate non-preferred debt such as credit cards. Secondly, your purchasing power increases as interest rates fall. As rates go down, you can qualify for a larger loan with the same monthly payment. As interest rates increase, housing prices decrease. This is one of the reasons you are seeing the Federal Reserve lowering interest rates today; they are trying to spur the real estate market. Unfortunately, it is not helping due to the massive amounts of surplus currently on the market and the high rate of foreclosures...but more on this later. Homes can and will depreciate but, over time, homes will appreciate in value. According to the National Association of Realtors® (NAR), houses have appreciated on average across the entire country at a rate of 7.25% since the early 1970s. This should be sufficient evidence that inflation is much higher than you are being told. As we go forward, we will assume an average appreciation rate of only 5%.

There you have it. You may not have all seven accounts on your home but, as you can see, of the seven accounts only two are positive (equity and appreciation); the rest are liabilities.

Let me ask you some very important questions.

Q. Is your home an asset or a liability?

A. This is the million-dollar question. I am sure that if I were to ask you what the average American's largest asset is, your answer would be their home. This, of course, is what you have heard for your entire life. First of all, your house is not your largest asset; the *equity in the house* is the asset. If you have an underlying home loan, the bank owns that portion of your home.

Equity in homes is decreasing at an alarming rate for two very obvious reasons. During the past three years, I am sure that you have become aware of the sub-prime loans that were handed out to just about anyone so long as they had a pulse. People were using their home equity just like an ATM. Whenever they had the urge to purchase something, they would simply pull it out of their home equity and consume the equity. This is what is causing a big problem in

America today: the consumption of home equity on wants, not needs. Keep in mind that many of the borrowers who were being permitted to borrow money to buy a house had absolutely no business buying a home in the first place and had no idea what an adjustable rate mortgage was, let alone realize that they would be forced to make higher payments in the very near future—payments they would never be able to afford. Once again, Wall Street's greed has stuck it to the greater good of the American public. Couple that with all the home loan fraud and you have the ingredients for a nightmarish ending. When money is so easily found to buy a home and initial interest rates are so low, a simple economic theory ensues: Higher demand for homes means higher prices on homes. This is exactly what we experienced across the nation in the not too distant past: an artificial increase in the values of homes.

Free economies are a beautiful thing unless you get caught up in all the hype. All markets will eventually correct themselves. Many people who did not understand that they would have to cough up larger payments in about two to three years didn't really mind because they figured that they would simply sell their homes for a huge profit and move on. When these mortgages did start to adjust, people could not keep their promise to the bank and the bank used the instrument they had to repossess the underlying collateral: the borrower's home (the instrument is a deed of trust or mortgage, depending on what state you live in). This is commonly referred to as foreclosing on the borrower. Many other people had no intention of making payments in the first place and figured it would be a great way to live rent-free for one or more years.

Today we are seeing a huge downward adjustment in the values of real estate in about half of the major U.S. markets. Again, this is simple economics. With all of the foreclosures, there is a glut of properties on the market or too much supply for the demand. The demand has gone down because lenders have tightened their lending criteria and we live in a less liquid environment. When supply is high and demand is driven down, you will have a natural retraction in prices. Truth be told, these prices are going to continue to adjust until supply and demand even out and as I write this, there is no telling when these two lines will actually meet.

Equity in homes in America is shrinking because of the poor financial education of consumers and because of supply and demand forcing values down. I think it is safe to say that the largest asset of the average American is no longer their home (equity). In a moment, I will tell you why a *home loan* can be the average American's largest asset, but back to the original question: Is your home an asset or a liability?

I have to agree with Robert Kiyosaki on this one. In *Rich Dad Poor Dad,*

Kiyosaki points out a not so clear point to the reader. Assets produce income and liabilities produce cash outflows. Now, assuming your home is 100% free and clear—that is, you have no home loan on the property—does your primary principal residence (the home you live in) produce income? Of course not! In fact, you are probably paying property taxes, homeowner's insurance, maintenance costs, and maybe homeowner's association dues on this home monthly or at the very least annually. Obviously, these are cash outflows, which define a liability.

Your home is certainly an asset on paper. Let me ask you another question: Do you think you can walk down to the local grocery store, fill your basket full of the essentials you need to live on, and, when you go to the checkout line, write an IOU based on your equity to the cashier? In other words, can you buy groceries with home equity? No, you cannot! Now, typically, at my seminar, someone will stand up and say that you can refinance your home to pay for these bills or use for cash flow, or sell your home, downsize and pocket the equity. Precisely, yes, you can—but the minute you pull the equity out of your home, it is no longer equity.

The equity in your home does not provide a return that you can tap into for income. Equity will never and has never produced income for people—unless, of course, you take the equity out of your home by putting a loan on the property. This could be a regular mortgage or a reverse mortgage but this would increase your debt load. In the case of a regular mortgage, it increases your monthly payment or outflow of cash. (Keep reading because this is what this chapter is all about.)

Over your working years, you try to accumulate assets that will produce income for you during retirement. Yet we are told that the average American's largest asset is the home (home equity) and it cannot produce income while you are living in it. This seems like a colossal waste of an asset to me.

Yes, your home equity is an asset on paper, yet it is an asset that is "dead"! It is useless to you for the most part, yet most people try to create more of it over their lifetime. Remember that the entire purpose of investing and building wealth is for income replacement during your non-working years. Equity does not provide income.

As you move along in this chapter, you will find that my recommendation is to increase your home loan and remove your equity, not to consume it but to conserve and reinvest the equity. You must understand that interest charged on home loans, coupled with the home interest tax deduction, is the cheapest money you can borrow. Instead of calling it an increase in debt, you must think differently; you must now call it "employment costs."

If you own a business and have employees, you know that this costs you monthly outflow of cash. The only reason you would hire an employee is if that employee can make you more money than you are paying him/her. If you are paying that employee ten bucks an hour (plus payroll taxes), that employee better be saving you or making you more than that or it is time to let him go. This is nothing more than employee costs. Now I am recommending putting your equity (money) to work for you so start thinking of it as employee costs. As long as you can produce a spread of money, or receive the same returns in a compounding tax-deferred or free environment, then you win in the long run.

To top it off, the moment you pull out your equity and create this spread, your net worth increases. Take a look at the following example:

Unlock Your Equity and Increase Your Net Worth on Day One				
ASSETS (Current)		**ASSETS** (1 year later)		
Home Value	**$300,000.00**	**Home Value**	**$300,000.00**	
		Equity Investment	**$100,000.00**	
		Gross Interest Earned	*$12,000.00*	
		Employment Cost	*-$6,000.00*	
		Net Gain	*$6,000.00*	
Liabilities		**Liabilities**		
Loan	**$200,000.00**	**Loan**	**$300,000.00**	
Net Worth	**$100,000.00**	**Net Worth**	**$106,000.00**	

1 year later (assumes no property appreciation)
Figure 25

In Figure 25 above, you have two homeowners with identical homes and identical home loans. The borrower on the left has a home with a fair market value of $300,000 and an underlying home loan of $200,000 (I use the term "home loan" because a mortgage is the recorded instrument used to give the lender the ability to foreclose). Disregarding all other assets, this homeowner has a home "net worth" of $100,000; this represents the borrower's equity.

Our second homeowner on the right understands this book and decides to refinance his home, take out the $100,000 of equity and reinvest it in a hard money loan secured by a deed of trust paying 12% annually. This person can take the $100,000 out of the home with an interest-only loan at 6%. This would cause the homeowner to have an *employment cost* of $6,000 per year. The $100,000 loaned out at 12% generates income of $12,000 per year. Disregarding tax deductions on the $6,000 (home interest deductions when pulling out equity is a bit tricky; you can typically only go $100,000 over the current loan to receive a deduction—talk to a professional tax consultant to fully understand) and taxes owed on the $12,000 passive income, the homeowner is left with $6,000. At the end of the year, assuming no property appreciation, our left side borrower has $100,000 net worth and our right side borrower has $106,000 net worth. With the equity pulled from the home and put to work in the right investment, the equity now becomes an income-producing asset.

Now, assume the property appreciates in value 5% over the year. The borrower on the left will have a net worth of $115,000 (5% appreciation on a $300,000 home is $15,000) but our borrower on the right has a net worth of $121,000. Remember that the $100,000 used to invest does not disappear; in the investment illustrated, the principal will have to be paid back to you at a predetermined time.

In light of the current state of real estate, let's look at an example that will really open your eyes. Let's take a look at these same borrowers but now let's assume that the property depreciates 15% over the year.

Unlock Your Equity and Increase Your Net Worth on Day One			
ASSETS (Current)		**ASSETS** (1 year later)	
Home Value	$285,000.00	**Home Value**	$285,000.00
5% Depreciating Market		**Equity Investment**	$100,000.00
		Gross Interest Earned	*$12,000.00*
		Employment Cost	*-$6,000.00*
		Net Gain	*$6,000.00*
Liabilities		**Liabilities**	
Loan	$200,000.00	**Loan**	$300,000.00
Net Worth	$85,000.00	**Net Worth**	$106,000.00

1 year later (assumes no property appreciation)
Figure 26

As you can see in Figure 26, the fair market value of the home has depreciated to $285,000. The homeowner on the left now has a net worth of only $85,000. The smart homeowner on the right still has a net worth of $106,000 at year's end. Really, this is simple math; his home depreciated to $285,000 but he already took out the $100,000 of equity and put it to work. Even though the home depreciated, the bank cannot call the loan due unless he is not making his payment. Keep in mind that $100,000 is still available and has only been repositioned into an outside investment. The investment is making the payment and earning a net difference of $6,000 by year's end. If this smart homeowner is forced to sell his home, he can easily bring money to the table and still come out $6,000 better off than the homeowner that leaves his equity in the home.

If you understand what was just presented to you, then you should understand that if you believe your home will go up in value, depreciate in value or remain the same, you are nonetheless better off pulling out your equity in all three scenarios—*and* you are liquid (covered below).

These examples should show you that equity in your home is only a paper asset with no real rate of return. Your home will appreciate in value at the exact same rate regardless of what the underlying home loan is. The market does not know anything about your home loan; appreciation is tied only to the home itself, not the home loan.

Q. Is your home equity safe?

A. The answer is a solid NO! Imagine that you are wealthy and you own a two-million-dollar home on the top of a cliff overlooking the Pacific Ocean in Southern California. Your home is paid off and you are living mortgage-free. You travel to work one rainy day and receive a call from the fire department. On the other end of the line, the caller gives you some very disturbing news. "Sir, we had to call to notify you that your home was built on top of a mudslide area and your home, along with everything inside of it, is now sitting in the Pacific Ocean." It's a call I hope nobody ever has to receive—yet it has been made on several occasions. You just had two million dollars of your net worth slide into the ocean with no way to recover it because hazard insurance does not cover mudslides. Or imagine you lived in New Orleans during Hurricane Katrina. You have heard the horror stories of people losing their homes and the insurance companies not paying...but why? First of all, understand that many of those homes were totally paid off or had a lot of equity sitting inside them. Now understand that it was not the hurricane that wiped those homes off the city grid but rather the flood caused by the barges breaking down around the lake. Alas, now you know why insurance companies are claiming that they do not owe these homeowners money; it wasn't the hurricane but the floodwaters that

90   *Moving at the Speed of Wealth*

destroyed their homes and standard hazard insurance does not cover floods—flood insurance covers floods.

Very conservative people invest only in very safe investments (only to lose in the end) and believe that home equity is the safest place of all. Yet I just showed you two real examples of people losing their entire investment in one massive stroke. Is home equity truly as safe as you believe it to be?

Let's take this a step further. Now imagine that you have a twin and you love each other to death and have been best friends since birth. You cannot be separated so you both decide to buy the exact same model home on the exact same street in the same subdivision. Your homes are identical and you both pay $300,000 for them. You decide to take out a 100% loan to value home loan and your twin makes a large down payment. In fact, your twin puts 50% down or $150,000. You had the $150,000 but attended a Speed of Wealth function and decided to keep your money growing and borrow the other $150,000. At a 6% interest-only loan, your payment is about $9,000 more than your twin's every year. Keep in mind that you also receive additional tax deductions on the $9,000 so your "true effective" out-of-pocket expense at the end of the year is less. You are starting to believe in Moving at the Speed of Wealth™ and understand that "lump sums of money grow larger than periodic payments." You totally retrained your financial wealth IQ and now understand that every time you send that additional $9,000 to the lender, you are doing nothing more than making a $9,000 annual contribution to your retirement fund. You understand that, although you are sending off an additional $9,000 to a lender, you have a lump sum of $150,000 already working for you in an investment.

Your twin decides to go it old school and takes out a 30-year amortized loan at 5.5% interest. The total monthly payment is $851.68 toward principal and interest (I do not include taxes and insurance because that would remain the same for both of you regardless of the type of loan). Your twin will pay a total of $306,604.80 back to the lender over the life of this loan. This means that your twin paid $156,604.80 in interest, which, in most cases, is tax-deductible. If you and your twin were both in the 30% marginal state and federal tax bracket, your twin would save approximately $51,680 in taxes over that thirty-year period (this is for illustration purposes only and you must understand effective tax rates to get a full understanding).

You, on the other hand, understand that you never want to have your primary residence paid off; you want the ability to pay off your home at any given moment. You decide to borrow $300,000 at 6% with an interest-only loan.

Secret of the Super-Rich #6

> **Important Note:** *I am only trying to make a point here. You will probably need to put down 20% to avoid mortgage insurance premium or take out a 10% second mortgage to avoid this premium. There are currently no 100% LTV loans, for the most part. You will also notice that your interest rate is a half percent higher than your twin's because, unlike in the past, lenders are charging more for interest-only loans. Also, it is very unlikely that either one of you will remain in your home for the full thirty years, and interest rates will be different on your next loan. The strategy is the same regardless, so learn the principles I am trying to teach you.*

Your interest-only payment is $1,500 per month, which is only $648.32 more than your twin's, but you have $150,000 liquid to reinvest. You will pay $540,000 back to the bank over thirty years and save $178,200 in taxes. You saved $126,520 more than your twin in taxes but by year thirty, you have paid $233,396 more to the lender than your twin has. Now it is important to hang in with me because the fun is about to really begin.

So that we can compare apples to apples, your twin decides to invest the difference between your payments every month in the same investment where you put your $150,000. Let's just say you make a hard money loan and receive a 12% annual return on your money. You both read this book and understand that you must own your own business and understand that we can set up a self-directed 401(k) for you so your money will grow tax-deferred and will compound annually.

At the end of year thirty, your twin's periodic monthly investment of $649 grows to an astonishing $1,999,552. That is a whole lot of money; of course, we have not factored in inflation. Lo and behold, your lump sum investment of $150,000 in this same investment has grown to $4,493,988. Your twin received total tax deductions of $77,101.20 over the thirty years (providing s/he stays in the same tax bracket and Congress does not change the rules). This gives your twin a total of $128,781.20 in tax deductions over thirty years when you add in the home interest deduction. You, on the other hand, received a home interest tax deduction of $178,200 on your interest-only loan and a one time tax deduction of $49,500 when you deposited your $150,000 into your self-directed 401(k) (a bit more complicated, but it can be done), for total tax deductions over the thirty years of $227,700. You still received better tax advantages.

Let's forget about taxes for now. Going back to the difference in growth of your $150,000 lump sum and your twin's $649 monthly periodic payments, it is clear who came out the winner. Yet both of you are out of pocket the exact same amount of money and you were both in the exact same investment.

Results Summary

Starting amount	$150,000
Years	30
Additional contributions	$0 per month
Rate of return	12.00% compounded annually
Total amount you will have contributed	$150,000
Total at end of investment	**$4,493,988**

Savings Balance by Year

Year	Additions	Interest	Balance
Start	$150,000		$150,000
1	$0	$18,000	$168,000
2	$0	$20,160	$188,160
3	$0	$22,579	$210,739
4	$0	$25,289	$236,028
5	$0	$28,323	$264,351
6	$0	$31,722	$296,073
7	$0	$35,529	$331,602
8	$0	$39,792	$371,394
9	$0	$44,567	$415,962
10	$0	$49,915	$465,877
11	$0	$55,905	$521,782
12	$0	$62,614	$584,396
13	$0	$70,128	$654,524
14	$0	$78,543	$733,067
15	$0	$87,968	$821,035
16	$0	$98,524	$919,559
17	$0	$110,347	$1,029,906
18	$0	$123,589	$1,153,495
19	$0	$138,419	$1,291,914
20	$0	$155,030	$1,446,944
21	$0	$173,633	$1,620,577
22	$0	$194,469	$1,815,047
23	$0	$217,806	$2,032,852
24	$0	$243,942	$2,276,794
25	$0	$273,215	$2,550,010
26	$0	$306,001	$2,856,011
27	$0	$342,721	$3,198,732
28	$0	$383,848	$3,582,580
29	$0	$429,910	$4,012,490
30	$0	$481,499	$4,493,988

Figure 27

Figure 20 shows you another huge advantage of reinvesting your money instead of using it as a down payment. Look very closely at year seven and move your eyes over to the last column that shows your accumulation. You will see that the number is **$331,602.** Holy bologna sandwich, Batman! You have the ability to pay off your home loan in its entirety by the end of the seventh year. You actually accelerated the payoff of your home by putting this money to work. In fact, although I don't condone it, if you are dead-set on paying off your principal residence, you will actually accelerate the payoff by pulling out your equity and reinvesting the money in almost every scenario.

Now, let's look at your twin's financial picture below.

Results Summary

Starting amount	$0
Years	30
Additional contributions	$649 per month
Rate of return	12.00% compounded annually
Total amount you will have contributed	$233,640
Total at end of investment	**$1,999,552**

Savings Balance by Year

Year	Additions	Interest	Balance
Start	$0		$0
1	$7,788	$497	$8,285
2	$7,788	$1,492	$17,565
3	$7,788	$2,605	$27,958
4	$7,788	$3,852	$39,599
5	$7,788	$5,249	$52,636
6	$7,788	$6,814	$67,238
7	$7,788	$8,566	$83,592
8	$7,788	$10,529	$101,909
9	$7,788	$12,726	$122,423
10	$7,788	$15,188	$145,399
11	$7,788	$17,945	$171,133
12	$7,788	$21,033	$199,954
13	$7,788	$24,492	$232,234
14	$7,788	$28,366	$268,388
15	$7,788	$32,704	$308,879
16	$7,788	$37,563	$354,230
17	$7,788	$43,005	$405,024
18	$7,788	$49,100	$461,912

Figure 28 (continues)

Year	Additions	Interest	Balance
19	$7,788	$55,927	$525,627
20	$7,788	$63,573	$596,987
21	$7,788	$72,136	$676,911
22	$7,788	$81,727	$766,426
23	$7,788	$92,469	$866,683
24	$7,788	$104,499	$978,970
25	$7,788	$117,974	$1,104,732
26	$7,788	$133,065	$1,245,585
27	$7,788	$149,968	$1,403,341
28	$7,788	$168,898	$1,580,027
29	$7,788	$190,101	$1,777,916
30	$7,788	$213,847	$1,999,552

Figure 28 (continued)

Because your twin is amortizing the loan, s/he is reducing the principal paid each year and, in turn, reducing tax deductions each and every year. Your twin will be able to pay off the home loan somewhere between the ninth and tenth years. Not only were you able to pay off your home loan sooner, but you received greater tax deductions and you were liquid, which brings us back to our original question: Is home equity safe?

Two years pass by and you are both doing fine. You both work for a small aviation company and arrive one day to work only to find the doors are locked for good. You are both out of a job. Your twin used every dime of savings as a down payment. Your twin cannot make the loan payment. The $150,000 that you did not use as a down payment can now be used to make the loan payment while you look for work.

Because your twin was putting about $649 per month aside in our investment, she has accumulated $17,565 in savings. Your twin's monthly payment is about $851.68 (not counting taxes and insurance) and she can continue to make the home loan payment for just less than twenty-one months before her savings is depleted. You, on the other hand, are very liquid and have accumulated $188,160 in your savings account. Your payment is $1,500 per month and your savings would allow you to make your home loan payment for almost ten-and-a-half years before you could no longer make them. With a little more time on your hands, you may be able to hold out for a better job than your twin...just a small point I felt like making.

You see, it doesn't matter that you have a higher loan payment. After twenty-one months, your twin cannot make the payment, period. You can.

Secret of the Super-Rich #6

That aside, what if neither of you could afford your loan payment and I was your banker? Who do you think I am going to foreclose on first? Your twin has $150,000 of equity and you have none. Chances are, as the banker, I am going to foreclose on the home with equity quickly and try to make some kind of payment arrangement with you. As a banker, I do not want the properties and I especially do not want a property that has no equity.

These are just three examples of why home equity is not safe. However, the story for the person who continues to think paying off the primary principal residence is a good idea gets worse.

Q. Is your home equity liquid?

A. The answer is, "Of course it is"—that is, if everything in your life is going exactly as planned. Once again, let's look at our twins above. We talked about your twin who used every dime of savings as a down payment on the purchase of a home. I showed you how your twin lost her job a few years down the path, which happens to thousands of Americans every year, often times with absolutely no warning. The payment on your home is about $18,000 a year or about $1,500 per month. You have your original $150,000 sitting in a side account earning interest (the purpose of this example is to show you how to not only make that payment but build wealth at the same time; hang in there with me…these points are important). Your side account of $150,000 will allow you to make your loan payment for 100 months while you find your next income-earning opportunity. Your twin is stuck and the pressure mounts.

Now, I know what you are thinking: Your twin can simply go down to the local lender, borrow out all of the equity and be in the same position you are in… Read on!

Your twin decides that she has great credit and a wonderful history with the lender and decides to go down to the local bank, where she has great rapport, to borrow back the original $150,000 down payment like you did originally. Let's stop here and discuss the four major criteria used when lenders make a decision to loan you money (and remember that, today, these criteria have been tightened):

- **Your willingness to pay:** This is your credit and we stated that your twin has great credit and a good history of making payments to the lender on time.
- **The collateral:** The value of the property being loaned

against. In our example, regardless of what is going on in the housing market, your twin has plenty of equity. If the value of the home is the exact same as when the loan was taken out, there is $150,000 in equity. In the old days, this would have been enough but with the recent sub-prime loan collapse, 'A' lenders care very little about this.

- **Your current debt:** This is called your "debt-to-income ratio" and is becoming a bigger factor in today's lending environment. Back in the day, you could have five, maybe more, investment property loans at any given time and lenders would have still loaned you money. Not today. If you have a primary residence loan and just one more investment property loan, it could be hard to find another loan. In years past, lenders were willing to stretch these ratios but today they are sticking really close to the guidelines unless you have very strong compensating factors (a long time at the current job, 800 FICO or better, long-time residence in the same place, a lot of assets—and I mean *a lot*). I never even talked about these criteria three years ago, but today I must bring it up and make sure you understand. If you think you are going to borrow yourself to a rental property empire, think again. The "new rules" have dampened that outlook.

- **Your ability to pay:** Here is the big one. Do you have the ability to make the payment each and every month? When your twin announces that she has just been laid off unexpectedly and that the money is needed for a buffer while she looks for a job, the lender will quickly show your twin the front door and tell her to come back when gainful employment has been found. And by the way, you have to have at least a year under your belt with your new employer. Your twin could come to my clients and borrow about $50,000 but will pay a minimum of 12% plus 2-5% points. All we care about is the equity in the home. Today, 'A' lenders' primary concern is that you have the ability to pay back the loan; if not, then there is no need to apply.

As you can see going by these four criteria, your twin is up the proverbial creek without a paddle and with no way to access this equity. Your twin is likely to lose the house along with the $150,000 down payment. And it can get worse. If the lender can only sell this home for, say, $130,000, your twin will also be liable for a deficiency judgment of $20,000 (the amount owed less the selling price). With this much equity, this is very unlikely but many folks with foreclosures pending today are faced with deficiency judgments—not to mention that your twin would receive a 1099 from the lender for the $20,000 debt relief and owe income taxes on that amount.

It just makes absolute sense to pull out your equity every few years and, as you will soon see, put it to work. If nothing else, you want the liquidity so that money is available in bad times or if a great investment opportunity rears its smiling face.

If after reading this chapter, you are still adhering to old, conventional wisdom and are just too darn gun shy to pull out your equity and reinvest it, then I at least want to urge you to refinance one last time with the mortgage accelerator loan. To summarize, this loan, when managed properly, will actually accelerate the payoff of your home loan. It is basically a first position home equity line of credit (HELOC). It is also tied to your bank account.

The interest on this loan is charged on a daily basis on the then-current principal amount due. Using this loan allows you to place your entire paycheck in your bank account, thus reducing your principal balance. You then pay your bills through this account and the balance on your loan increases. You need to think like any well-run business and get in the habit of paying your bills on the very last day they are due. This little bit of principal reduction each and every month will literally shave years off of your loan and save you a boatload of interest.

More importantly, you are able to get a line of credit up to 90% of the value of your home and pay off the underlying current mortgage. Let's say your home is worth $300,000 and you owe $200,000. You can borrow up to $270,000 and pay off the $200,000, leaving you with a line of credit of $70,000 (liquidity). If you do not use this $70,000, then you are not charged interest on it but you have it at your disposal for any purpose, no questions asked.

If you are the type of person who holds certificates of deposits (CDs) or money market accounts, we suggest you cash them in and place them into this special account. You will be receiving the effective interest rate charged on your loan as a return on investment and be liquid.

Of course, we do not want you to ever pay off the loan on your primary principal residence, but we want you to have *the ability* to pay off the loan at any given moment. So why would we recommend this acceleration loan? Because it stands to reason that if you are accelerating your loan, you are creating equity faster and this is equity you can pull out to reinvest. This loan

98   *Moving at the Speed of Wealth*

is available through Speed of Wealth Lending and you can learn more at *www.SpeedofWealth.com* or contact a Speed of Wealth specialist to answer your questions.

Q. Does home equity have any tax advantages?

A. Nope! You are in the unfortunate position of probably having to pay property taxes. The equity you may be sitting on has no tax advantages whatsoever. Your *home loan* has tax advantages. Most Americans are able to deduct the interest paid on their home loan over the course of a year. If you are in a traditional amortized loan, whether thirty-, twenty-, fifteen-, ten-year, etc., you are actually paying less in interest each year and, consequently, are systematically reducing your tax deductions every single year. This may sound like good news to you because you are slowly paying off your mortgage but as I continue with this chapter, you should come to realize that paying off your home loan and having your home free and clear is not financially wise.

I recommend interest-only loans because they allow you to take full advantage of tax deductions each year and the savings in monthly payments can be redirected to a side account to build your wealth. If you have no intentions of reinvesting your monthly savings, then forget it and do what all the conventional wisdom preaches: Amortize your loan and pay it off. Here is an example.

You have a choice. Let's assume you are buying (or refinancing) a $300,000 home and making a 10% down payment for a total new loan amount of $270,000 (for now, let's forget about mortgage insurance premiums and just assume you can get a first mortgage in this amount). Choice one is to take out a thirty-year amortized loan at 5.5%. Choice two is to borrow $270,000 on an interest-only loan with a rate of 6%.

The monthly principal and interest payment on your amortized loan is $1,533. If, on the other hand, you borrow using the interest-only loan as a tool to build wealth, your monthly payment will be $1,350. You save $183 per month and the interest rate you are being charged is half a percent higher. Now, what do you do with this extra $183 per month? Well, I would suggest dumping it into a properly designed indexed life insurance contract to build a banking system. You may want to consume it and use it to pay extra bills (if this is the case, then you are not in the wealth-building mindset yet). Or you can put it into a self-directed IRA or a self-directed 401(k) plan (if you own a business of any kind—and you should).

You decide to build wealth using a self-directed IRA. You invest this savings

Secret of the Super-Rich #6

monthly into your account and invest in an opportunity that pays 12% annually. Remember that your money will now grow tax-deferred.

Results Summary

Starting amount	$0
Years	30
Additional contributions	$183 per month
Rate of return	12.00% compounded annually
Total amount you will have contributed	$65,880
Total at end of investment	**$563,818**

Savings Balance by Year

Year	Additions	Interest	Balance
Start	$0		$0
1	$2,196	$140	$2,336
2	$2,196	$421	$4,953
3	$2,196	$735	$7,884
4	$2,196	$1,086	$11,166
5	$2,196	$1,480	$14,842
6	$2,196	$1,921	$18,959
7	$2,196	$2,415	$23,571
8	$2,196	$2,969	$28,735
9	$2,196	$3,589	$34,520
10	$2,196	$4,283	$40,999
11	$2,196	$5,060	$48,255
12	$2,196	$5,931	$56,381
13	$2,196	$6,906	$65,484
14	$2,196	$7,998	$75,678
15	$2,196	$9,222	$87,095
16	$2,196	$10,592	$99,883
17	$2,196	$12,126	$114,205
18	$2,196	$13,845	$130,246
19	$2,196	$15,770	$148,212
20	$2,196	$17,926	$168,334
21	$2,196	$20,340	$190,870
22	$2,196	$23,045	$216,111
23	$2,196	$26,074	$244,381
* 24	$2,196	$29,466	$276,042
25	$2,196	$33,265	$311,504

Figure 29 (continues)

Year	Additions	Interest	Balance
26	$2,196	$37,521	$351,221
27	$2,196	$42,287	$395,703
28	$2,196	$47,625	$445,524
29	$2,196	$53,603	$501,323
30	$2,196	$60,299	$563,818

Figure 29 (continued)

As you can see in Figure 29 above, you have the ability to pay off your home in year twenty-four; you have cut six years off the life of your mortgage. On top of that, your side account is liquid and you have access to your money during the entire course of the loan, giving you more peace of mind.

In addition, you saved more money by reducing your taxes further. If you were to take out an amortized loan, you would have paid approximately $269,794 in interest by the end of the twenty-fourth year. If you were in the 25% federal marginal tax bracket, your tax savings would have been $67,449, which is real money to you. On the other hand, if you used the interest-only strategy, you would have paid $441,504 in total interest with a tax savings of $110,376. This is almost $43,000 more money in your pocket over the course of twenty-four years than you could have received with an amortized loan.

Your argument might be that debt is bad and why would you ever want to pay more interest. This is your grandparents speaking through you. You are now Moving at the Speed of Wealth™. You need to quit being so concerned about expenses and debt. If you are better off, who cares?

By taking out the interest-only loan and reinvesting the difference in payment between the two strategies, you are much better off financially. You spent the exact same money out of pocket in each year. With an interest-only loan, you had the ability to pay off your home loan six years earlier and you remained liquid for peace of mind.

To take it one step further, if you were only able to receive an average return of 8% on your money in a tax-deferred compounding environment, by year thirty your side bucket would have grown to $259,423. You are less than $11,000 shy of paying off your home but the additional tax savings has more than made up for this, especially if you reinvest those tax savings. More importantly, YOU REMAINED LIQUID! Come on now, can't you get an average of 8% returns? That's child's play.

Q. Does home equity have a rate of return?

A. Herein lies the big question. It is said that the largest investment the average American family has is their home. What they really mean is the *equity* in the home. The bank owns the other portion until the loan is paid off. I have preached for years that the biggest asset the average American family has is *not* their home equity but rather their home loan! You cannot manage the value of your home other than maintaining it and possibly doing some remodeling (be careful, you can actually spend more on remodeling than it will return to you). Like most investments, the value of your home is dictated by economic conditions. However, you can manage your home loan and home loans come with an additional benefit, in most cases: Interest paid on home loans is tax-deductible (there are some IRS rules that dictate how much can be deducted; make sure to check with a competent tax specialist when making decisions based on tax deductions—you will see later that I never make investment decisions based on taxes).

Assume now that your home is worth $300,000 and you have an underlying loan on it of $150,000. Although the real estate market adjusts from time to time (much like it is doing as I write this), we know that over time, homes will appreciate in value.

As a side note, I want to reiterate that, on average, homes appreciate at the same rate as inflation. It is also important to understand that times have changed. It used to be that the improvements on land appreciated. In other words, the homes were appreciating and the land they sat on was not of much value. The truth is that with the changing landscape in America, it is now the land that is appreciating. Let me explain. There is a current movement of more and more people moving back into the inner city. This is a trend that is holding true throughout the nation. You can now go into any city, travel toward downtown and find buyers scooping up old homes and scraping them. Once they remove the old structure, they are then building a bigger, (more often than not) two-story home on them. This is an indication that the land (location) is more valuable to the buyer than the home itself. (I want you to keep this paragraph in mind as we continue our education process.)

Let's get back to our example. Your home is worth $300,000 and you owe $150,000 to the bank, so you have $150,000 of equity in your property. According to a study done by Ibbotson, homes have appreciated in value an average of 7.25% across the United States since 1973. For our example, let's be conservative and say that your home will, over time, appreciate on average 5% per year.

Here is the burning question. If you were to take out your $150,000 of home equity by refinancing your home and have a 100% loan on your house, would your home still appreciate 5% on average? The answer is, "Of course it would." On the other hand, if you paid off your home loan and had no loan on your home, would your home appreciate more than 5%? The answer is, "Of course not." Your home will appreciate at the same rate regardless of the underlying home loan. In fact, your home has no idea that you even have a loan on it.

Since this is the case, you now know that the amount of equity in your home has absolutely no bearing on the appreciation of your home—so your home equity, the asset that experts say is the largest asset of the majority of Americans, has absolutely no rate of return. This is exactly what the pundits say: Equity has no rate of return. But does it?

The truth is that home equity does have a rate of return but it is pathetic. To illustrate, I must tell a true story so that you can understand very clearly.

Back in 2004, I met with a sixty-two-year-old pre-retiree to discuss her retirement planning. Remember, what you are about to hear is a true story. She had worked part-time for the school district for her entire adult life and was set up to receive about $1,000 per month from her government pension on top of about $1,000 in Social Security benefits. Her total before-tax income would be reduced at retirement by 50%. She was only to receive $2,000 per month to survive on but I discovered that she owed $50,000 to several different credit card companies. The average rate she was being charged was an outlandish 15%. Before you gasp, understand that the fastest-growing segment with credit card debt in America today is seniors over age sixty-two.

Coincidentally, the only other money that she had managed to save was $50,000 that she had stored in a fixed rate annuity (yuck!) that was earning about 3% annually at the time (interest rates were very low in 2004; by the way, did you know that low interest rates are great for consumers but really crappy for investors? Just thought I would throw that out there.). In other words, she was earning about $125 per month on her annuity before taxes. Mind you, she was not taking this income out but letting it continue to grow tax-deferred because this was her "retirement savings," as she put it.

At the very same time, her minimum monthly payment on her credit card was $500. She was paying $6,000 per year on credit card charges and, at this rate, would never have the credit card debt paid off in her lifetime.

I made a very simple suggestion to her that I am sure you, the educated reader, would have suggested as well. I suggested that she cash in her $50,000 annuity and pay off the credit card debt and tear up the damn cards. I went on to explain that if she was paying 15% on the credit card balance (monthly

Secret of the Super-Rich #6

outflow of cash), the minute she paid off that card, she was receiving a 15% return on her money. I explained that if she was not paying 15%, then it was a return of 15%—that's pretty simple. I said that she was currently only receiving about 3% in annuity or $125 per month. Her net advantage was $375 per month ($500 credit card payment minus the $125 earnings).

Well, you would have thought I was the devil himself. She came unglued and insisted that I leave her house. She went on to say that the annuity was her retirement savings and she could not believe that someone with my credentials and background would recommend that she deplete her retirement account.

You will learn as you work with me and continue your education with me that I can be very brash. I tell it like it is and you can accept it or ignore it; after all, it's your money. I never say anything to offend anyone unless, of course, it should offend them. I leaned into her and simply said, "Lady, you do have a retirement plan and it's called Social Security. I hear the government doesn't pay that well!" I politely left, never to contact or hear from her again. Rest assured, if she did contact me, I would not have worked with her. I am at the point in my life where I can be very choosy when deciding who I want to give my time to.

You may have thought that story had nothing to do with home equity but it does. I mentioned that many planners will tell you that home equity has no rate of return when, in fact, it does. If you borrow money and pull out your equity, you now have a monthly payment. If that interest rate is 6%, this is outflow of cash annually. Remember that in most cases, you can borrow up to $100,000 and take a home interest deduction. So depending on your tax bracket, again your true effective rate is lower than that 6%. Let's just say your effective rate is 5%. If you are not paying 5%, then it is a return on your money of 5%.

However, as you will learn as you continue reading, you must factor inflation into the mix. And you will learn as you read on that inflation is much higher than what we are being told by our government. In fact, some would say it is closer to 12% than the 3% being reported, I think it is around 8%. If you are receiving a 5% return on your equity and you factor inflation into the formula, you are truly losing 3% on equity each year. This, of course, is when you keep the appreciation of your home out of the formula. You cannot use appreciation in the formula because I have already proved that the equity in your home has no bearing on the appreciation of your home.

I only explain this to you to shut up my critics out there. Other planners are always trying to beat up on people who understand more than they do.

Good planners research what they learn, come to their own conclusion and will rebut using the facts.

For our discussion, let's just assume that, in truth, because homes will appreciate at the same rate regardless of whether there is a home loan on them or not, your home equity has no rate of return.

Remember the old, conventional wisdom: "The largest asset (investment) of the average American family is their home!" If this were true, and it is not, then the largest investment for the average American family has no rate of return, is not safe, is not liquid, has no tax advantages and produces absolutely zero income! Sounds like very sound financial planning to me.

Would you put money in any investment that has no rate of return, is not safe, is not liquid, has no tax advantages and will never produce any income? Of course you wouldn't, yet that is what hundreds of thousands of Americans are currently doing by trying to pay off their home loans in the shortest amount of time possible.

How to Use Equity Arbitrage to Build Tremendous Wealth

If you are still reading up to this point, I guess I have wakened the sleeping financial giant within. I know that you agree with my logic and everything I pointed out makes sense. After all, this is just simple math. Let's assume that you have some equity in your home, it doesn't matter how much, and you now agree that you should never pay off your primary residence and should strongly consider the mortgage accelerator loan or an interest-only loan. This is where the fun begins!

Remember, to be a wealth magnate, you must be disciplined as well. Speed of Wealth is not here to increase your monthly cash flow; we are here to show you how to reposition assets to maximize the asset potential. If you want more cash flow each month, we can do that as well, but that does not build wealth. The best way to create extra cash flow is to start your own part-time home-based business even if you can only make an extra $200-$500 per month. The extra tax savings add to your cash flow. This, however, is for another chapter.

Let's now turn our attention to building wealth using The Speed of Wealth Equity Arbitrage Strategy.™

Take a look at the following real-life example of one of our students. In Figure 23, you have a wealth-builder who has a home with a fair market value of $400,000. He took out a thirty-year amortized loan six years ago in the amount of $250,000 and is paying an interest rate of 5.5%. At the end of the sixth year, his current loan balance is $226,720.58 (he paid off a whopping

Growth on Spread of Payments Using Equity Arbtrage

Home Loan Fair Market Value:	$400,000.00
Original Loan Amount:	$250,000.00
Current Loan Amount:	**$226,720.58**
Current Type of Loan:	30 **Amortized**
Current Interest Rate:	5.50%
Current P&I Payment:	$1,419.47
New Loan LTV:	80.00%
New Loan Amount:	$320,000.00
Equity to Use in Arbitrage:	$93,279.42
Type of Loan:	**Interest Only**
Interest Rate:	6.00%
Monthly Payment:	$1,600.00
Marginal Tax Bracket:	30.00%
New Investment:	**Trust Deeds**
Monthly Returns:	17.00%
Payment Difference:	$126.37
After Tax Return on Deed of Trust:	$925.02
Monthly Spread on Payments:	$798.65
Return on Investment:	10.50%

Figure 30

$23,279.42 in six years). We will call this guy "Mr. Smith." Mr. Smith understands the Speed of Wealth movement and decides to take my advice. He decides to refinance his home into an interest-only loan at 6% (notice he doesn't care that his rate is going up) and take out as much equity as possible.

We recommend going to 80% loan to value (80% of the fair market value of the home) for a new loan of $320,000. Mr. Smith's payment goes up to $1,600 per month; his old payment was $1,419.47. At first glance he has to come up with an additional $180.53 per month. Speed of Wealth does not want you to increase your outflow unless, of course, you need to in order to reach your financial goals.

Mr. Smith will receive a check at closing (his equity) in the amount of $93,279.42. I then show him an investment opportunity in which he is collateralized by real estate by deeds of trust at a very low loan to value. This opportunity is paying 17% annually and pays Mr. Smith monthly. This income will be taxed as ordinary passive income and he is in the 30% marginal federal tax bracket. In this example, Mr. Smith will collect a gross check of $1,321 monthly on his $93,279 at 17%. After holding back taxes due, he will have a net after-tax monthly positive cash flow of $925.

Now, remember, his payment increased $180.53 per month due to taking out

COMPOUNDING VEHICLE

Year	Growth on Spread
1	$10,366.97
2	$22,640.34
3	$37,170.69
4	$54,373.04
5	$74,738.76
6	$98,849.58
7	$127,394.17
8	$161,187.87
9	$201,195.96
10	$248,561.21
11	$304,636.53
12	$371,023.64
13	$449,618.79
14	$542,666.94
15	$652,825.87
16	$783,242.12
17	$937,640.83
18	$1,120,432.20
19	$1,336,837.38
20	$1,593,037.69
21	$1,896,351.12
22	$2,255,441.37
23	$2,680,565.36
24	$3,183,866.13
25	$3,779,719.74

Figure 31

a larger loan and I don't want Mr. Smith to build wealth with any more out-of-pocket expenses. Mr. Smith takes his after-tax positive cash flow monthly check of $925 and pays the increase of payment of $180.53, leaving him an excess of about $799 each month. This is an investment strategy and I want to encourage Mr. Smith not to consume this extra $799 but to reinvest the money. So Mr. Smith takes my advice and reinvests the $799 monthly into the same 17% deeds of trust.

Assuming he uses a tax-deferred instrument such as an individual retirement arrangement (IRA) or self-directed 401(k), his money will grow larger. The chart on the left shows how his $799 per month invested at 17% compounding annually would grow.

By year ten, Mr. Smith has an additional $248,561.21 in assets and it cost him absolutely nothing out of his pocket. How does this work? Remember, the investment he put his equity into paid monthly and he paid the increase in his home loan payment directly from the after-tax proceeds he received. He then took the difference and reinvested the money as shown in Figure 31. The equity Mr. Smith used for this investment did not disappear. It is still sitting there and Mr. Smith can use it to pay off that portion of his new mortgage at any time. In other words, he is in no worse shape than he was before he took out his equity with his new loan. In fact, by the end of year one, Mr. Smith is $10,366.97 better off than he was in his original position.

Take a look at year twenty. The spread of $799 has grown to almost $1.6 million and by year twenty-five, he has created an additional $3.779 million of wealth with absolutely no money out of his pocket.

He also has the ability to pay off his entire loan balance on his house between the eleventh and twelfth year. He accelerated the payoff of his home by pulling out the equity and putting it to work. Let's assume Mr. Smith takes my advice and never pays off his home. His interest-only payment is $1,600 per month and it never goes away because he is not reducing the principal balance. By the end of year twenty, he has almost $1.6 million in his side bucket plus the original $93,279 of principal sitting in the investment. His equity spread can produce an additional $270,816.29 of before-tax income twenty years down the road ($1,593,037 x 17% interest = $270,816.29). Do you think he gives a darn about the $1,600 monthly house payment that is still tax-deductible (providing Congress doesn't change the rules)? Heck no! This is truly "Moving at the Speed of Wealth™"!

I know what you're thinking: "How in the world can you find an investment secured by real estate that pays 17%? That's too good to be true and my daddy always said if it is too good to be true, it probably is." This mentality is what is keeping you from the big wealth. Truth be told, I can show you an investment just like that today. As a member of The Speed of Wealth Gold Club™, you will be introduced to these opportunities all the time; your job is to be educated enough to take action—action that creates wealth. To learn more about the club, visit *www.SOWGoldClub.com* and become a member.

But since you don't believe 17%, what would happen if Mr. Smith only received 8%? Do you think you can do at least that well? Take a look at the chart below:

Growth on Spread of Payments Using Equity Arbtrage

Home Loan Fair Market Value:	$400,000.00
Original Loan Amount:	$250,000.00
Current Loan Amount:	**$226,720.58**
Current Type of Loan:	30 **Amortized**
Current Interest Rate:	5.50%
Current P&I Payment:	$1,419.47
New Loan LTV:	80.00%
New Loan Amount:	$320,000.00
Equity to Use in Arbitrage:	$93,279.42
Type of Loan:	**Interest Only**
Interest Rate:	6.00%
Monthly Payment:	$1,600.00
Marginal Tax Bracket:	30.00%
New Investment:	**Trust Deeds**
Monthly Returns:	8.00%
Payment Difference:	$126.37
After Tax Return on Deed of Trust:	$435.30
Monthly Spread on Payments:	$308.93
Return on Investment:	8.00%

Figure 32

COMPOUNDING VEHICLE

Year	Growth on Spread
1	$3,846.21
2	$8,011.66
3	$12,522.84
4	$17,408.44
5	$22,899.55
6	$28,429.82
7	$34,635.69
8	$41,356.65
9	$48,635.65
10	$56,518.38
11	$65,055.59
12	$74,301.33
13	$84,314.58
14	$95,158.86
15	$106,903.22
16	$119,622.34
17	$133,397.15
18	$148,315.27
19	$164,471.57
20	$181,968.85
21	$200,918.39
22	$221,440.73
23	$243,666.41
24	$267,736.82
25	$293,805.06
26	$322,036.95
27	$352,612.07
28	$385,724.91
29	$421,586.10
30	$460,423.75

Figure 33

As you can see in Figure 32, Mr. Smith was only able to receive 8% in his side bucket but it still created a monthly spread of about $309 that he could reinvest at only 8% every month. Remember that he has created liquidity for himself as well. By the end of year twenty-six, Mr. Smith can pay off his home (cutting four years off the life of the loan), enjoy greater tax deductions and, as I have said, remain more liquid. If he waits until his original loan was scheduled to be paid off (year thirty), Mr. Smith can pay off his $320,000 mortgage and still have an additional $140,000 sitting in the bank.

You are going to have to put up a pretty strong argument to start going back to your traditional thinking. Every scenario I showed you has you coming out better when you *separate* your equity from your property and reinvest it.

At this point, I want to stress that it doesn't matter how much equity you have in your home. I use different numbers in this book to make illustrations. If the principles work with $100,000, then the same principles work with $10,000 or any amount. To take out all of your equity, you may have to take on a home equity line of credit (HELOC). If you have good credit and job history, this should not be difficult—but be aware that the interest rate is typically higher. So what? As long as you can create arbitrage (spread between what you are paying and what your money is earning in an investment), you win. You may not be able to take tax deductions on the home loan. So what? As long as that after-tax spread is still positive, you win.

When applying these principles, the interest rate you pay on a home loan is not as important…just create spread. I am not saying not to get the best possible rate but more often than not it is to your advantage to pay a slightly higher interest rate and allow the lender to pay closing costs with the additional interest rate (if your lender says they cannot do that, find another lender). We have an in-house mortgage company licensed in all states that knows what we do. Go to *www.SpeedofWealth.com* to learn more.

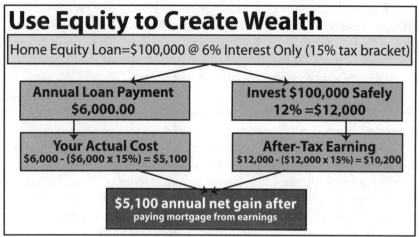

Figure 34

Figure 34 breaks these principles down to the core. If you were to borrow $100,000 from home equity with a 6% interest-only loan and you are in the 15% tax bracket, your annual payment would be $6,000, right? Wrong! In most cases, this annual payment is tax-deductible, making your true effective out-of-pocket cost only $5,100. Now you place that $100,000 into an investment that pays 12% annual and you earn $12,000 a year, right? Wrong! Because we are using a portion of the $12,000 to pay the additional monthly payment on our mortgage, we cannot put the investment into a tax-deferred environment. Therefore, your $12,000 becomes taxable at the end of the year, leaving you with $10,200.

Remember: Of that $10,200, $5,100 went to make the additional increase in your payment, leaving you with $5,100 of free money. Here comes the big question. What is the return on your investment?

Most people answer 12% or 100% or just throw out a number. The answer is, drum roll, please... **YOU RECEIVED AN INFINITE RETURN ON YOUR MONEY!**

That's right! Your return cannot be measured because you have no money out of pocket to make this additional $5,100. It's just like free money. Do you currently have any investments with that kind of return? The only other investment that can do this is real estate. You must be able to take out a 100% loan and the rents you collect must cover all expenses... forever. If you can pull that off, you will receive infinite rates of returns on your real estate but this seldom, if ever, happens.

110   *Moving at the Speed of Wealth*

I know this has been a long chapter but hang in there with me for just a little bit longer. I have shown you how to take that spread of money and put it into an IRA or self-directed 401(k) plan to build tremendous wealth. Now I want to show you what happens when you put that spread of money into the right life insurance product that is structured correctly.

For this example, I will assume you are a fifty-five-year-old male in good health and you do not use tobacco. Remember that I showed you about putting the extra $799 into our 17% investment? Now I will show you about putting that $799 into a life insurance contract and using it as a banking system. Life insurance is a very poor investment but it makes for a very good investment tool.

The policy I will illustrate shows an average return of 9%. This type of policy (indexed universal life) credits your side account with the upside of the S&P 500 Index® with no downside risk. This illustration shows a two-year crediting cycle with a cap of 30%. In other words, they will credit your side account once every two years with the upside of the market and they will not credit you more than 30%. Again, I am illustrating at an average return of 9% credited to your account value.

Knowing that life insurance is not a great investment (although I would put it up against almost any mutual fund any time), why would I recommend parking your monthly payments within a policy? I recommend this for a few reasons.

First, this offers you diversification. Life insurance is traditionally one of the safest places to put your money. Although life insurance companies have and will continue to fail, the number is small compared to banks. Secondly, with current tax laws, life insurance provides a great tax shelter. Your money grows tax-deferred; it can come out tax-free by making policy loans that are never repaid and the remaining balance transfers tax-free to your heirs. This sounds a whole lot like a Roth IRA but with more bells and whistles. My primary reason for recommending life insurance to park your payments is that you are building a personal banking system. Look below at the illustration and find the column titled "Surr Cash Value." This represents the "surrender cash value" of your policy and the amount of money you can borrow from the policy. You can see that by the second year, you can start to borrow from the policy and reinvest the money. The policy will continue to appreciate at an average of 9% over time, as if you had never taken any money out. If you look to year eleven, you will see that I illustrate taking out a policy loan in the amount of $12,192. You will see that the "Surr Cash Value" column reduces in size but the "Account Value" column continues to grow.

Secret of the Super-Rich #6

This works much like pulling out equity from your home; the home will continue to appreciate at the same rate regardless of the underlying home loan. When you make a policy loan; the insurance company loans you the money out of the company's general account and charges you an interest rate tied to bonds. They then collateralize your policy for the amount of the loan plus interest. This sounds a whole lot like a home loan to me. The difference is that you do not have to pay back the loans and you are not on a payment schedule. It's your money and it's entirely up to you when and how you want to pay back the loan.

End of Year	Age	Model Premium	Times Per Year	Annual Premium	Cash From Policy	Annual Outlay	Non-Guaranteed Assumed			
							Surr Cash Value	Surr Charge	Account Value	Death Benefit
1	56	800	1	9,600	0	9,600	0	11,385	6,975	246,545
2	57	800	1	9,600	0	9,600	4,103	10,626	14,729	246,545
3	58	800	1	9,600	0	9,600	12,698	9,867	22,565	246,545
4	59	800	1	9,600	0	9,600	22,457	9,108	31,565	246,545
5	60	800	1	9,600	0	9,600	32,335	8,349	40,684	246,545
6	61	800	1	9,600	0	9,600	43,648	7,590	51,238	246,545
7	62	800	1	9,600	0	9,600	55,166	6,831	61,997	246,545
8	63	800	1	9,600	0	9,600	68,403	6,072	74,475	246,545
9	64	800	1	9,600	0	9,600	81,977	5,313	87,290	246,545
10	65	800	1	9,600	0	9,600	98,282	4,554	102,836	246,545
		0		96,000	0	96,000				
11	66	0	1	0	12,192	-12,192	94,290	3,795	111,124	233,505
12	67	0	1	0	12,192	-12,192	90,318	3,036	120,340	219,559
13	68	0	1	0	12,192	-12,192	86,242	2,277	130,421	204,644
14	69	0	1	0	12,192	-12,192	82,298	1,518	141,669	188,691
15	70	0	1	0	12,192	-12,192	78,349	759	154,023	171,630
		0								
16	71	0	1	0	12,192	-12,192	74,688	0	167,851	153,382
17	72	0	1	0	12,192	-12,192	70,341	0	183,020	133,866
18	73	0	1	0	12,192	-12,192	66,448	0	200,000	112,993
19	74	0	1	0	12,192	-12,192	62,882	0	218,758	90,669
20	75	0	1	0	12,192	-12,192	60,122	0	239,874	72,116
		0		96,000	121,920	-25,920				
21	76	0	1	0	12,192	-12,192	57,792	0	263,080	70,946
22	77	0	1	0	12,192	-12,192	56,179	0	288,777	70,618
23	78	0	1	0	12,192	-12,192	54,972	0	316,780	70,812
24	79	0	1	0	12,192	-12,192	54,719	0	347,766	72,107
25	80	0	1	0	12,192	-12,192	55,049	0	381,509	74,125

Figure 35

In the illustration above, I show this person pulling out $12,192 per year in policy loans that s/he never repays. You will see the "Surr Cash Value" column depleting until age eighty, when it starts to grow again. This is caused by the internal "arbitrage" within the policy. If you are borrowing at bond rates (in this illustration, I am showing the policyholder borrowing at 6.5%) while the same money is

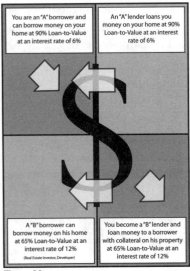

Figure 36

being credited with the upside returns of the market (in this case, I am illustrating a 9% average annual return), then you are creating 2.5% arbitrage within the policy—not to mention that you had life insurance protection the entire time.

In truth, using the monthly "spread" on your house payment to fund an insurance policy only makes sense if:

You have at least ten years before you want to use the policy for income.

You have no place else to invest $800 per month. For example, it is hard to find a trust deed that only requires $800 per month and mutual funds stink.

If you need a place to park the $800 per month, I would highly recommend parking it into a properly structured indexed life insurance product. But not just any indexed life product—it must be a specific type of policy, and most life insurance agents have no clue about what I just shared with you. A Speed of Wealth specialist can help you determine whether a policy is best for your situation and structure the policy properly to meet your objectives.

Important Note: *The illustration I used above is for illustration purposes only and there are no guarantees of the outcome. Life insurance does offer guarantees but I do not have the space or time to go into every detail of the policy in this book. The illustration shows the non-guaranteed assumed performance of the policy based on historical data, which, of course, is no guarantee of future performance. For a more accurate and complete understanding of the policy, please have a professional design one specifically for you and review it carefully.*

Now You Are the Banker

I have outlined in this book exactly what banks do to make huge profits. They borrow at a lower interest rate, then they can loan it out and make arbitrage. It really is that simple; take a look at the illustration above.

You are an 'A' borrower and can borrow from an 'A' lender up to 90% of the value of your home. You get the best rates at 6% (of course, interest rates change).

Secret of the Super-Rich #6

113

You borrow money from an 'A' lender at 6% and become the 'B' lender, whereby you will loan money out to 'B' borrowers (and these are not deadbeats). Your 'B' borrower is typically a real estate investor or developer and will gladly pay you 12% or more on your money.

You just created 6% arbitrage and began to build wealth. (See how cool my dollar sign is in the middle of the illustration, showing you the flow of the money?) You created a banking system and created "free" money.

Don't worry—The Speed of Wealth has all kinds of good borrowers who are willing to pay these interest rates and collateralize the land. I want you to go to Bermuda and relax while you build wealth. Let us handle the dirty stuff.

So, with all you know now, here is the biggest question up to this point. If I can show you how to get 12%, 15%, even 17% returns on your money in a nice, safe investment that pays you consistently and predictably, how many of you would go out right now and pull out not only all of your equity but your parents' equity as well? If you don't have your hand up, then I did a very poor job convincing you. Remember, I specified if I could make you feel "warm and fuzzy" on these investments that pay these returns and you were very confident in the investment, how many of you would pull out your equity?

I know a few of you are not raising your hand because of the conditioning you received throughout your entire life. No offense but women, in particular, are very difficult to separate from their equity. This is a security blanket to them. Not that they don't understand the principles I have just taught you, but they tend to be a bit more conservative than men. After all, we die sooner.

That's all right. I can show you how to take other assets you own and receive these types of returns, not to mention safe investments with 25% annualized returns or better, all backed by real estate. I bet I got your attention! But I also recommend that you continue your education and let me show you some really neat tricks. Join The Speed of Wealth Gold Club™ today, enjoy what I have to teach you on an ongoing basis and learn some of my advanced strategies. I am on a mission to bring back Middle America and I am starting with you!

All I ask is that you listen to me with an open mind and do not dismiss anything I share with you until you have thoroughly mulled it over. The next step is to get your friends, neighbors, relatives and co-workers involved. All you have to do is hand them this book when you are finished (though I prefer they buy their own book), and let them make up their own minds.

I can tell you that people who grasp what I teach will cross the finish line in a much better position than where the road is leading them today because I know the safe shortcuts.

Chapter Seven

Secret of the Super-Rich #7

Super-Rich People Know How to Pay off Their Home Loans Early, with No Change in Lifestyle and No Out-of-Pocket Money—but Choose Not to

- No expensive software to buy
- No need to refinance your home
- No bi-weekly plans
- No fees to set up
- No change in lifestyle
- No effect on your current cash flow whatsoever!

Massive Home Loan Payoff Acceleration Strategy!

First of all, I want to make it very clear that I don't believe you should ever pay off your home loans. You can read all about my opinions in the previous chapter. However, I do understand the appeal of paying your home loan off. This might give you a sense of security.

No offense, ladies, but you are even more aggressive when it comes to paying off your home loans.

A quick recap of why you should never pay off your home loan:

1. You cannot spend home equity: Once you have paid off your home loan, you are left with home equity (the difference between what you owe on your home and what the fair market value of your home is). When was the last time you saw anybody go to

the store and buy groceries with home equity? You may reply you can easily take out a loan and spend it, but—ah-ha!—it is no longer home equity. You now have a loan on your property.

2. Home equity has a very small rate of return: If it is true that the average Middle American's largest asset is their home—more specifically, the equity in their home—then why do people insist on having the majority of their assets in an environment that has very little rate of return? The truth is that the rate of return is equivalent to what you would pay, after tax deductions, in interest on a home loan. Today, depending on your tax bracket, your effective return would be anywhere between 3.5 - 6%. Home equity has no rate of return if you can earn a higher interest rate than this paltry interest you are being charged on your home loan…and, of course, you can!

3. Your equity is not liquid: Sure, you can take out your home equity when everything in your life is hunky-dory—but when you need the equity the most, it is unavailable to you. You must remain liquid.

4. Equity is not safe: Just ask people living in New Orleans what happened to all the equity in their homes when Hurricane Katrina flooded them away. Homeowner's insurance doesn't cover floods.

Enough of the soap box speech. You have already had this explained to you in the previous chapter in more detail, but you are reading this chapter because you want to pay off your home as soon as possible.

Since this is what the majority of Middle Americans want, then I will give it to them.

Many of you have undoubtedly heard of mortgage acceleration loans or companies like United First Financial (UFirst). I am about to refute many of the claims these companies make and provide you with a much easier solution.

First, let me speak about the UFirst program. I must admit that, when looking at the plan from the surface, it could easily get you excited. The plan, in a nutshell, involves no refinancing of your current loan. You are required to take out a home equity line of credit (HELOC) on your home. Understand that both the UFirst Financial program and the plan I am about to share with you require you have equity and you take out a HELOC.

Now, I do not profess to be an expert on the UFirst program. In fact, all I have seen is a presentation offered by one of the company's associates and it did not take me long to realize what was going on.

This is how I see it working. You take out a HELOC and the first thing you do is pay for the web-based software in the amount of about $3,500 with your cash. I have no problem with people earning money; in fact, I earn a lot of money, but not at the expense of something you could do on your own without this cost.

Once you have established this line of credit, you begin to deposit all of your paychecks into paying down this HELOC. Understand you must have a HELOC with check-writing capabilities. When it is time to pay your bills each month, you simply cut the checks from this line of credit.

In theory, what happens is that whatever is left over (your savings) sits inside this account and reduces the interest you are paying on the loan. What the representatives will tell you is that you track all of this activity with the web-based software and at certain intervals the software will tell you exactly how much and when to send a payment off to your underlying first mortgage.

I appreciate the approach and truly believe that United First Financial has good intentions. Unfortunately, for the vast majority of Americans, you will fail (not that they have not had some success stories).

Here are the problems with this program, as I see it. First of all, America has a negative half-percent savings rate today. The majority of Americans are living paycheck-to-paycheck, barely able to make ends meet. This means there will be no "extra" money left over at the end of each paycheck cycle. You bring in a paycheck and 100% of it goes toward paying bills.

This program is nothing more than a strategic plan to send extra money to principal on your loan whenever possible. It does not take $3,500 worth of software to tell you when you can afford to do this, but in the defense of UFirst, most Americans truly need an executable plan or they fail. After all, I have been saying it for years: The only good feature of a qualified retirement plan [401(k), 403(b), basically a work-sponsored plan] is that it is a forced savings account. Your money comes right out of your paycheck so you do not have a chance to spend it.

With the UFirst plan, you do have a chance to spend it. More importantly, you have a huge line of credit via your HELOC and the temptation to consume that equity can be overwhelming.

With all that said, if you want to pay off your home loan early, it does not take a rocket scientist or any expensive software program to tell you how to do it: Just send extra money to your lender as often as you can and you will dramatically reduce the lifetime of your loan and dramatically reduce the interest you pay on that loan.

Here is an example. Let's assume that your home is worth $300,000; you have a $250,000 thirty-year amortized loan and you are paying 5.5%. You made a $50,000 down payment when you purchased the home. Your monthly principal and interest payment equals $1,419.47. Obviously, if you make this payment on time for thirty years, you will pay off your home loan in year thirty and spend $261,010.10 in interest expense.

Don't forget that most of you receive a home loan interest deduction on your taxes and let's just assume you save 20% of the interest you paid over the lifetime of this loan on taxes. You saved $52,202.02 in taxes that you would have ordinarily sent to Uncle Sam for a net interest cost on this loan of $208,808.08 (total interest paid of $261,010.10 minus tax savings of $52,202.02).

That is still a whole lot of interest to pay. Fair enough. Now, let's assume you have this same loan but decide to pay an extra $300 per month toward your principal. In other words, you are sending a total of $1,719.47 to your lender each month ($1,419.47 principal and interest payment plus an extra $300 after tax money).

If you are consistent in this pattern, you will pay off your home loan in twenty years and one month and pay only $130,224.76 in net after tax deduction interest. On the surface this sounds like a screaming deal, but let's look a little closer.

Let me first ask if you would put your money in an investment that:

- Had a dismal return (let's say 4.5%)?
- Reduced your tax deductions every time you invested?
- Locked in your money so that you could not retrieve it (in other words, it is no longer liquid)?
- Was not safe—in fact, every time you contributed to this investment, your money became less safe and the person you sent the money to became safer?
- Produced no income for you in retirement once you loaded this investment with as much money as you could?

The truth be told, every time you send money to your lender, the scenario I described above is happening to you. Chances are you said you would never invest in an investment like the one I described. Yet that is exactly what you are doing by sending extra payments to your lender.

I have been telling my students for years: You never want to pay off the home you live in; you only want *the ability* to pay off your home at any given time.

As for the second challenge of this problem, aside from the fact that Americans just don't have extra money left over, let's look at another reality. The reality is that the chances of you staying in this home for a full thirty years are very slim.

The good news is that by sending an extra $300 each month to pay off or repay your home loan, you have created more equity and when you sell, you will walk away with more cash. Essentially, the only way to recapture the $300 you sent each month is to sell or refinance your home, which is, of course, what you are trying to avoid in the first place.

Using our $300 a month example, you have reduced the amount you owe on your loan to $181,019.73 by the end of year seven (the year you are likely to sell). Assuming your home appreciated in value an average of 5% over that same seven years and your home was worth $300,000 when you bought it, it would sell for $422,130. Forgetting about costs to sell the home, you would walk away from the closing table with $241,110.27. Not bad at all!

But, wait! You paid $144,435.48 in payments over that same period. You paid $85,821.59 in interest over this same time period. So you saved about $17,164.32 in taxes (at 20%) for a grand total out of pocket of $127,271.16. Don't forget that you made a $50,000 down payment, so now your total out-of-pocket cost is $177,271.16.

It may seem like I'm getting a little bit off course, but bear with me. It will all come together soon. Back to my example, by looking at Figure 26, you can see that you made $241,110.27 from an investment of $177,271.16, so you have a true profit from the sale of your home of $63,839.11. When you divide your profit by your total out-of-pocket costs of $177,271.16, you come up with a return on investment of 36.01%. To determine the internal rate of return, you must divide your return by seven years. Your internal rate of return (or averaged annual return) on this great investment was 5.14%!

Of course, in reality it is much lower than that because we did not factor in property taxes, homeowner's insurance, mortgage insurance premium (if any), sales costs, and the granddaddy of them all, maintenance costs. Less than 5.14% is probably better than your mutual funds, but that's another story.

Okay, there you have it. That is what you can look forward to and the drawbacks of paying off your home early by sending an extra $300 to the principal each month. I know the idea of paying off your home loan gives you a warm, tingly feeling, but it just does not make financial sense.

INTERNAL RATE OF RETURN AFTER SEVEN YEARS OF SENDING $300 EACH MONTH TO PRINCIPAL

Sale Price of Home:	$422,130 (again, 5% appreciation and disregarding sales costs)
Minus Payoff of First Mortgage:	$181,019.73
Net Proceeds:	$241,110.27
Plus Side Account Balance:	$0
Out-of-Pocket Costs:	$127,271.16 plus $50,000 down payment for total of $177,271.16
Profit:	$63,839.11
Return on Money (profit divided by out-of-pocket costs):	36.01%
Internal Rate of Return (return divided by seven years):	5.14%

Figure 37

Having *the ability* to pay off your home loan early, on the other hand, makes a ton of sense.

If I were your parent, here is exactly what I would recommend. Take out the home equity line of credit (HELOC) and reinvest the money where you can earn more interest than you are paying and it is secured by real estate (of course, we are talking about arbitrage again).

From here forward, I am going to assume that you have read the chapter on investing in hard money loans. I am going to show you how to pay off your home loan in as little as nine years with no expensive software, no change in lifestyle, no bi-weekly mortgage plans, no costly refinance, and no extra money out of your pocket, and provide you with more liquidity and maximum tax deductions. Wow, that was a mouthful!

Believe me when I say you can receive between 12 and 18% returns on your money and it is secured by real estate. In fact, you will receive a monthly paycheck from this investment but understand that because we pulled out equity, this money is not in a tax-deferred instrument. The money you receive will be taxed at the end of the year. WHO CARES?

Here is a little trick I bet you never knew. If you want to accelerate the repayment of your home loan, receive better tax advantages and remain liquid, **then pull out your home equity** and invest the money safely, so long as you create spread between the interest rate you are paying and the returns you are receiving. The key is to avoid what most Americans do, and that is to consume their home equity. You must reinvest this equity safely.

Figure 38 below shows an example of pulling out $50,000 of equity using a HELOC loan. I am keeping all other parameters on your current home loan the exactly the same. You have a thirty-year amortized $250,000 loan and you are paying 5.5%. Your monthly payment is still $1,419.47.

The interest rate you are going to pay in this example on the HELOC is 8% and you choose an *interest-only* loan with a term of twenty years. Make sure you check with your own accountant, but in most cases you can take out up to $100,000 and still receive the interest deduction on taxes on this new line of credit.

Your monthly payment is now $333.33 on this new line of credit because you took out the entire $50,000 at once. If you are able to take a tax deduction, your true effective payment would be $266.67 (assuming you are paying a 20% effective tax rate; remember that the entire payment is tax deductable because it is all interest).

HELOC	$50,000.00	
Interest Rate:	8.00%	
Type of Loan:	Interest Only	**Tax Deduction**
Term:	20	Yes
Payment:	$333.33	$266.67
Effective Tax Rate:	20%	
Return on Equity:	17%	
Monthly Payment:	$708.33	
After Tax Payout:	$566.67	
Arbitage:	$300.00	
After Tax Return:	13.60%	

Figure 38

Now, put this $50,000 in an investment that is safe and secure, earns 17% and is paid out monthly. Each month you will receive a check for $708.33, which is taxable. After setting aside the money you will need for taxes, you are left with $566.67. You take this $566.67 and make the payment of $266.67, leaving you $300 extra money each month.

You could send this $300 off to the principal on your mortgage but I already showed you why that is a mistake. Instead, you should let the money compound and reinvest it in the same investment, which has an after-tax return of 13.60%.

I know that this involves a lot of numbers and only you anal people are following me here, but even if you are not anal, stay with me. All you need to understand is that you created spread on your money and you are going to let this "spread" continue to enjoy compound growth at an after-tax return of 13.60%.

Let's fast-forward. At the end of nine years and eleven months, your "side account" has grown to $259,374.07 and the total principal you still owe is $257,293.38 (underlying first mortgage and the $50,000 second one combined). You have the ability to pay off your entire home loan, which seems like a much quicker way than sending off an extra $300 each month. In fact, it's over ten years quicker and you remained liquid!

The reality, however, is that you will probably sell this home at the end of

Sale Price of Home:	$422,130 (again, 5% appreciation and disregarding sales costs)
Minus Payoff of Both Mortgages:	$267,517.33
Plus Side Account Balance:	$196,606.51
Net Proceeds:	$351,219.18
Out-of-Pocket Costs:	$98,762.04 plus $50,000 down payment for total of $148,762.04
Profit (net proceeds minus out-of-pocket costs):	$202,457.14
Return on Money (profit divided by out-of-pocket costs):	136.09%
Internal Rate of Return (return divided by seven years):	19.44%

Figure 39

the seventh year. The numbers don't lie and we will use the same numbers we used earlier.

Looking at Figure 39, you will find that your home has appreciated to $422,130. You still owe, between the first and second mortgage, $267,517.33. You only spent $119,235.48 out of pocket on the first mortgage, but you enjoyed the luxury of $20,473.44 in tax deductions for a grand total out-of-pocket cost of $98,762.04. Remember that your investment covered the payments on the HELOC so you have zero out-of-pocket expenses there. You took the spread and put it into a side account.

Did I mention that your side account has grown to $196,606.51? Look at the math in Figure 39.

Once again, I am comparing apples to apples and disregarding property taxes, insurance, sales costs, and maintenance; but isn't a 19.44% IRR better than the 5.14% IRR that you received by paying an extra $300 each month?

My method did not change your lifestyle: You had the extra $300 each month to spend any way you wanted.

Again, let's look at the IRR if you paid an extra $300 each month toward principal:

Sale Price of Home:	$422,130 (again 5% appreciation and disregarding sales costs)
Minus Payoff of First Mortgage:	$181,019.73
Net Proceeds:	$241,110.27
Plus Side Account Balance:	$0
Out-of-Pocket Costs:	$127,271.16 plus $50,000 down payment for total of $177,271.16
Profit:	$63,839.11
Return on Money (profit divided by out-of-pocket costs):	36.01%
Internal Rate of Return (return divided by seven years):	5.14%

Figure 40

124 *Moving at the Speed of Wealth*

What is your internal rate of return (IRR) if you did nothing but pay as promised on your 30-year amortized loan and sold your home in seven years (Figure 41)? You sell the home for $422,130. You made $119,235.48 in payments but saved $20,473.44 in taxes for a net out-of-pocket cost of $98,762.04 plus your $50,000 down payment for a grand total out-of-pocket cost of $148,762.04.

Sale Price of Home:	$422,130 (again 5% appreciation and disregarding sales costs)
Minus Payoff of First Mortgage:	$217,517.33
Net Proceeds:	$204,612.67
Plus Side Account Balance:	$0
Out-of-Pocket Costs:	$98,762.04 plus $50,000 down payment for a total of $148,762.04
Profit (net proceeds minus out-of-pocket costs):	$55,850.63
Return on Money (profit divided by out-of-pocket costs):	37.5%
Internal Rate of Return (return divided by seven years):	5.36%

Figure 41

What! Just a cotton-picking minute here! Do your eyes deceive you? If you did nothing but make your payment as promised, you have an internal rate of return of 5.36%. If you paid an extra $300 per month to pay down your loan, you have an internal rate of return of 5.14% when you sell the house. How could this be true?

It must have a lot to do with the tax advantages of home loans, wouldn't you guess? The truth be told, if you think you might sell your home within this seven-year window, then you are better off not making extra principal payments at all. In fact, if you took that extra $300 and put it into a self-directed IRA and could receive this same 17% I have been talking about, it would grow

Secret of the Super-Rich #7 125

to $46,188 after seven years. Now your internal rate of return is 9.79%.

Once again, sending extra payments to your principal is about the biggest financial mistake one can undertake.

Even if you do not believe it, I can show you how to receive 17%; your $300 extra compounding in an IRA at only 8% grows to $33,498. This gives you an internal rate of return of 8.6%!

But neither compares to my strategy where you received a whopping 19.44% internal rate of return with **NO EXTRA MONEY OUT OF YOUR POCKET!**

Now, all I have to do is convince you that you can earn 17% safely and securely in today's environment. But I will take it a step further. If I can only show you how to receive 12%, you can pay off your home in less than fourteen years. At only 10%, you can pay off your home in less than sixteen-and-a-half years and still remain liquid.

If you could only receive an after-tax return of 6.4%, you would still pay off your home in twenty years, just as if you were sending an extra $300 per month, but you remain liquid.

Not to beat up on the good faith of UFirst, or any other company promoting these types of programs, but all you are doing is paying extra to your principal whenever the "software" gives you the green light. I have just proven that of all three strategies available to you, this is the absolute worst one you could undertake.

On the other hand, if you truly believe you are going to stay in the same home for thirty years and you love the safety of having your home paid off, then, by all means, pay extra money to your principal and hope you never have problems making your payment. Just because you paid extra to your loan does not mean the lender will show leniency or apply your pre-payments if you cannot make your payment to the loan. All you did by making additional payments was increase the safety of the lender's position. Common sense tells us that if the lender is safer, you must be less safe.

This has been an educational piece of the unconventional ways Moving at the Speed of Wealth™ shows people like you how to build wealth.

In my opinion, you should never, ever…ever, ever, ever send extra payments to your lender. You would probably be better off renting and reinvesting the savings (between rent and a home loan payment) in a side account; at least you would be liquid.

When you are liquid and you lose your job, you can always pull from this side account to make the payments while you get back on your feet.

Look, it should be obvious to you that conventional financial wisdom is just not working so you must take an unconventional road. This road is much harder to take but will get you to the high ground much more quickly. It means you step out of your comfort zone and see the bigger picture.

When you are ready, the teacher will appear. I would like to be that teacher. To get started on your unconventional financial journey, visit me at *www.SOWGoldClub.com* and begin your education in earnest. Take your time. Change can be hard over time, but even harder overnight. All I ask is that you come to me with an open mind and willingness to at least look at other points of view.

Chapter Eight

Secret of the Super-Rich #8

Super-Rich People Understand that Lump Sums of Money Grow Larger than Monthly Periodic Payments!

This concept is so obvious but is often overlooked by Middle America. In this brief chapter, I will show you how to build more wealth with the exact same amount of money out of your pocket and by using the exact same investment vehicle you are currently using.

Most Americans are attuned to making periodic payments to their retirement accounts on a monthly or annual basis. This could be a monthly contribution to a work-sponsored qualified retirement account such as a 401(k), 403(k), SEP, etc., or to an individual retirement arrangement (IRA). After all, you can budget this and know it's what you need to be doing to make your golden years your fun years.

You will typically make these deposits and take the tax deduction, which, of course, is real money in your pocket (or income), and let your money grow tax-deferred. One of the problems with these accounts is that you are limited as to how much you can contribute on an annual basis.

The contribution limits are illustrated in the following chart:

IRA Contribution Limits

YEAR	AGE 49 & BELOW	AGE 50 & ABOVE
2002-04	$3,000	$3,500
2005	$4,000	$4,500
2006-07	$4,000	$5,000
2008	$5,000	$6,000

Figure 42

You can see in Figure 42 that if you are age forty-nine or below, the maximum contribution you can make to an IRA is $5,000 in the year 2008. If you are fifty or older, you can make "catch-up contributions" and they stretch the maximum contribution to $6,000. You do not have to make the entire contribution at once; you can make it throughout the course of the calendar year. It is also important to note that contributions do not roll over. In other words, if you are fifty years old and only contributed $3,000 in 2007, you cannot roll over the other $2,000 and add it to the $6,000 for the 2008 calendar year. Basically, it is use it or lose it. After 2008, the contributions will raise $500 per year and, depending on the rate of inflation, the maximum contribution limits could be adjusted.

For 2008, the maximum amounts you can contribute to your 401(k) plan, as set by the IRS, are shown below:

2008 401(k) Contribution Limit: $15,500
2008 Catch-Up Contribution Limit
(only for those over fifty): ......an additional $5,000

If you are over fifty, you can make an annual contribution of $20,500. It is also very important to understand that the administrator of each plan and your employer can also impose limitations to contributions but cannot exceed the IRS guidelines. Every qualified plan has different rules and regulations governing the employees of each company.

You see, the government is in a quandary and speaks out of both sides of its mouth. In one sentence, the government will complain about the low savings rate of U.S. citizens and how this will impact government spending on entitlements in the future. On the other hand, the government must rely on consumer spending to strengthen the economy.

Secret of the Super-Rich #8

If you are planning on enjoying the same standard of living in retirement as you do now, then you cannot only rely on these plans to get you where you need to be. You must also start your own personal savings and investing plan, which, after all, is what Moving at the Speed of Wealth™ is all about.

One of the strongest strategies available today for Americans is the self-directed 401(k) plan. At Speed of Wealth, we strongly urge members of The Speed of Wealth Gold Club™ to start their own part-time, home-based or second business. Because we are teaching you all to become personal bankers, this is the first logical business to start. If your name is John Smith, you can, for example, set up a corporation (of any type) named John Smith Holdings Company, LLC. Because you are lending money to others and generating a profit, this is a true business. Holding companies have different rules and regulations, so oftentimes it's better to just start another business all together.

Back to the subject of self-directed 401(k) plans. A huge advantage of setting up your own business is that now you can open up a self-directed 401(k) plan for yourself and reap the benefits. The first major benefit is that you can make larger contributions. You are an employee of your corporation and can make a personal contribution of $15,000 of your own money that is, of course, tax-deductible. Your company can also make a contribution to your personal plan of an additional $29,000 that is tax-deductible to your business for a grand total of $44,000 for the year (2006). Take a look at some of the other great advantages.

- Unlike a typical plan at the workplace, your self-directed plan can hold real estate and real estate-related investments.
- A self-directed 401(k) can use its 401(k) funding as a down payment for a real estate purchase, with the self-directed 401(k) financing or borrowing the balance. The use of debt financing for real estate is not subject to UBIT (unrelated business income tax).
- When a self-directed 401(k) sells real estate or other investments, the capital gains are deferred through the 401(k), like any other 401(k) investment. *The headaches of 1031 exchanges are never necessary (which is MY FAVORITE ADVANTAGE).*
- Ownership of the property in a self-directed 401(k) allows you, as manager, to have direct, hands-on control

of any investment decisions over self-directed 401(k) assets, including control of the checkbook. Custodian involvement and hassles are eliminated, regardless of whether the investments are in securities, real estate or other assets.

- Since you control and handle all self-directed 401(k) transactions and act as the "custodian," then there are no expensive annual fees.
- Litigation threats, which accompany investments such as real estate, are substantially reduced. This is done by isolating the investment inside a title-holding company or trust-holding company, and away from the rest of your 401(k) funds and estate.
- It continues to provide deferral of income and gains inside the 401(k).

There are many more benefits to these types of plans, including a full menu of investment strategies that are not typically allowed within an IRA or work-sponsored plan. Contact Speed of Wealth for more details on self-directed 401(k) plans. We work with a very competent specialist who can walk you through the entire process. You can learn more by viewing a recorded webinar once you become a member of The Speed of Wealth Gold Club™ at *www.SOWGoldClub.com.*

The purpose of this chapter is to show you how lump sums of money grow larger than periodic payments. You can see that by utilizing a work-sponsored qualified retirement plan or an IRA, you are limited to contributions. We also know that if at all possible you want your money to grow tax-deferred or tax-free and compound.

Important Note: Although every financial planner in the world would argue that if you buy mutual funds within your IRA or work-sponsored qualified retirement plan, the money grows tax-deferred and compounds. But let's step back for a moment and challenge that assumption. Yes, it is true that all earnings on your money are tax-deferred. However, those earnings in mutual funds are represented by the NAV (net asset value) of the fund. This is a price per share determined by the fund's total assets minus liabilities divided by outstanding shares. If the underlying stocks within the mutual fund increase in value, the assets increase, thus increasing the NAV. Fair enough, but is this compounding? This is simply the increase in value and here is my argument. Net asset values of funds often go down in price, so is this negative compounding? In fact, if your mutual fund portfolio lost 50% of its value, you would need a 100% return just to get back to even. When I think of tax-deferred compounding, I think of earning interest: interest on principal, interest on the interest I have earned previously, and interest on the money that I would have ordinarily sent to Uncle Sam in (taxes), which is tax-deferral. I may be stupid compared to all of these highly educated financial planners, accountants, lawyers, etc., but I do not see how mutual funds compound when the value can just as easily go down. You are not truly earning interest within a growth mutual fund (income and money market funds are an exception). The value of the fund increases only if the underlying stocks increase in value, which fluctuates from day to day. Call me old-fashioned, but I think of compounding only on an interest-based investment. Although real estate can fluctuate in value, the appreciation of the property is directly tied to the previous value of the property; this is compounding. The price increase in stocks is not tied to any interest or inflationary movement, such as real estate. When the dollar goes up or down in value, is this compounding? I am sure that some day, someone will prove me wrong but this is my opinion and I am sticking to it. I challenge you to come up with your very own conclusions.

Now that you have a little bit of background associated with tax-deferral, compounding and how your qualified plans and IRAs work, I can now make my point.

We now know that if you are under fifty years old, the maximum contribution you can make to your IRA in 2008 is $5,000. If you divide this by twelve months, you can maximum fund your IRA by putting roughly $417 per month into your plan (you should always try to fund your plan toward the beginning of the year and not wait until the end of the year). We see that $417.67 per month times twelve months is $5,000. At the end of the year, most Middle Americans are able to deduct this $5,000 on their income tax form. This money comes right off the top of your earned income.

Remember that the last dollar in is taxed at your marginal tax bracket and deductions come off the top of your income, reducing your marginal tax bracket or effective tax bracket. Assuming you are in the 25% federal marginal tax bracket, you would save $1,250 in taxes ($5,000 contribution times 25%), which, of course, is real money to you (income).

If you are like typical Middle Americans, you will put that money into

132 *Moving at the Speed of Wealth*

mutual funds and if you are lucky, and I do mean lucky, you can average over time about 8%. (I have seen numerous studies suggesting that you are earning less than that by far and what's really scary is that according to a study done by J.P. Morgan, most investors believe they average 13.1% returns. This is laughable if you are investing in mutual funds, but believe what you will.)

The following chart shows you how your "periodic" payments of $417 will grow over time in a tax-deferred compounding environment like your IRA. Remember, this is if you could receive 8% returns each and every year. If you are a student of mine, then you know that it is the losses in your plan that kill you. (I mentioned above that if your portfolio loses 50% in value, you will need 100% returns to get to even. Of course, you could buy shares of the mutual fund at a lower cost when you lose money and this is dollar cost averaging, but I would just as soon not lose any money!)

This chart shows your money compounding on an annual basis with no starting balance.

Results Summary

Starting amount	$0
Years	30
Additional contributions	$417 per month
Rate of return	8.00% compounded annually
Total amount you will have contributed	$150,120
Total at end of investment	**$591,145**

Savings Balance by Year

Year	Additions	Interest	Balance
Start	$0		$0
1	$5,004	$214	$5,218
2	$5,004	$632	$10,854
3	$5,004	$1,083	$16,941
4	$5,004	$1,570	$23,514
5	$5,004	$2,095	$30,614
6	$5,004	$2,663	$38,281
7	$5,004	$3,277	$46,562
8	$5,004	$3,939	$55,505
9	$5,004	$4,655	$65,164
10	$5,004	$5,427	$75,595
11	$5,004	$6,262	$86,861
12	$5,004	$7,163	$99,028

Year	Additions	Interest	Balance
13	$5,004	$8,137	$112,169
14	$5,004	$9,188	$126,360
15	$5,004	$10,323	$141,688
16	$5,004	$11,549	$158,241
17	$5,004	$12,874	$176,118
18	$5,004	$14,304	$195,426
19	$5,004	$15,848	$216,279
20	$5,004	$17,517	$238,799
21	$5,004	$19,318	$263,121
22	$5,004	$21,264	$289,389
23	$5,004	$23,365	$317,759
24	$5,004	$25,635	$348,398
25	$5,004	$28,086	$381,488
26	$5,004	$30,733	$417,225
27	$5,004	$33,592	$455,822
28	$5,004	$36,680	$497,506
29	$5,004	$40,015	$542,524
30	$5,004	$43,616	$591,145

Figure 43

Looking at year thirty, you can see that you have accumulated $591,145. This is not bad considering you only contributed a total of $150,120 for a total return on your money of 294% or an IRR of 9.79% (294% divided by thirty years)—this is the power of compounding. Your true return is higher than the 8% and this IRR goes up a bit with every passing year.

So, how much money do you have for retirement in thirty years? Before you answer that question, remember that this is your individual retirement arrangement (IRA) and that you have deferred taxes, not eliminated them. It's hard to say how you will withdraw the money or what tax bracket you will be in, but let's assume you are still in the 25% tax bracket and that you withdraw all the money at once.

There is a difference between marginal tax bracket and effective tax bracket. If you do not have any other income during the year in which you withdraw this entire amount, not all of it will be subject to the 25% rate. But let's assume you do have other income and all of this money is subject to the marginal tax bracket (chances are you will not withdraw all of this money at once, but you will pay more in taxes by taking the money out over time). After the one-time withdrawal,

134   *Moving at the Speed of Wealth*

you are left with $443,329. This is the true value of your plan, not the $591,145—that's a difference of $147,786 (taxes owed) and you only saved $37,500 in tax deductions over that same thirty-year time span. Crazy, isn't it?

Now, let's put this to the "lump sum of money" test. I will assume that you have some equity in your home and you can borrow $83,333 out on an interest-only loan at 6%. Coincidentally, your monthly payment happens to be $417. At the end of the year, you have paid $5,000 in interest on this new loan.

This interest is all tax-deductible for most Middle Americans. And guess what? This tax deduction is the exact same as you would have received from your IRA above. You will save $1,200 in taxes. This, too, comes right off the top of your income. In both your IRA and your payments to your lender, you are out of pocket the exact same amount of money at the end of the year: $5,000 - $1,200 savings in taxes for a total out-of-pocket expense of $3,800. Assuming you put this lump sum of cash ($83,333) in the exact same mutual fund to which your periodic payments were going and you averaged 8%. Let's see what happens by looking at the following chart.

This time you are putting in a lump sum with no additional payments. The account is compounding annually. We are comparing apples to apples here to prove that lump sums of money grow larger than periodic payments!

Results Summary

Starting amount	$83,333
Years	30
Additional contributions	$0 per month
Rate of return	8.00% compounded annually
Total amount you will have contributed	$83,333
Total at end of investment	**$838,551**

Savings Balance by Year

Year	Additions	Interest	Balance
Start	$83,333		$83,333
1	$0	$6,667	$90,000
2	$0	$7,200	$97,200
3	$0	$7,776	$104,976
4	$0	$8,398	$113,374
5	$0	$9,070	$122,444
6	$0	$9,795	$132,239
7	$0	$10,579	$142,818
8	$0	$11,425	$154,244

Secret of the Super-Rich #8

Year		Additions	Interest
9	$0	$12,339	$166,583
10	$0	$13,327	$179,910
11	$0	$14,393	$194,302
12	$0	$15,544	$209,847
13	$0	$16,788	$226,634
14	$0	$18,131	$244,765
15	$0	$19,581	$264,346
16	$0	$21,148	$285,494
17	$0	$22,840	$308,334
18	$0	$24,667	$333,000
19	$0	$26,640	$359,640
20	$0	$28,771	$388,412
21	$0	$31,073	$419,484
22	$0	$33,559	$453,043
23	$0	$36,243	$489,287
24	$0	$39,143	$528,430
25	$0	$42,274	$570,704
26	$0	$45,656	$616,360
27	$0	$49,309	$665,669
28	$0	$53,254	$718,923
29	$0	$57,514	$776,436
30	$0	$62,115	$838,551

Figure 44

Wow, look at the difference! The lump sum of money, in the exact same investment, has grown to $838,551. Keep in mind that you still have a home loan in the amount of $83,333 because you only paid interest on this loan and did not reduce the principal. Knowing that, you will now pay off the home loan and you are left with $755,218. Compare that to the growth of $591,145 that you received making a $417 monthly payment. You have $164,073 more money with the exact same amount of money out of your pocket, the same tax benefits and in the same investment, but not in a tax-deferred IRA.

In fact, a good place to put this lump sum of cash is into a properly structured life insurance product. Many of you absolutely hate life insurance but that is because you have not been fully educated on how you can use it to create an unbelievable banking system (when using the right product that is structured properly). A life insurance contract is much like a Roth IRA (if you do not understand what a Roth IRA is, continue your education with us), only with more bells and whistles.

Of course, you could go directly into one of the opportunities that we recommend to you. If you do not have a self-directed IRA, then you cannot participate in these powerful opportunities. As we continue to educate you, I will be showing you the power of a self-directed 401(k) plan that beats everything else, hands down.

Let's take a look at how this lump sum of money would grow if I could show you how to receive a safe, reliable 17% return. If you do not reposition this money into a qualified retirement plan or IRA, it will not grow tax-deferred and I have already told you that you cannot dump this large of an amount into these plans [however, you could get a good portion of it into a self-directed 401(k)].

We can assume that if you are earning 17% outside of a tax-deferred plan, you will have to pay ordinary passive income tax on the interest you earned. For argument's sake, let's just say that your effective tax bracket is 20%. This would reduce your effective return to 13.6% [17% x 80% (100% - 20% taxes) = 80%].

I want to take this lump sum idea a little bit further. In our next example, you take our advice and open up a self-directed IRA and invest $417 per month into this great investment that offers 17% returns safely (truth be told, very few investments outside of mutual funds will accept a monthly payment).

Your other choice is to pull out the $83,333 from home equity and invest it directly, but this money is not in a tax-deferred plan so you will be taxed on earned interest annually, and we will use my example above so your effective return is 13.6%. Look at the difference in the two charts below.

Results Summary

Starting amount	$83,333
Years	30
Additional contributions	$0 per month
Rate of return	13.60% compounded annually
Total amount you will have contributed	$83,333
Total at end of investment	**$3,820,911**

Savings Balance by Year

Year	Additions	Interest	Balance
Start	$83,333		$83,333
1	$0	$11,333	$94,666
2	$0	$12,875	$107,541

Secret of the Super-Rich #8

Year	Additions	Interest	Balance
3	$0	$14,626	$122,166
4	$0	$16,615	$138,781
5	$0	$18,874	$157,655
6	$0	$21,441	$179,096
7	$0	$24,357	$203,454
8	$0	$27,670	$231,123
9	$0	$31,433	$262,556
10	$0	$35,708	$298,264
11	$0	$40,564	$338,828
12	$0	$46,081	$384,908
13	$0	$52,347	$437,256
14	$0	$59,467	$496,722
15	$0	$67,554	$564,277
16	$0	$76,742	$641,018
17	$0	$87,178	$728,197
18	$0	$99,035	$827,231
19	$0	$112,503	$939,735
20	$0	$127,804	$1,067,539
21	$0	$145,185	$1,212,724
22	$0	$164,930	$1,377,654
23	$0	$187,361	$1,565,015
24	$0	$212,842	$1,777,858
25	$0	$241,789	$2,019,646
26	$0	$274,672	$2,294,318
27	$0	$312,027	$2,606,345
28	$0	$354,463	$2,960,808
29	$0	$402,670	$3,363,478
30	$0	$457,433	$3,820,911

Figure 45

In Figure 45, you can see that after-tax growth with compounding interest grows to $3,820,911 by the end of year thirty. Now, pay very close attention: You have already been taxed on this money so you no longer owe taxes; all this money is principal and can come out tax-free. If you pull the interest you earn from this $3,820,911 as income, it will be taxed as ordinary non-wage income annually.

But wait a minute—your periodic payments were inside an IRA so you did not have to pay taxes as you went along. Your effective return was 17%, not

13.6%. Surely, with this better return, your money had to grow larger. Take a look below.

Results Summary

Starting amount	$0
Years	30
Additional contributions	$417 per month
Rate of return	17.00% compounded annually
Total amount you will have contributed	$150,120
Total at end of investment	**$3,530,963**

Savings Balance by Year

Year	Additions	Interest	Balance
Start	$0		$0
1	$5,004	$450	$5,454
2	$5,004	$1,377	$11,835
3	$5,004	$2,462	$19,300
4	$5,004	$3,731	$28,035
5	$5,004	$5,216	$38,255
6	$5,004	$6,953	$50,212
7	$5,004	$8,986	$64,201
8	$5,004	$11,364	$80,569
9	$5,004	$14,147	$99,720
10	$5,004	$17,402	$122,126
11	$5,004	$21,211	$148,341
12	$5,004	$25,668	$179,013
13	$5,004	$30,882	$214,899
14	$5,004	$36,983	$256,886
15	$5,004	$44,120	$306,010
16	$5,004	$52,471	$363,485
17	$5,004	$62,242	$430,732
18	$5,004	$73,674	$509,410
19	$5,004	$87,049	$601,463
20	$5,004	$102,698	$709,165
21	$5,004	$121,008	$835,177
22	$5,004	$142,430	$982,611
23	$5,004	$167,494	$1,155,109
24	$5,004	$196,818	$1,356,931

Secret of the Super-Rich #8

Year	Additions	Interest	Balance
25	$5,004	$231,128	$1,593,063
26	$5,004	$271,270	$1,869,337
27	$5,004	$318,237	$2,192,579
28	$5,004	$373,188	$2,570,771
29	$5,004	$437,481	$3,013,255
30	$5,004	$512,703	$3,530,963

Figure 46

Looking at year thirty in Figure 46, you can see that your periodic payment is growing at a full 3.4% better rate than our previous example, which grew to $3,530,963. That's $289,948 less than our lump sum at a lower effective return. But it gets much worse. Your $3,530,963 is in an IRA and every single dime, principal plus interest earned, is subject to non-wage income taxes when withdrawals are made. And you must take withdrawals, whether you want to or not, by age 70½.

Using the same 20% effective tax rate, you are left with only $2,824,770.40 if you pulled it all out at once, which, of course, you would not do because it would put you into the highest marginal tax bracket and all the money would probably be subject to a much higher marginal tax bracket.

The lump sum will produce more income if you just live off of the interest than your periodic payment model would—and when you pass away and leave this money to your heirs, the lump sum model passes tax-free [unless, of course, you have an estate tax issue, which is easily handled using an irrevocable life insurance trust (ILIT)].

The money you pass on to your heirs in an IRA is still a tax burden to them. However, I am sure they would still be very happy to receive this money even after taxes.

Of course, we would like to see you use a lump sum and put it into a tax-deferred vehicle, and we can get most of the money into one as long as you are educated and willing to start a small business with the intent to earn a profit. We have the experts to show you how to create a self-directed 401(k) that, with some very careful planning, could allow you to put more than half of the $83,333 into a tax-deferred vehicle.

If you can receive 17% annually in a tax-deferred investment, who cares what taxes are due down the road? Take a look at the following table.

Results Summary

Starting amount	$83,333
Years	30
Additional contributions	$0 per month
Rate of return	17.00% compounded annually
Total amount you will have contributed	$83,333
Total at end of investment	**$9,255,350**

Savings Balance by Year

Year	Additions	Interest	Balance
Start	$83,333		$83,333
1	$0	$14,167	$97,500
2	$0	$16,575	$114,075
3	$0	$19,393	$133,467
4	$0	$22,689	$156,157
5	$0	$26,547	$182,703
6	$0	$31,060	$213,763
7	$0	$36,340	$250,103
8	$0	$42,517	$292,620
9	$0	$49,745	$342,365
10	$0	$58,202	$400,567
11	$0	$68,096	$468,664
12	$0	$79,673	$548,337
13	$0	$93,217	$641,554
14	$0	$109,064	$750,618
15	$0	$127,605	$878,223
16	$0	$149,298	$1,027,521
17	$0	$174,679	$1,202,200
18	$0	$204,374	$1,406,574
19	$0	$239,118	$1,645,691
20	$0	$279,768	$1,925,459
21	$0	$327,328	$2,252,787
22	$0	$382,974	$2,635,761
23	$0	$448,079	$3,083,840
24	$0	$524,253	$3,608,093
25	$0	$613,376	$4,221,469
26	$0	$717,650	$4,939,118
27	$0	$839,650	$5,778,768

Year	Additions	Interest	Balance
28	$0	$982,391	$6,761,159
29	$0	$1,149,397	$7,910,556
30	$0	$1,344,795	$9,255,350

Figure 47

Figure 47 illustrates the magic of compounding tax-deferred; the $83,333 has grown to $9,255,350 by the end of year thirty, $1,925,459 by year twenty and over $400,000 by the end of only the tenth year. How does that compare to your current financial plan?

You have achieved this all because you learned the techniques that the rich have hidden from Middle America for centuries. This is no more than a reprogramming of your financial wealth IQ. Keep in mind that in our example above, your out-of-pocket costs were exactly the same but with very different results.

Maybe you do not have home equity to pull off this not-so-magical trick. Where else can you turn to get this lump sum of cash? Before I go into places you can look to pull out a lump sum, I must retrain your mind and get you in the correct mindset. First of all, America's savings rate today is a negative half-percent. That's right: Americans are spending more than they are saving. It doesn't take a mathlete to figure out that you cannot build a retirement plan when you do not save money. I suspect that if you are reading this, then either you are a saver or you are ready to save.

That being said, it should be obvious that the more you save, the more retirement income you will be able to produce. If you listen to representatives at Charles Schwab®, they will tell you straight up that each and every American needs to have $245,000 saved by retirement for every $1,000 per month income they want in retirement. Imagine that you are in retirement. If you are married, you may be lucky to receive $2,000 per month in Social Security benefits. Most of you are not going to be able to rely on a pension unless you work for the government.

I would suspect that the dual income your family produces today is in the neighborhood of $75,000 per year or more. That's $6,250 per month in before-tax income. And if you think you will need less income in retirement than you need during your working years, you have been sold a bill of goods.

Assuming you can receive $2,000 from Social Security, you are still $4,250 short of maintaining the same standard of living that you currently enjoy (and

142   *Moving at the Speed of Wealth*

I would bet that you would prefer a better standard of living in retirement than you enjoy today). Going by the Schwab model, you would need $1,041,250 saved for retirement.

I personally think Schwab is off the mark a bit. If true inflation is closer to 8%, you will need returns on your money consistently of about 13% for the Schwab model to hold up. If you are receiving 13%, you can only withdraw the difference between your returns and true inflation to maintain the same standard of living throughout retirement without the fear of outliving your money. (This is covered in the chapter on inflation.)

The point is that most of us need to make more contributions to retirement than we are making today. We need to pay ourselves first (after all, there are 300-page books that will tell you to save more and invest for the long term).

Here is the mental shift you must make. If you pull out a lump sum of money from the sources I am going to show you below, then you will have a monthly payment associated with it in almost all cases. I will show you how to offset these payments, but if my offsets don't work for you, then my advice is to suck it up and find a way to make the payments.

If you were to pull out $83,333 of equity, your payment with an interest-only loan at 6% would be $417 per month. Even though you are making that payment to a lender, you need to tell yourself every time you send off that payment that it is a retirement contribution. You see, you already have the $83,333 working as a lump sum to grow your retirement; you are essentially just making the contributions to retirement after the fact.

If you can wrap your mind around this concept, it won't hurt as badly when you send those payments in. You have to overcome the psychology of all the conditioning you have had up to today. Start thinking like wealthy people do and you will soon join them on their financial scale.

The following are some ideas of where you can find a lump sum of cash:

- **Equity**—We just talked about using equity and have covered the use of equity. This is obviously the first place you want to turn to, especially if you are making contributions to an IRA.
- **Parents' Equity**—I have a wide variety of reports available for seniors who have equity in their homes. Suffice it to say that equity in your parents' home is as bad as equity in your home, but they have an opportunity that people under sixty-two years of age don't. If you are a

Secret of the Super-Rich #8

senior age sixty-two or over, you can take out a "reverse mortgage" on your home, pull out this dead asset and put it to work with no monthly payment. After all, your parents' plan is probably to leave you the house, so just talk to them about this program and get your inheritance now to start building for your future (you can tell your parents that if they don't help you, you won't be able to build a retirement plan and you may be forced to move back in with them...this should pique their interest).

- **Car**—Perhaps you have a car that is paid for, free and clear. Today, you can refinance a car at extremely low interest rates and pull out a lump sum to put to work for you. It doesn't matter what the size of the lump sum is—just get a lump sum working for you.
- **RV, Jet Ski, Boat, Snowmobile, Etc.**—If you own any type of property that the banks will collateralize and make a loan on, then borrow money against it to get a lump sum. (See the car example above.)
- **Personal Signature Loan**—If you have a good credit score and assets, you may be able to borrow up to $250,000 on a personal signature loan alone. If you need help finding a lender like this, log onto *www.SpeedofWealth.com*, become a member of The Speed of Wealth Gold Club™ and we can guide you in the right direction.
- **Business Loan**—If you own a business, you may be able to borrow money. (See the personal signature loan above; it is essentially the same.)
- **Student Loan**—I really don't know much about student loans but I do know that they come with low interest rates and, best of all, are not payable until six months after you graduate, in most cases. If you can afford tuition, fees, housing, books, etc. during your first year in college, go ahead and take out a student loan and put it to work. The next year, simply take out another student loan to pay your expenses and continue to let the original loan work for you. Let's assume you attend college for six years and are resigned that you must take out a $10,000 student loan each year to pay your way. You are fully aware that at

144   *Moving at the Speed of Wealth*

the end of the sixth year, you will owe $60,000 plus interest. You are going to college to help you attain a high-paying job and you are resigned to the fact that you will be paying off student loans for quite some time once you are in the "real world."

Not so fast! If you take your original $10,000, you can open up a self-directed 401(k) since there is no rule that a college student cannot own a business. In fact, we can show you businesses that are perfect for college students that they can work very few hours a week on right from their dorm room, apartment or any other living quarters.

Anyway, you invest this original lump sum student loan in an investment that generates 17% returns, and by the end of the sixth year it will have grown to $51,303. Now, when you start your career, you are only saddled with a loan balance of $8,697 plus the interest owed on the other student loans. Can you take a deep breath and relax already? By the way, the same holds true for parents who are planning on paying for their child's college tuition. If you can create arbitrage between the interest rate being charged on a student loan and where you can invest your money, take out the student loans and continue to let your money grow. Wait until the loans become due and then pay them off with all your newfound wealth (more about this in the chapter on opportunity cost).

- **Credit Cards**—If you have great credit, I am sure you are bombarded with offers of 0% on credit cards. It is not hard to create arbitrage when you are being charged 0%. Borrow from the credit card but do not consume it. Reinvest the lump sum and let the money grow. Most 0% offers are good for only one year but if you make the payment each month, the interest rate it will jump to is typically below 8%. If you use this strategy, make sure you read the fine print. If you make just one mistake, the issuer will jack up your interest rate in a millisecond. Many fortunes have been built starting with just a credit card, including my own.

Now that we have found places to find lump sums of money, you will notice that most of them carry a monthly payment. Let's see how we can handle that monthly payment and still build tremendous wealth.

1. **Suck it up**—Heck, you probably need to be contributing a lot more to your retirement plan anyway. You can borrow on a car for as low as 0% today, though typically more like 4.5% to 6%. Assume you borrow $30,000 against your car at 6% amortized over a five-year period. Your monthly payment would be $579.98 but you put the $30,000 in an investment that pays 17% annually.

   At the end of five years, you have paid a total of $34,799 but your $30,000 has grown to $65,773. You have a profit of $30,974 ($65,773 growth minus what you spent, $34,799 = $30,974). Your returns are 89% or an internal rate of return of 17.8% over the five years.

   The cool part is that at the end of five years, you have no more payments and your money will continue to grow. In just five years more, a total of ten years, your money has grown to $144,205 compounding annually at 17%. Now you have an internal rate of return of 31.4%. So, sometimes you just have to suck it up and make the payments.

2. **Redirect your IRA contributions**—I already gave you an example of this but let me explain a little more. Instead of sending monthly payments to an IRA account, redirect them to make the loan payment…it really is that simple. Of course, if the loan is not a home loan, it is not tax-deductible. So what? You still win the game in the long run.

3. **Redirect contributions you are making to your work-sponsored 401(k) plan**—There is an entire chapter in this book on The Speed of Wealth 401(k) Arbitrage Strategy.™ Once you read that chapter, you will have an entirely new outlook on your qualified retirement plans.

   Don't get me wrong: I like IRAs and qualified retirement plans but only when they are self-directed. You are lucky if you are averaging 8% or more returns in your work-sponsored plan! Once you read the chapter on 401(k) arbitrage, you may never contribute to one of these plans again. Take a look at number 1 above. Do you think that if you just contribute $579.98 per month to your plan for five years, it will grow to $144,205 in ten years?

Heck, let me show you what happens when you add in your employer matching (I know this is your strongest argument). Let's say you contribute $579.98 per month and your employer adds another $500 for five years. Because you are limited to invest in mutual funds, you are going to be lucky to receive an 8% average return. After five years, your money has grown to $79,214. That is only $13,481 more in growth than the car example above. Yet your employer contributed an extra $30,000 to the plan.

The point is that with my strategy, you have freed up over $65,000 that is not constrained by all the rules and regulations of a qualified plan. Again, read the chapter on 401(k) arbitrage; it will slap you across the face and wake you up.

4. **Start your own business**—We would be happy to show you a simple business to start that will allow you to increase your annual tax deductions. This increase in tax deductions, on things you are already paying for, can easily save you enough money at the end of the year to offset these monthly payments. Again, you will need to speak to a professional tax advisor, but suffice it to say that Uncle Sam is generous to business owners. In fact, it is our belief at Speed of Wealth that every American should own his or her own home-based business and preferably one that makes money. The business we can show you can easily produce the extra money you would need each month to make a loan payment (without much effort on your behalf) using the tax benefits alone. If you would like more information on this great business opportunity, please email Donna McKelvy at *dmckelvy@comcast.net*. She would be happy to give you a short presentation that will excite you to no end.

On top of that, if you start the correct part-time home-based business, you should be able to generate an extra $200 - $500 or more each month to offset these additional monthly payments. Heck, you may be able to generate enough to not only offset the payment to pull out a lump sum of money but also to generate some additional monthly cash flow.

It doesn't take much to generate an extra $500 per month other than time. What's your hobby? Do you like to fix things around the house? Then let the neighborhood know that you can do handyman work for them and generate some revenue. Collect aluminum and paper and recycle; you are paid for this effort. The only thing holding you back is laziness! I am not talking about taking on a part-time job at 7-Eleven; I am talking about doing what you want to do. I routinely speak at corporations and colleges about building wealth and getting paid for what you love to do. But, remember, if you have any asset you can borrow on, you are better off using a lump sum of money to grow richer rather than putting away your extra income each month. Use the extra income to make the payment.

5. **Refinance your home into an interest-only loan**—Again, there is an entire chapter in this book discussing this very topic, so read it. Proper use of home equity coupled with the right type of home loan can make you wealthy beyond your wildest dreams.

6. **Increase the deductible on your insurance**—Trust me, you do not want to make a claim anyway. During my wife's real estate career, she had a client who lost a $500 necklace in her home. She thought it was stolen by someone looking at the home as a buyer (it happens frequently). She had no deductible and made a claim. The insurance company paid the claim and promptly dropped her coverage. No other insurance carrier would touch her without tripling her annual premium. Insurance should be used for major losses, not minor ones, so go ahead and increase those deductibles; you will save money, which can be used to offset these payments.

7. **Use equity arbitrage, IRA arbitrage and annuity arbitrage**—All of these are strategies discussed in this book, so I will leave it up to you to read those chapters. There is some pretty intense stuff in those pages and you will start to discover the ways in which very wealthy people think differently.

The point is that you need to use your imagination or just suck it up. I understand that monthly cash flow is a hot topic for most American families but if you do not do something today, wait and see how much of a topic monthly cash flow becomes during retirement…it ain't a pretty picture.

I want to make one last point regarding using lump sums of money to build wealth before we move on. A lump sum of money will always beat periodic payments but your money will grow exponentially larger as you receive better returns.

You need to quit thinking that so much risk is associated with good returns. Read Robert Kiyosaki and Donald Trump's book *Why We Want You to Be Rich*. There is a great chapter in the book regarding risk and what it really is. Remember that wealthy people expect at least 15% returns on their money. You need to believe you can receive these types of returns as well.

Take a look at the charts below to see how your lump sum compares to periodic payments as your returns rise. I am comparing a $375 monthly payment to a $75,000 lump sum of cash.

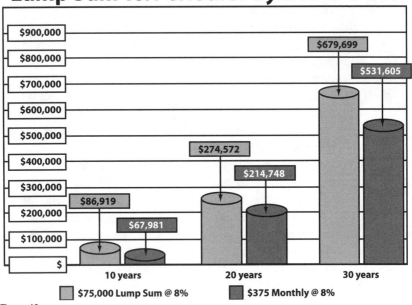

Figure 48

The above chart compares the lump sum to the periodic payment if you can receive an 8% return on your money, and the lump sum reflects money left over after paying off the underlying loan of $75,000. You can see that you have more growth at all three intervals and, by year twenty, you are ahead of the game by $59,824. Keep in mind that I am showing this without you spending any more money monthly than you are currently doing.

If I can show you how to receive better returns safely, and, of course, I can, then you can see in Figure 37 what a 12% return will do for you. By the end of year twenty, you are better off by $303,525, again with no extra money out of your pocket. That's exponentially better than what your money grew to when receiving only 8%, but you still won the battle at 8%.

Look at the huge jump when I show you how to receive 15% on your

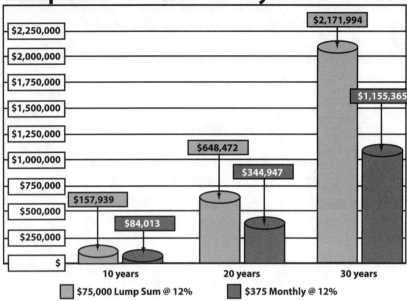

Figure 49

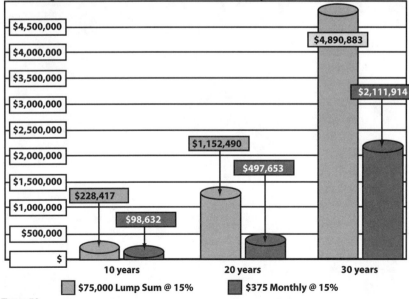

Figure 50

money consistently and safely. By the end of only ten years, you are ahead of the periodic payment schedule by $129,785 after paying back the loan—and remember that both the periodic payments and the lump sum are in the exact same investment.

By the end of year twenty, you beat the periodic payments by $654,837 and look at year thirty! Your lump sum outperformed the periodic payments in the same investment by over $2.7 million.

It is very easy to summarize this chapter. If you want to be "Moving at the Speed of Wealth™", then use lump sums of money whenever possible, and let us show you how to receive better returns on your money! This is another wake-up call and I don't care who you are: If you want to build massive wealth, then use this strategy. After all, wealthy people do.

Chapter Nine

Secret of the Super-Rich #9

Super-Rich People Have a Great Understanding of Opportunity Costs

By the time you are finished with this chapter, I would be surprised if you ever paid cash for a car or other large-ticket items again. I am about to shock you by sharing with you what I believe to be a huge wealth destroyer in America.

We go through our lives living by the old conventional wisdom that was passed down to us by our parents. In case you were wondering where your parents received their financial knowledge, it was probably from their parents. So here you sit in the twenty-first century, living off of ideas that may have been true fifty years ago but no longer apply.

I know that you have been conditioned to "pay cash for everything," to "never be in debt," and that "debt will destroy you"—then I come along and tell you that debt, in some cases, is good. Let me ask you a simple question: If you had $30,000 in the bank and wanted to buy a car for $30,000, you would probably have two choices, right? You could pay cash or finance the car. Because you are a firm disbeliever in debt, you pay cash. Now, let's explore this subject and discover if you made the right decision.

You absolutely must understand that you pay interest on everything you buy. If you finance something, obviously you pay interest; if you pay cash for something, you lose the interest you could have earned on that money and this is called opportunity costs.

152 *Moving at the Speed of Wealth*

For the examples I will use throughout this chapter, here are my assumptions. First, you are thirty-five years old and you plan on buying a brand new car every five years until you are sixty-five. Secondly, I will not take into account inflation or interest rate movements. Third, you are only going to buy a $30,000 car every five years and the car will depreciate 50% over that five-year period. Fair enough? Let's get started.

First, you are faced with a choice. You can pay cash or finance this car at 6% amortized over a five-year period. You, of course, do not believe in debt so you opt to pay cash for the car. You just happened to have $30,000 sitting in a savings account.

Let's walk through Figure 51. Another assumption I want to make is that you did not inherit this $30,000; you had to save it over time.

If you pay cash, what is your loan amount? Well, of course it is zero. You have no loan— you can see that in the first row in the table below. Next, you will notice that you have a $452.50 payment each month. Pause…

"Wait a minute," you say. "I don't have a loan so I don't have a payment!" Oh, but you are wrong. Remember, I said you did not inherit this money and that you had to save it. If you were to put away $452.50 into a bank account paying 4% a year, in five years you would have saved $30,000, enough to pay cash for this car.

Not that this fact has anything to do with what I am showing you in this chapter, but I wanted to make sure that you understood this. Sure, you did not take on debt but you still had to make monthly payments to save money. The difference is that you pre-paid for your car rather than financing and paying after the fact. Let's move on with our illustration.

Since you have no loan on this car, you will see that you have $0 loan costs, which is good. Now, here comes the biggie. If you would have let your money sit in a tax-deferred environment that compounded annually and received only an 8% return, your $30,000 would have grown to $301,880 by the time you retired at age sixty-five (thirty years down the road). Subtract the original principal of $30,000 and you had an "opportunity cost" of $271,880.

No worries, the car has some value at the end of five years; it is worth $15,000 using our earlier assumptions. So in those thirty years' time, you lost $256,880 of potential growth on your money at only 8% in a compounding environment. Just in case you were wondering, that is a *negative* 28.54% internal rate of return each year.

Let's take a longer look at this and see what happens when you use this plan to buy five cars with cash over that thirty-year span. You know you lost $256,880 that you could have had for retirement on the car you bought at thirty-five. I will

Item	Pay Cash
Loan	$0
Payment @ 6% Remember, this is simple interest	$452.50 (each month in bank @ 4% for 5 years)
Loan Costs	$0
Growth @ 8% This is in a compounding account	$0
Opportunity Costs @ 8%	$271,880** ($30,000 would have grown to $301,880**)
Loan or Cash Recapture	$0
Car Residual Value	$15,000
Net Gain or Loss	($256,880)
Return on Money	-856%
* If you had the $30,000 to reinvest. **30-year opportunity costs. For illustration purposes only, not guaranteed.	

Figure 51

go ahead and deduct the $15,000 depreciated value of the car and not factor inflation into our equation.

I am assuming you could have received an 8% annual return compounding annually in a tax deferred/free account. If you cannot get 8% returns on your money, you really need help.

Let's look at Figure 52 and see what you missed out on.

Pretty scary, considering you did exactly what you were told to do by your parents and grandparents...but let me make it even more frightening. If you could have financed these cars at 6%, you would be paying back $34,626 to the bank every five years. The total finance charges would have been $173,130, excluding resale of

Age	Opportunity Costs
35	$256,880
40	$190,454
45	$124,829
50	$52,768
55	$29,080
Total By Age 65 (retirement)	$654,011

Figure 52

154 *Moving at the Speed of Wealth*

the car. You would have been ahead by $480,881 if you would have financed. Remember: simple interest versus compounding growth with a little bit of arbitrage. It is all starting to fall together now, isn't it?

Now I really want to blow your mind. Let's assume we have a thirty-five-year-old man who has no money to his name so he has no choice but to finance the car. The following chart shows his numbers.

Item   Pay Cash

Item	Pay Cash
Loan	$30,000
Payment @ 6% Remember, this is simple interest	$577.10
Loan Costs	$34,626
Growth @ 8% This is in a compounding account	$0 Remember, he does not have $30,000; he is broke.
Opportunity Costs @ 8%	$0
Loan or Cash Recapture	$0
Car Residual Value	$15,000
Net Gain or Loss	($19,626) Loan costs minus car residual value
Return on Money	-11.34% Negative Internal Rate of Return… expected!

Figure 53

So our broke thirty-five-year-old borrows $30,000 at 6% interest amortized over five years for a monthly payment of $577.10. He did not have the $30,000 to start with so he has no growth on this non-existing money and no opportunity costs. He does not recapture any principal (more on this later) and his car is worth $15,000 at the end of five years.

When you subtract the car's residual value ($15,000) from his total payments ($34,626), you have a net loss of $19,626. Negative $19,626 divided by what he paid ($34,626) gives you a negative annual internal rate of return of 11.34%. This is to be expected when you are financing or paying cash for a depreciating asset.

This guy only lost $19,626, and if you multiply that by five cars, you have a total loss of $98,130 over a thirty-year period. This broke guy did better than the guy who paid cash for the cars. But it gets even worse.

Let's assume that instead of trading in his cars at the end of each five-year period, he sells the car independently and reinvests his $15,000 in this account that compounds 8% annually.

Our broke guy sold the cars for $15,000 and reinvested the money in an annual compounding 8% account; the money grew to $274,648 (imagine what you can do if you get 12% or more). He paid $34,626 every five years to finance these cars, which, multiplied by five cars, adds up to total payments over the years of $173,130. This guy who started out with nothing, nada, zero is ahead of the game by $100,000 because he took my advice and quit trading in his cars.

Either way, you may have eliminated the so-called stress of having a car payment by paying cash for you car, but you are not Moving at the Speed of Wealth™. Your fears are keeping you back from building wealth. I have said it before and I will say it again: You don't know what fear is until you retire with very little money in the bank, even if you are debt-free.

Years to Compound	Growth on $15,000 @ 8% compounding annually
25	$102,727
20	$69,914
15	$47,583
10	$32,384
5	$22,040
Total by age 65 (retirement), selling the cars and reinvesting the money	$274,648

Figure 54

Enough said about the two methods of buying a car. Do you think I might have even a better way to purchase your car? Sure I do. I wouldn't leave you hanging, so let's look now at the best way to buy a car. I actually have a better method and the best method, so follow along.

Let's make our assumptions now for the rest of this discussion. You have some home equity, your home will continue to appreciate at 5%, and you can take out a HELOC (home equity line of credit) at 8% amortized over five years. We will also assume that you have $30,000 in the bank so you could pay cash if you wanted to (although I just showed you why you wouldn't). One more assumption: Your home is worth $300,000.

Okay, look at the Figure 55 and follow along:

Item	Pay Cash
Loan	$30,000
Payment @ 8% 5-year amortized loan (HELOC)	$608.29
Loan Costs	$36,497.40
Home Loan Interest Tax Deduction (20% assumption)	$1,299.48
Net Loan Costs (loan costs minus tax deductions)	$35,197.92
Growth on $30,000 @ 8% - This is in an annually compounding tax-deferred account	$14,080
Property appreciation @ 5% annually on $300,000 home (remember that homes can, and do, depreciate as well)	$82,884 ($300,000 compounding for five years at 5% annual appreciation)
Opportunity Costs @ 8%	$0
Loan or Cash Recapture	$30,000 (Of the $36,497.40 you paid back on the loan, $30,000 was principal so it created the same equity position you had before you took out the loan; in other words, you recaptured the principal of this car purchase.)
Car Residual Value	$15,000
Net Gain or Loss	$106,766.08 (appreciation on house plus gain on $30,000 plus car residual value minus net interest cost of $5,197.92)
Return on Money	60.66% internal rate of return...expected! (Read on; this is a little misleading.)

Figure 55

Secret of the Super-Rich #9 157

You will notice you have a 60.66% IRR on your money but this is a little deceiving. I will explain. You borrowed $30,000 from your home equity using a HELOC and you amortized it for five years at 8%. This resulted in a monthly payment of $608.29. Over the course of five years, you paid the lender back a total of $36,497.40. Obviously, this is your monthly payment of $608.29 times sixty months.

Most of you readers would be entitled to a home interest tax deduction (again, check with your accountant). You paid a total of $6,497.40 in interest and assuming a 20% effective tax rate, you save an additional $1,299.48 in taxes; this is real money to you because it is money you would have ordinarily sent to Uncle Sam but kept. If you subtract this real money from what you paid back to the lender, your true after-tax net out-of-pocket cost was $35,197.92. Are you keeping up with me? Again, I use numbers just to complement my strategies; the most important point is that you understand the principle I am trying to teach you.

It was assumed that you had the $30,000 and could have paid cash but chose to finance your car this way instead. That being the case, you let your $30,000 continue to grow tax-deferred and compound annually at 8%. The growth on this $30,000 in five years was $14,080.

Here is where it gets a little tricky. I am showing you property appreciation of 5% and, of course, property can depreciate (but mutual funds can lose money as well). This is a 5% increase on the value of your home, the entire $300,000 value of your home, which compounds over five years for a total appreciation of $82,884.

Now I'll explain why the internal rate of return is a little skewed. When I calculated the IRR, I used the property appreciation as well. Here is the kicker: Your property would have appreciated by the exact same amount even if you did not take out this HELOC. (I talk about it in the chapter on equity.) Your property will appreciate at the same rate whether your home is 100% paid off, 100% mortgaged or anything in between.

If you want a more accurate IRR, add the growth on your $30,000 of $14,080 plus the car's residual value of $15,000 for a total of $29,080. Divide this number by how much money you have put into this investment, which is the net after-tax loan cost of $35,197.92, which equals 82.62%, and divide that number by the five years for an IRR (16.5%).

Important Note: *Remember that you recaptured the $30,000 principal as you paid back the HELOC. You now have that money available as*

158   *Moving at the Speed of Wealth*

> *equity in your home again. This is very important to remember when calculating your returns.*

My goodness, you beat the stock market by purchasing your personal depreciating car the proper way. Did you ever think you could have that kind of return on your money when purchasing a car, or did you always think buying a car was just a losing proposition?

Before I move on to another solution, let me point out the negatives to buying cars the way I just described. First of all, you have a monthly payment on your HELOC that must be paid to the bank, regardless of your current situation. That's no big deal; if you financed a car, you would have a monthly payment to a car finance company that also must be paid monthly. However, if you pay cash, you have no monthly obligation.

A second pitfall is that you financed a car using your home as collateral. The money you borrowed is secured by your house. If, God forbid, something happened to you and you were forced to file bankruptcy, you could not walk away from this obligation. You need to keep your house. Sure, when you finance a car, the loan is secured by the car, but which is easier to walk away from: a car or your home?

I get a gut-wrenching feeling every time I hear a commercial suggesting you refinance your house to pay off high-interest credit cards. Do you realize that by doing this you are turning a non-secured debt into a secured debt? We are all just one lawsuit away from bankruptcy, so be very careful. A better approach would be to pull out your equity, invest as a hard money lender secured by trust deeds, and use the monthly payment to pay off your credit cards. At least you still have your principal in tact.

If you choose to finance your cars the way I have just described, make sure you do it exactly the way I laid it out. Do not take out a home equity line of credit with a twenty- or thirty-year amortization schedule; make sure you only do it for a maximum of five years. If you amortize it for longer, the payment will be smaller but, and this is a big but, when you go to buy another car, you are still paying on your previous car.

Oh, and by the way, unless you own a business, quit leasing cars. I know they suck you in with those low payments but you will never win the money game. On the other hand, if you own a business, leasing is a very strong alternative.

An even better way to buy the car is to use a properly structured life insurance contract. Keep in mind that we are using the insurance policy as a banking system but it does take a few years to capitalize and to have enough equity in your policy to borrow from.

Let's take a look at what happens when you redirect a current asset into a policy. We'll assume you have $100,000 sitting in a money market, certificate of deposit, bonds or other cash-equivalent type of account, generating a low return on your money.

Instead of letting your money sit in these investments, which are presumed to be very safe, reposition the cash into a very safe indexed universal life policy. Going back to our discussion on life insurance, make sure you maximize the premium and minimize the death benefit. Remember that we must fund it for five years so we will reposition the $100,000 over a five-year period or $20,000 a year in premium.

Just to keep on course with my earlier examples, I will show a non-smoking male in good health funding a policy starting at age thirty-two.

Looking at the illustration below, you will see that from day one this thirty-two-year-old male has covered his family with $711,356 worth of death benefit. This is another great benefit from the banking system—you receive life insurance to protect your family or help with estate taxes at any age.

Look down at year three and you will see that our Speed of Wealth candidate has accumulated $45,677 in surrender cash value. This is enough to borrow $30,000 to purchase his car. He simply calls the insurance company and tells them he wants to take out a policy loan in the amount of $30,000 on the variable loan option, and he receives a check within ten days. He then walks it down to the car dealership and pays cash for the car.

End of Year	Age	Model Premium	Times Per Year	Annual Premium	Cash From Policy	Annual Outlay	Non-Guaranteed Assumed			
							Surr Cash Value	Surr Charge	Account Value	Death Benefit
1	33	20,000	1	20,000	0	20,000	3,632	13,309	16,941	711,356
2	34	20,000	1	20,000	0	20,000	24,536	12,422	36,957	711,356
3	35	20,000	1	20,000	0	20,000	45,677	11,534	57,211	711,356
4	36	20,000	1	20,000	0	20,000	70,379	10,647	81,026	711,356
5	37	20,000	1	20,000	0	20,000	95,495	9,760	105,255	711,356
6	38	0	1	0	0	0	105,957	8,873	114,830	711,356
7	39	0	1	0	0	0	113,214	7,985	121,199	711,356
8	40	0	1	0	0	0	125,453	7,098	132,551	711,356
9	41	0	1	0	0	0	134,026	6,211	140,237	711,356
10	42	0	1	0	0	0	149,432	5,324	154,756	711,356
				100,000	0	100,000				

Figure 56

Assuming that the current average AAA corporate bond rate is 6%, this is what the insurance company will charge him to borrow the money. Just as in our example of financing the car, his monthly payment back to the insurance company would be $577.10.

160   *Moving at the Speed of Wealth*

This next statement is very important for you to absorb. He is *not required* to make that payment. It's not like it is when borrowing from a car finance company or home equity, where he is required to make that payment every month. If he has a bad month, he can skip the payment; in fact, he never has to pay it back, although we strongly encourage him to be disciplined and do so. By making the payments, you ensure yourself of having enough in your banking system to borrow from your insurance policy five years down the road for your next car.

Let's fast-forward to age sixty-five.

End of Year	Age	Model Premium	Times Per Year	Annual Premium	Cash From Policy	Annual Outlay	Non-Guaranteed Assumed			
							Surr Cash Value	Surr Charge	Account Value	Death Benefit
26	58	0	1	0	0	0	669,105	0	669,105	923,365
27	59	0	1	0	0	0	722,447	0	722,447	968,079
28	60	0	1	0	0	0	807,335	0	807,335	1,049,536
29	61	0	1	0	0	0	871,914	0	871,914	1,116,050
30	62	0	1	0	0	0	974,501	0	974,501	1,227,871
				100,000	0	100,000				
31	63	0	1	0	0	0	1,052,468	0	1,052,468	1,305,060
32	64	0	1	0	0	0	1,176,300	0	1,176,300	1,435,086
33	65	0	1	0	0	0	1,270,437	0	1,270,437	1,524,524
34	66	0	1	0	0	0	1,419,994	0	1,419,994	1,689,793
45	67	0	1	0	0	0	1,533,642	0	1,533,642	1,809,697

Figure 57

Looking at the illustration above, you will see that by age sixty-five, our car buyer's original $100,000 has grown to $1,270,437 (assuming a 9% average return and, again, we know that nothing works on averages). He has paid back all of his payments on the five cars he had bought over thirty years, so he is out of pocket $577.10 for thirty years times twelve months for a total of $207,756.

Remember that I recommend selling the car independently and reinvesting the proceeds. Using our example earlier in this chapter, we know that at an 8% compounding tax-deferred growth on $15,000 every five years for twenty-five years grows to $274,648.

By repositioning money into an insurance policy, this guy is ahead of the game by $1,237,329 ($1,270,437 growth in policy plus $274,648 growth on selling cars minus $207,756 car payments minus $100,000 original investment). On top of that, in a perfect world, if everything goes as planned, this policy would cash flow a tax-free income stream of $178,644 for this person forever, starting at age sixty-five.

There are two programs I know of that use an insurance policy as a banking system, Infinite Banking™ or Bank on Yourself™, both of which are not telling the whole truth (probably because the people touting it do not fully understand). I am going to tell you the truth. You can basically accomplish the same goal by leaving your money invested where it is and not moving it to an insurance policy. I showed this in our first solution. You do not need an insurance policy to start your own banking system. The promoters of these plans believe that the insurance policy is the only way to achieve the goal but it simply is not true. They talk about recapturing interest and all kinds of cool stuff, but if you create arbitrage, you are better off.

So why use an insurance policy? First of all, if you have money sitting around in cash equivalents or equity, it is a great place to receive better returns with the safety you may desire. Another great reason is that the insurance policy gives you flexibility. You do not have to make your payments if you do not want to. The other methods I discuss require you to finance either from a car finance company or HELOC, which requires you to make a payment each month come hell or high water.

But perhaps the best reason of all is that you do not stop by borrowing from your policy to purchase cars. Just because you borrow money from your policy to purchase a car does not mean you cannot borrow the remaining balance to reinvest. Think about it. If you can do this well by using a banking system to buy a depreciable asset, what do you think happens if you borrow from your plan to buy an appreciable asset, such as real estate, or make hard money loans? You got it—you get richer.

Truth be told, I don't always recommend borrowing from the policy to buy cars; I would rather see you borrow to reinvest. There are other reasons to use an insurance policy to build wealth.

College Funding

Since we are on the subject of opportunity costs, let's take a look at what a college education really costs parents. Let's assume that you are forty-five years old and your first child is off to a college that charges $20,000 per year. This would include tuition, books, fees, and room and board. Of course, this may be a little low but, again, we are talking about principles.

Many parents and/or grandparents are intent on not only sending their children to college but also paying for it. This is admirable, but let's see if there is truly a better way to pay for this education.

First of all, if you are forty-five and spend $20,000 on tuition, you cost your retirement plan a whole lot of money. Your kids better get a good education because they may have to take care of you during your retirement years. (I see this everywhere today. Kids take care of their parents and blow their

162   *Moving at the Speed of Wealth*

retirement savings so the next generation must take care of their parents and so on. This is a vicious cycle that must be stopped.)

If you could have received a meager 8% return on your money in a tax-deferred compounding annually environment, let's take a look at the chart below to find out your opportunity costs. We will assume you would spend $20,000 a year for a four-year education and you plan on retiring at age sixty-five.

Age and Investment	Growth by age 65 at 8% tax-deferred compounding annually
45 - $20,000	$93,219
46 - $20,000	$86,314
47 - $20,000	$79,920
48 - $20,000	$74,000
Total - $80,000	$333,453
Important Note: Just because I want you to start thinking about better returns, this same college investment would have grown to $1,074,700 if you could have received 15% on nice, safe, secured hard money loans in a tax-deferred annually compounding environment, such as a self-directed IRA or self-directed 401(k). That is an expensive college education!	

Figure 58

Looking at the chart above, you can see that the "true" cost of this college education is $333,453 (take a look at the important note—this education could have cost you over one million dollars) in opportunity costs. Pretty sick when you stop and think about it, wouldn't you agree?

What if, instead, you created a banking system using a life insurance product, or took out your home equity at age forty-five and invested it?

First of all, my recommendation is to make all attempts to help your child receive a scholarship, federal grant or, at the very least, student loans to pay for college. Let's assume that you can take out student loans to pay for the entire cost of college. You will be borrowing $20,000 a year, but keep in mind that student loan interest rates are relatively low. Your payments are deferred until six months after graduation but the interest compounds while they wait for the pay back period.

Assuming you could borrow at 6%, your child would owe $92,742 in student loans after four years of college. I am sure you have heard of plenty of kids starting out in life saddled with these large student loans. When it is time

Secret of the Super-Rich #9 163

to pay back the loan, the monthly payment would be $664.43 if amortized at 6% over twenty years.

Important Note: I am not professing to be an expert on student loan rules and regulations (that's for another book). Once again, I am trying to make a point. The key is to find a loan that can be deferred during the time your child is in college. One way to achieve this is to build up a life insurance policy's surrender cash value and borrow from the surrender cash value to pay for college.

Keep in mind that the federal government insures student loans and if your child defaults on the loan or makes late payments, the consequences can be devastating for a long time to come. Your child, just starting out in life in his or her early twenties, does not need this kind of pressure.

There are many challenges with the "college savings plans" available to you. These accounts have many rules and regulations and I personally would not touch one knowing I have life insurance available to me with much fewer rules. Again, these plans are beyond the scope of this book, but I would be happy to address it in the future.

There are many ways to fund this insurance policy. If you are tucking away money monthly in one of the college savings plans mentioned above, you could tuck away money into a life insurance contract just as well. If you have saved enough money to pay for college, you could maximum fund the plan. For our example, let's assume that you started tucking away $300 a month into a life insurance policy, starting when your child was born and continuing for the next eighteen years. Your child was born when you were twenty-seven.

By looking at Figure 47, you can see that you have accumulated $111,104 by the age of forty-five, just in time to send your kid to college. You have a couple of choices you can make here: You can borrow from your policy and defer the payments until your kid graduates and finds a job (I encourage you to make your child pay back the loan, but this is your call; remember, if your kid has a rough time making the loan payment, it just doesn't have to be made).

You could borrow on student loans and continue to leave your policy alone until the student loans are due in four-and-a-half years. At this point, you have continued to let your money grow and you have accumulated $160,119 in surrender cash value. Now, you could simply borrow from your policy, pay off the student loans and pay yourself back loan payments. Remember that your policy will continue to be credited interest (in this case, 9% before cost of

End of Year	Age	Model Premium	Times Per Year	Annual Premium	Cash From Policy	Annual Outlay	Non-Guaranteed Assumed Surr Cash Value	Surr Charge	Account Value	Death Benefit
1	28	300	1	3,600	0	3,600	0	5,286	2,390	355,307
2	29	300	1	3,600	0	3,600	151	4,934	5,085	355,307
3	30	300	1	3,600	0	3,600	3,283	4,581	7,864	355,307
4	31	300	1	3,600	0	3,600	6,853	4,229	11,082	355,307
5	32	300	1	3,600	0	3,600	10,517	3,876	14,393	355,307
6	33	300	1	3,600	0	3,600	14,709	3,524	18,233	355,307
7	34	300	1	3,600	0	3,600	19,010	3,172	22,182	355,307
8	35	300	1	3,600	0	3,600	23,934	2,819	26,753	355,307
9	36	300	1	3,600	0	3,600	29,017	2,467	31,484	355,307
10	37	300	1	3,600	0	3,600	35,069	2,114	37,183	355,307
				36,000	0	36,000				
11	38	300	1	3,600	0	3,600	41,695	1,762	43,457	355,307
12	39	300	1	3,600	0	3,600	49,322	1,410	50,732	355,307
13	40	300	1	3,600	0	3,600	57,292	1,057	58,349	355,307
14	41	300	1	3,600	0	3,600	66,449	705	67,153	355,307
15	42	300	1	3,600	0	3,600	76,056	352	76,408	355,307
16	43	300	1	3,600	0	3,600	87,063	0	87,063	355,307
17	44	300	1	3,600	0	3,600	98,268	0	98,268	355,307
18	45	300	1	3,600	0	3,600	111,104	0	111,104	355,307
19	46	0	1	0	0	0	121,669	0	121,669	355,307
20	47	0	1	0	0	0	133,266	0	133,266	355,307
				64,800	0	64,800				
21	48	0	1	0	0	0	146,058	0	146,058	355,307
22	49	0	1	0	0	0	160,119	0	160,119	355,307
23	50	0	1	0	0	0	175,642	0	175,642	355,307
24	51	0	1	0	0	0	192,710	0	192,710	355,307
25	52	0	1	0	0	0	211,545	0	211,545	361,743

Figure 59

insurance and expenses) on the entire $160,119, as if it never left the policy. You can pay back the loan any way you choose. You do not have to amortize it; you can make bigger payments, smaller payments, and the flexibility is the best part of this strategy.

Of course, you would be borrowing from your plan during the four years of college to reinvest the money. Nothing changes here. Just to reiterate, borrowing from a life insurance policy is a lot like borrowing home equity to reinvest. The differences are big, however.

When you borrow from home equity, your home will continue to appreciate regardless of the new loan. I have been using a 5% average appreciation rate but we all know that your home can depreciate as well. The life insurance policy cannot depreciate more than the cost of insurance and expenses. The returns you receive are tied to the upside of the stock market with no downside risk. If the market is down, you are simply credited with a 0% return. However, the policy has a minimum guarantee; your home does not. Also, on average, the policy will appreciate more than your home and is safer and liquid.

Secret of the Super-Rich #9

Another big downside to borrowing from your home is that you are put on a repayment schedule. This could be an amortized loan or interest-only loan. It really doesn't matter. You are obligated to make a payment each and every month or you are in default. With an insurance policy, when you borrow from the equity you have built up, you repay the loan at your own pace and schedule. Clearly, it is in your best interest to repay the loan as if it were a set schedule but, hey, things change in life and things happen.

The interest rate that the insurance company will charge you is very close to home interest rates. Both are tied to bonds; however, in most cases, the interest you pay on home equity loans is tax-deductible whereas the interest rate charged on the policy loan is not.

Both the account value in your insurance policy and the appreciation on your home will continue on the full amount whether you have a loan against it or not. This is the power of both strategies.

Now, let's look to see what would happen if you maximum funded your policy using $100,000 at age forty to prepare for the college expenses. You will put $20,000 in the policy each year for only five years and be done.

End of Year	Age	Model Premium	Times Per Year	Annual Premium	Cash From Policy	Annual Outlay	Non-Guaranteed Assumed			
							Surr Cash Value	Surr Charge	Account Value	Death Benefit
1	41	20,000	1	20,000	0	20,000	3,490	13,536	17,026	492,786
2	42	20,000	1	20,000	0	20,000	24,489	12,634	37,123	492,786
3	43	20,000	1	20,000	0	20,000	45,698	11,731	57,429	492,786
4	44	20,000	1	20,000	0	20,000	70,463	10,829	81,292	492,786
5	45	20,000	1	20,000	0	20,000	95,636	9,926	105,562	492,786
6	46	0	1	0	0	0	106,161	9,024	115,183	492,786
7	47	0	1	0	0	0	113,459	8,122	121,581	492,786
8	48	0	1	0	0	0	125,743	7,219	132,962	492,786
9	49	0	1	0	0	0	134,337	6,317	140,654	492,786
10	50	0	1	0	0	0	149,774	5,414	1545,188	492,786
				100,000	0	100,000				

Figure 60

I do want to point out that it is very important to have life insurance while your family is young (personally, I think it is important throughout your life but especially when you have young children). So not only are you achieving your goals, but you also have life insurance to protect your family in the event of an untimely death.

By maximum funding the policy, you have enough to borrow for college at the exact right time. If you wait until your child graduates, you have accumulated $134,337 of surrender cash value; this is more than enough to pay off the student loans if you choose to wait.

End of Year	Age	Model Premium	Times Per Year	Annual Premium	Cash From Policy	Annual Outlay	Non-Guaranteed Assumed			
							Surr Cash Value	Surr Charge	Account Value	Death Benefit
1	41	20,000	1	20,000	0	20,000	3,490	13,546	17,026	492,786
2	42	20,000	1	20,000	0	20,000	24,489	12,634	37,123	492,786
3	43	20,000	1	20,000	0	20,000	45,698	11,731	57,429	492,786
4	44	20,000	1	20,000	0	20,000	70,463	10,829	81,292	492,786
5	45	20,000	1	20,000	0	20,000	95,636	9,926	105,562	492,786
6	46	0	1	0	0	0	106,161	9,024	115,185	492,786
7	47	0	1	0	0	0	113,459	8,122	121,581	492,786
8	48	0	1	0	0	0	125,743	7,219	132,962	492,786
9	49	0	1	0	0	0	134,337	6,317	140,654	492,786
10	50	0	1	0	100,000	-100,000	43,391	5,414	155,188	386,403
				100,000	100,000	0				
11	51	0	1	0	0	0	48,805	4,512	166,490	379,613
12	52	0	1	0	0	0	60,973	3,610	184,980	372,389
13	53	0	1	0	0	0	67,959	2,707	198,748	364,704
14	54	0	1	0	0	0	83,078	1,805	221,140	356,528
15	55	0	1	0	0	0	92,076	902	237,933	347,831
16	56	0	1	0	0	0	110,890	0	265,097	338,579
17	57	0	1	0	0	0	121,499	0	285,549	328,736
18	58	0	1	0	0	0	143,933	0	318,455	318,264
19	59	0	1	0	0	0	157,712	0	343,373	307,125
20	60	0	1	0	0	0	185,832	0	383,344	300,835
				100,000	100,000	0				
21	61	0	1	0	0	0	203,571	0	413,691	319,405
22	62	0	1	0	0	0	238,514	0	462,045	358,405
23	63	0	1	0	0	0	260,901	0	498,700	380,589
24	64	0	1	0	0	0	304,085	0	557,063	426,639
25	65	0	1	0	0	0	332,210	0	601,335	452,477

Figure 61

Now, I want to show you something very exciting.

In the illustration above, you see that you borrow $100,000 from the plan to pay off the student loans at age fifty. Without making one single payment on the loan back to the insurance policy, you still have equity in your plan of $332,210 at the age of sixty-five (this, of course, is not guaranteed and is based on historical performance, which is no guarantee of future performance.) I am using a 6% loan rate, which will fluctuate annually. This loan rate could be higher or lower in any given year. Again, we are working off averages but you can see the power of utilizing and managing a properly structured indexed life contract.

In this example, you started by repositioning $100,000 into your policy with the sole purpose of helping with your child's (or grandchild's) college education. You still have tripled your money twenty years down the road after paying for this college education and making no loan repayments. I call that powerful—and in case you were wondering, yes, you can still borrow from the plan to reinvest during that same twenty years.

A final strategy would be to borrow the $100,000 and reinvest the money. I would recommend hard money loans. If you could receive 13% after-tax returns on your hard money loans, this $100,000 would generate $13,000 annually. You could take this money, pay your child's (or grandchild's) student loan payment and take the difference to pay back the loan in your policy (or use it for income, or reinvest it). The possibilities are endless.

One final note to make is that the college savings plans available to you have very strict rules. Depending on which plan you choose, you could receive tax deductions and the money grows tax-deferred, but if your child does not use the money to attend college the rules change dramatically. With a life insurance policy, you have all the freedom you would ever want. And, let's face it, just because you want your kid to go to college and have saved the money does not necessarily mean your kid will go.

Again, I want to point out that this book is not about buying life insurance. I have said it many times: Life insurance is a poor investment but a great investment tool if you use the right product and the right company and if it is structured properly. My intent in this book is to educate you and I feel the American public has been misled regarding life insurance.

I don't think anyone would argue that hundreds of thousands of Americans have built some tremendous wealth through the home they live in (poor IRR, but still wealth). You need to think of a life insurance contract like you do a home. It is a place to store money and you can use this "equity" that you are building up to build tremendous wealth.

The neat thing about a home is that you can leverage, or borrow, the money to build wealth. Guess what? You can borrow money to create a sound life insurance policy as well. (This is too deep to discuss here, but if you contact us we will be glad to show you how.) The easiest way to achieve this is to borrow the equity from your home and reposition the cash into a life policy. Once your policy has been capitalized, you borrow from the policy equity to reinvest. Your money is growing in three columns at the same time. Your home continues to appreciate, your policy continues to appreciate and the investment into which you placed your policy loan proceeds hopefully appreciates. That, my friend, is truly Moving at the Speed of Wealth™.

In case you have not figured it out yet, if you can borrow from this plan to buy cars, reinvest or pay for college, then it makes sense to borrow from this plan to buy business equipment as well.

If you own a business, there are some really neat tricks for which you can use a life insurance contract. Did you know that life insurance is one of the few investments that you cannot use IRA money for? I wonder why... Could it be because of all the tax advantages associated with it? Of course it is, but did you know that you can use a life insurance contract inside a self-directed 401(k) plan that you set up for your business?

You sure can and we will discuss that later when I talk about owning your own business. Oh, heck, why don't we just dive into this fact in the next chapter?

Chapter Ten

Secret of the Super-Rich #10

Wealthy People Understand that You Must Absolutely, Positively Own Your Own Business to Build Tremendous Wealth

This is perhaps the most important chapter in the book. You need to read it and let it sink in. What I am about to share with you will make all the difference in your goals of financial independence and I am going to break it down so that you will have no excuse not to follow my advice.

Make no mistake: If you do not own your own business, you are already behind the eight ball. Now, don't freak out on me yet. I am not saying you have to quit your current job and invest all of your money on the gamble that you can start a business that will replace and overcome your current income. I am saying you can easily start your own home-based business into which you put very few hours and that can easily make you wealthy even if you don't net a whole lot of profit.

One of the reasons I am considering self-publishing this book is the fact that when you use publishers, they are not big on the author promoting themselves and/or their services. Let's face it: I am in the self-promotion business—writing books does not make up the bulk of my income. My business of setting people up in a life insurance contract, introducing alternative investments, setting up self-directed IRAs and 401(k) plans for people, providing home loans, speaking, and selling Internet tools, books, courses, bootcamps and my network marketing business are what pays me collectively

169

(how is that for multiple streams of income?). But understand that everything I do is still focused on my core business of educating and helping Middle America build wealth faster.

As always, I like to ask you questions. So here is the big question for this chapter: Would you be willing to trade $480 for $4,000? Would you be willing to trade five hours a week and maybe $1,000 in order to receive $24,000 or more annually? Just what are you willing to trade to increase your income: your time, your money, other people's time and money?

Here is the plain truth of the matter: Americans are just not willing to put in the work needed to increase their wealth or income. We as a society have become very complacent and content just showing up. After all, we are Americans and we are entitled to the better life.

Well, you better take a look around you. The middle class is disappearing quickly and most of us go by the theme "out of sight, out of mind." In other words, we walk around with blinders on and our fingers crossed, hoping and praying that everything will work out in the end. The bad news is that it ain't turning out better in the end. More and more Americans are relying on their families and the government to get them through retirement and that's just to exist as a pauper.

I am not willing to just exist! I was given one very short life and I want to make the most of it. My father was self-employed and owned his own construction company here in Denver. What I learned very early on was that, although my dad made his own rules and schedule, he worked harder than the other parents on the block. He built a comfortable life for his family, with no formal education on how to do so.

If my dad knew then what he knows now, he would have been much better off. You see, things have changed, believe it or not. We now have the technology and tools to build massive wealth without lifting a hammer or pounding the street.

Home businesses in America are being created at record rates and those that take advantage fare much better. Depending on what statistics you look at, it is estimated that there are between 18 and 38 million home-based businesses in the United States alone. The U.S. Bureau of Labor Statistics estimates that number to be closer to 18.3 million.

According to the Office of Advocacy (Small Business Administration), the number of households that have a home-based business exceeds 12% and that is an old statistic. According to the Home-Based Business Institute, about 70% of all home-based businesses will last over three years, compared to only 29% of business ventures outside of the home.

Now, here is the real shocker—and you had better get your piece of the pie.

Entrepreneur magazine estimates that $427 billion (that's billion with a "b") in revenue is generated each year by these home-based businesses. And according to the SBA's Office of Advocacy, in the year 2000, nearly 20,000 home-based entrepreneurs grossed more than $1 million from home. Recent studies indicate that the average income for home office households is $63,000 and a good slice of these home-based entrepreneurs have other jobs as well.

According to the Small Business Administration, today more than half (53%) of the small businesses in the U.S. are home-based. Here are some other jaw dropping statistics:

- In the U.S., 1,500 jobs are eliminated daily.
- According to the U.S. Bureau of Labor statistics, mass layoffs reached a ten-year peak in the first quarter of 2005 (it is much worse today).
- In January 2005 alone, 2,564 different large layoffs, affecting 239,454 workers, occurred.
- Every eleven seconds, someone starts a home-based business.
- It is estimated that a home-based business is started every ten seconds in the U.S. In the last fourteen years alone, the number of home-based businesses has risen from 6 million to 32 million and shows no sign of slowing down. There are literally hundreds of home-based business ideas to choose from.
- There is a 95% survival rate in year one and an 85% success rate over a three-year term.
- Spare time turns into full-time for 50% of home-based business owners.
- Female-owned businesses are being created at about twice the rate of male-owned businesses.
- **Finally, *40 - 44% of all home-based businesses require less than $5,000 for startup.***

Why can't the average family with dual income get ahead financially? Many times, when you have a job, you do not factor in costs associated with that job. Let's take a look at some and I will leave the best for last:

- Average childcare costs: $7,000 per year. Owning a home-based business gives you the luxury of keeping your child home during the pre-school years and tending to his or her needs. On top of that, you can save, on average, $7,000 per year and that cost is increasing rapidly.

- Gasoline: $1,200 per year. This is a very old statistic but factor in all the gasoline you consume driving to and from work on a daily basis. Factor in all the time you waste sitting in a lane that is not moving (remember that time is money). Today, with gas prices at four dollars per gallon, I challenge you to record how much money you spend on gasoline alone getting to and from work each day for one month—be prepared to be shocked. This doesn't even include the wear and tear on your vehicle.
- Dry cleaning, pantyhose, and business wardrobe: hundreds to $2,000 yearly. Working from home gives you the luxury of working in your pajamas if you choose. With today's technology, there is no reason to ever pay for expensive suits and dry cleaning again. I used to go out on the road and perform live seminars, which cost me a fortune. Today, although I still do live events, I have scaled that way back. In fact, most of my seminars and educational presentations are done over the World Wide Web in the form of webinars. I can also pick up the phone and do a live teleseminar or teleclass any time and, in either case, you will never know where I am, what I am wearing, or even if I have a large pizza sitting in front of me. I currently have an office with over 3,500 square feet. I just don't need it anymore. I can help out all of my students right from the comfort of my own home, saving me about $8,000 in rent each month.
- Eating out for lunches: $2,000. Only $2,000, my rear end! My wife and I routinely go out for lunch every workday at an average cost of $20 (including tip). Multiply that twenty dollars by five days for fifty weeks and it equals $5,200 every year. When I work from home, I can make a tuna salad sandwich for less than a buck.
- Auto maintenance (oil, tires): $1,500. Although you will have costs to maintain your vehicle even when you work from home, it will more than likely decrease dramatically

Secret of the Super-Rich #10

because you have reduced the wear and tear on your vehicle by letting your car sit in the garage or driveway.

- Parking: $1,800 (or five dollars per day). Depending on where you work, you may have to pay for parking and this adds up over time.
- Shuttling the kids. I have talked about the extra gasoline consumption but have you ever stopped to think how much more you consume when you have to leave work to pick up your kids, who more than likely are somewhere closer to your home, and then drive them somewhere else? How much more wear and tear does this add to your vehicle when you could have left from home and saved miles shuttling them to and fro.
- And now for the granddaddy of them all…drum roll, please—taxes! For four months and a week, or three hours out of every eight-hour day, you're working for Uncle Sam. (The average American family of four with a median income of $47,012 will pay $10,250 in federal taxes and another $6,110 in state and local taxes for a total "tax liability" of $16,360.)

Let's add that all together. If you are making a median income of $47,012 and your spouse is making the same, you are grossing $94,024 per year. Assuming you have two kids in daycare, after a very conservative deduction of the expenses mentioned above, you are left with about $30,304 to handle all of your other bills. And you wonder why it is so hard to save money!

Besides the obvious costs above, let's take a long look at this tax issue. Remember the question I asked you to open up this chapter: "Would you be willing to part with $400 if you could earn $4,000?" I am positive you said yes without any hesitation.

Here is how easy it is to accomplish this. In just a few paragraphs, I am going to share with you two business opportunities that you can start and run for a total of less than $400 per year. You can operate any one of these businesses right from your home office.

Now that you are a business owner, you are entitled to business expense tax deductions. Chances are that you could easily save $4,000 per year in taxes or more every single year you operate your business.

You see, when you work for somebody else, your taxes work something like this:

- Earn
- Taxed
- Spend what's left

When you own your own business, and you have a very good accountant and record keeping system, your income resembles something like the following:

- Earn
- Spend
- Taxed on what's left

Folks, imagine if you could just reinvest the tax savings alone for retirement—$4,000 per year invested in a tax-deferred environment [an IRA or your own self-directed 401(k)] compounding annually at 12% (I already showed you how to get 12% safe and secure with hard money loans) would grow to over $78,000 in just ten years. By year thirty, it will grow to over $1 million. This is nothing more than found money.

Keep in mind that a business you start should eventually make you extra income that you could split and, say, use half for enjoying a more fruitful life and invest the other half. For every home-based business opportunity I will introduce to you, it should not take you more than five to ten hours a week to earn money, if you are willing to work and are coachable.

I am not an accountant and do not want to go deep into the rules that allow you these benefits, but suffice it to say that you must start a legitimate business with a profit motive. Then you can enjoy tax deductions on many of the bills you are already paying. Let me give you an example.

I have twin fifteen-year-old daughters; one is a "barn rat," the other is a "mall rat." I love them both equally for different reasons. My "mall rat" loves to play tennis, gets straight A's and, you guessed it, loves to shop for the finer things a girl can have. You, as a doting parent, would ordinarily pay for those things. My children, on the other hand, pay for their luxuries and it is a tax deduction for me.

You see, whenever my daughters need extra income, they come into my office and I put them to work. They do real work, listening to their iPods while they stuff envelopes or put together courses with their friends. At the end of the day, I pay them and that is 100% tax-deductible to me. Of course, there is a limit as to how much I can write off—but are you seeing the bigger picture?

Listen to me carefully. You can easily save $4,000 or much more each and every year that you would ordinarily send to Uncle Sam simply by starting your own home-based business and structuring it properly.

Let me provide you with a partial list of available deductions as a home-based business entrepreneur. First of all, understand that you have many more available deductions to you than the everyday taxpayer; the government offers these deductions because business is what pushes a free capitalist society. Our government, love it or hate it, really does promote entrepreneurship.

Of course, you must meet the requirements set forth by the IRS before you are able to take any deductions but, believe me, these are easy requirements and are easy to set up. Make sure you consult with a qualified tax consultant before starting on your own. If you are starting to get to know me, you probably have come to the conclusion that I have a red personality. Simply put, this means I am a leader and don't think I need anybody's help. At first I set up my own businesses and later found out about the thousands of dollars in taxes I paid, which I didn't have to.

As I age, I have realized that I do need others to help me complete my objectives, just like you do. The following list of tax-deductible items is taken from *some* of the categories of the IRS's Schedule C.

Advertising	Bad debts from sales/services	Car and truck expenses
Commissions and fees	Cost of goods sold	Depletion
Depreciation and section 179 expense deduction (my favorite)	Employee benefit programs	Expenses for business use of your home (another favorite)
Insurance (other than health but even this can be deductible)	Interest a) Mortgage (paid to banks, etc.) b) Other (really nice deduction)	Legal and professional services
Office expenses	Pension and profit-sharing plans (another favorite of mine)	Rent or lease a) Vehicles, machinery and equipment b) Other business property
Repairs and maintenance	Supplies	Travel, meals, and entertainment
Utilities	Wages (less employee credits)	Other expenses
Many more that a qualified tax pro can help you find!		

Figure 62

176   *Moving at the Speed of Wealth*

Your first thought is that you would have to spend money on your business in order to get a tax deduction. I have mentioned once before that it is better to pay twenty-five cents for every dollar you earn than to save twenty-five cents for every dollar you spend. But this simply is not the case here.

Suppose you have a 2,000-square-foot home. You choose one 200-square-foot room from which to conduct your business. This room is strictly used for business. This space is 10% of the entire square footage of your home.

Remember, this is just for illustration purposes; make sure to consult a qualified tax pro. Using the above formula, 10% of your mortgage payment, hazard insurance, water bill, gas, electric, home maintenance, snow removal, yard care, etc. would be tax-deductible at the end of the year. This is money you are currently spending, but now a portion of it is tax-deductible.

Also, do you own a computer? If you use it for your business, you can depreciate it over a scheduled time period, providing you with a "phantom" tax deduction. Depreciation is my favorite tax deduction because it is phantom. You do not have to spend money in order to get the deduction. Unlike real estate, there is no depreciation recovery on these items. Oh, how sweet it is!

Warren Buffet is on record speaking in front of a crowd of wealthy people and blasting the current tax code. He goes on to say that he paid a lot less as a percentage of his income than his house cleaner did (paraphrased, of course).

That is because wealthy people understand that you must absolutely own your own business. In fact, you should own several and use business entities to hold your assets within (that is an entirely different subject on asset protection, which is covered in a later chapter).

There are some reasons I can think of for people not starting their own businesses:

1. They are lazy and think it is costly and difficult to set up business entities.
2. They don't know what to offer.
3. They think too BIG and assume it is costly and painstaking to start a business.
4. They assume that they don't have enough time.
5. They assume it takes a lot of money to start a business.

All of these assumptions are, of course, fabricated in their minds. An educated person will soon find out that starting, operating and earning a nice profit with a home-based business is perhaps one of the easiest things to accomplish once you have the desire.

Secret of the Super-Rich #10

As for issue number one, no, it is very easy to set up these entities and the initial costs are tax-deductible to boot. On top of that, the taxes you save will more than cover any initial costs.

As for issue number two, I am going to unveil two possible businesses you could start today all for under $400 that could make you a boatload of money.

Business Number One: "The Speed of Wealth Affiliate and Super Affiliate Program"

This is perhaps the biggest no-brainer on the face of the planet. If you are enjoying this book and believe what I am sharing with you, then don't you think you should share it with others? Hopefully you have already joined us for a live webinar, seminar, teleseminar, workshop or some other function, or perhaps you have viewed the recordings of these events at *www.Speed-ofWealth.com* (you must be a member of The Speed of Wealth Gold Club™ to view most content; to learn more and to join, visit www.SOWGoldClub.com). If you like our investment opportunities, don't you think you should share them with people you care about?

If the answers to the above questions are yes, then I believe you should be paid to refer people to us. Look at it this way: Last year I spent over $150,000 promoting live seminars across the country. With what I have to teach people, I refuse to spend money any longer. I should be paid to share my knowledge and strategies. However, that would only happen in a perfect world and this just isn't a perfect world.

Because I am trying to help Middle Americans in all areas of their lives, it only makes sense for me to redirect that marketing budget to you. You see, I am going to spend money to market my services no matter what. In fact, any business owners that tell you they are not in the marketing business are doomed for failure. Nothing happens unless I market and marketing costs money.

On top of that, there is no better marketing or advertising than word of mouth (remember this as we go into our next two options). Adding up one plus one, I came to the conclusion that I should pay my students "affiliate commissions" and "finders' fees" to refer people to the club—people who take action.

In the last two months alone, I have paid over $50,000 to just one of my affiliates. This is not a full-time job and it never should be. In fact, once you become an affiliate, I will shoot you out a "Quick Start" manual that explains the easy steps you need to take to get set up. You are never asked to sell or talk to anybody about our program if you do not want to.

178 *Moving at the Speed of Wealth*

The program is really quite simple: You will be given instructions on how to purchase a domain name (website address) and how to forward that domain name to a special website with a special code. Your job is to direct people to your personal domain name. Once they do, they are redirected to one of the Speed of Wealth main websites. If that person orders my free report, this book or any course, or becomes a club member, he or she is tagged to you forever.

Once we have captured the names and the email addresses of the visitors that are tagged to you, they will be invited to our ongoing webinars, teleseminars, live seminars, live workshops, and live bootcamps. Once we have built credibility and trust, chances are good that the person will dip his or her toe into one of our investment opportunities. You are paid a preset fee on the money collected for these opportunities (only available to Gold Club member Super Affiliates). On top of that, you are paid a whopping 100% of all book sales made to your referred person.

You are also paid varying commission on other products offered by Speed of Wealth. For example, we pay a 50% commission to our affiliates who refer people to join The Speed of Wealth Gold Club™. This club currently has membership dues of thirty-four dollars each month or $348 for annual prepay, a sixty-dollar discount (these fees are soon to go up, so if you have not joined, do so now and lock in the lower dues at *www.SOWGoldClub.com*). This is a chance for you to earn an ongoing residual income. If you refer 100 people who become members of the club (not hard when I show you how to do it), you are paid $1,700 every month that the new members remain members.

Once a person is tagged to you, he is tagged forever. It doesn't matter when they take action—you are paid. Why spend over $150,000 in marketing when I can redirect that money to my students? It just makes a ton of sense for me to enrich your lives for helping me build my business.

You can learn more about this exciting program at *www.SpeedofWealthAffiliate.com*. While you are there, you might as well sign up to become a "Certified Affiliate." Once you fill in your information and click "Enroll," you will automatically be sent an email with paperwork that must be completed. This should take you about ten minutes. You simply return the completed paperwork to us and once we approve you, I will send you another email with the "Quick Start" manual attached.

Remember that we are more powerful as a group than as individuals. Share your good fortune with friends, relatives, neighbors, co-workers or whomever and get paid. Just an extra $500 or more a month can make a big difference in your wealth-building process.

The bottom line is that if you like what I do at Speed of Wealth and want to share it with others, then you might as well get paid in the process. There is no fee to enroll and you can set up a company just for this purpose and enjoy tax benefits as well.

Business Number Two: Get Involved in the Right Network Marketing Company and Build Principal-less Interest; Leverage Other People

Before you dismiss this section, I want you to sit back and really think about a few things. Have you ever referred a friend to a restaurant or movie? If so, did you get paid for it? Of course not. Network marketing (or MLM, multi-level marketing) has a well-deserved negative stigma surrounding it. The minute you mention network marketing to most people, they run for the hills. And it is easy to see why.

At some point in our adult lives, we have all been approached by a friend or acquaintance about some network marketing product they are pushing (I don't think there is a person alive today who has not listened to the Amway pitch). That's fine, we will listen. After all, it is a person we know and we want to give them the benefit of the doubt.

You listen to the pitch and decide whether or not you want to get involved. When your answer is no, the fun begins. It is at this point that you are about to jeopardize your friendship. You have said no but the person that pitched you just doesn't give up. Every time you are near this person, they pitch you again and again, over and over! It gets to the point where you start to avoid that person like the plague.

I want you to read on because you are about to learn that times have changed and network marketing, when promoting the right product, is easier than ever. On top of that, we never even want you to approach your friends or relatives.

A large percentage of people reading this book have probably either tried or looked at network marketing. A large percentage of those people have failed miserably because they do not understand the bigger picture.

This book is not about network marketing but if you read any *Rich Dad* or even Trump's books, you will find that they are big advocates of network marketing as well. There are hundreds of books and e-books on the subject but I want to point out some of the obvious factors and let you make a decision.

First of all, many people who have failed or never tried network marketing will call it a "pyramid scheme." This one just makes me roll on the floor laughing.

Do you understand that every business organization, including your federal and state governments, is nothing short of a "pyramid scheme"?

Let's look at the corporate structure. At the very top of the pyramid sits the president or CEO of the company. Below the CEO are vice presidents of the company. Below vice presidents, you have sectored or regional managers. Under them is second, third or fourth level managers. As you go down the pyramid, the number of people in that particular category gets wider and wider and the pay decreases more and more.

Now comes the really shady part of the corporate structure. In every instance, the person directly above you does not want you to achieve success. In fact, they will often take credit for your work. This is because they do not want you replacing them. In a corporate pyramid, it is in everyone's best interest to keep people down. If you currently work in the corporate world, then you know exactly what I am talking about. Do you think the government is structured any differently?

What people are more than likely referring to is illegal "ponzi schemes." These are the pyramids where people bring in money and it floats up the pyramid. Everyone above you receives a piece of the money and the person at the top gets the benefit of a little bit of money from a whole lot of people. "Ponzi schemes" have no product and nothing backing the money. For a corporation, the government or a network marketing company to work, there must be a viable product backing it.

Network marketing is based on nothing more than word-of-mouth advertising. Much like my affiliate program, the company has decided to market its product solely through word of mouth. Instead of spending millions of dollars on traditional advertising, they choose to pay what they would ordinarily pay to advertising agencies to you.

You are involved every day in network marketing. Every time you recommend a restaurant or a movie to a friend or acquaintance, you are networking. The difference is that you do not get paid to do so. So why is it so hard for people to open up and become associated with a product that they really like and share it with other people?

The minute you get paid for recommending a product to a friend, you want to clam up and this just does not make sense to me. All of a sudden, you think you are bugging your friends and relatives. If you like a movie and tell a friend or relative, you don't feel bad at all...you just don't get paid.

You will tell a virtual stranger whether or not you liked a movie or restaurant but when it comes to "pitching" a product that you like and believe in, you won't say a word if you are paid.

Secret of the Super-Rich #10   181

So what is the key to becoming a successful network marketer? It is really quite simple: You must get involved in a company that offers a product or service that you truly believe in. The other trick is that you must understand a simple cliché: Some will, some won't, so what...next! In other words, just because you firmly believe in a product or service does not mean everyone you come across will share that same passion. In fact, the majority of people that you come across will not share that passion, so move on.

One of the bad raps with networkers is that some of them can become a downright nuisance. If someone says no, then move on and be done with it. You will find with my investment opportunities that I introduce the opportunity to everyone in my database. Some will, some won't, so what...next! Either they like the opportunity or they don't. All I can do is bring it to their attention and let them make a gut level decision as to whether or not it is right for them. I don't ever pick up the phone and call people. I never try to persuade them if they have said no. I try to educate them and let them make an educated decision and that is all you should be doing with a product or service that you represent through networking. And for crying out load...be patient.

People move at their own pace and more often than not someone will decide to join your crusade when a change has happened in their life—for example: losing a job, or seeing someone get promoted over them who did not deserve it.

The truth is that if you do things right, you should never have to approach your friends or family. In fact, if you do things right, people should come to you...when they are ready.

Let me briefly explain the difference between the corporate pyramid and the network marketing pyramid. As I said earlier, if you are within the corporate pyramid, the person above you will do everything he or she can to keep you down.

With network marketing, it is just the opposite. Anyone who you sponsor is below you but you have a vested interest in that person doing better than you. After all, you are paid on their production so you do everything in your power to help them pass you.

Every new person who joins a network marketing company is essentially the CEO and at the top of the pyramid. Sure, there are people above you but you have just branched out and created a brand new pyramid with you on top. What you do with that position is entirely up to you and, make no mistake, many of these networkers make corporate CEO-type of money. I am talking about millions a year, but that is the minority, not the majority. All I am trying to do is help you make an extra $500, $1,000 or more each month.

I will be introducing you to the company and product I am involved with, as well as the autopilot system I use to allow me to build a huge network with very little effort. But for now let's assume you put in one full year, working part-time and passively, and you work your way up to making a mere $1,000 each month.

Here is the shocking truth: If you are like most Americans and have an unfounded fear of investing your money in what is perceived to be a risky environment, you will probably put your money in a CD or money market account. While I write this chapter, these accounts are paying about 3%.

Your network marketing company is generating you $12,000 a year before you even roll out of bed. Now, pay really close attention to this next sentence. At a 3% return, you would have to have $400,000 in one of these accounts to generate that kind of income!

So I ask you: Do you think it is harder to build a network marketing downline that will produce these results or to save $400,000 (and keep in mind, my students have the opportunity to plug into our autopilot system, where you never have to approach a soul)? The answer is that networking is much easier when you know what you are doing and you work *smart* for a couple of years. My wife, Donna, created a residual income of over $2,000 in only six months and she works full-time with me.

Every time Donna recruits someone new to the business, the new person goes underneath one of her downline members. In other words, she is helping her downline grow their business as well. What a great feeling—helping others make money while you help yourself (sounds like the Speed of Wealth mantra)!

Truth be told, I make very, very good money and we don't need this extra $2,000 but I have to show up every day to create income (excluding any income I choose to take from my investments; right now, I take no money from my investments—I choose to let them grow). With networking, once I have put in the time, I can go on cruise control and just be there to help my downline earn more money.

Again, this is not a book about network marketing but I want you to look at it from a different point of view. I hope I have achieved that, and keep in mind: It is a viable business that offers tremendous tax benefits as well…as long as you are trying to make a profit.

I believe in the company and product that my wife and I are involved in so much that about a month ago I decided to devote 50% of my time building this business. This is great news to you because I am very good at marketing.

Let me explain. I absolutely love helping people build massive wealth by educating them and introducing them to safe, high-return investments. I will never close Moving at the Speed of Wealth™. There is a desperate need for the public to learn unconventional methods of becoming financially independent. By now you know that one of these methods is to own your own business. I can help you by showing you how to grow your current assets faster, but many of you need to accumulate more assets. If you are not where you need to be, it only stands to reason that you need to generate more income and reduce your taxes. Once you have more income, it makes it a lot easier to save more money. It really is that simple.

Knowing this, it only makes sense for me to help you increase your income, passively and easily. You see, most of all of the aspects of Speed of Wealth are on autopilot. I have products and investment opportunities already created (although I continue to produce more quality educational products), and 80% of all of my marketing is done by using the Internet. You may be one of the people who was introduced to me in this manner. We simply direct people to a specific website and offer you a FREE report or encourage you to join our FREE online newsletter. Essentially, I am building a huge list of people who have raised their hands and said that they are interested in learning more.

At this point, my "SYSTEMS" take over. You are then emailed a series of educational lessons automatically. This is designed to build trust and credibility. I will often send out a broadcast email and/or a recorded phone call to invite you to a webinar, teleseminar, live seminar, workshop or bootcamp.

The point is that, as the old cliché goes, "When the student is ready, the teacher will appear!" We do not push anything down your throat; we wait until you are ready to take action. Obviously, you took action if you are reading this book.

Again, hang in there with me for a moment; all of this will make sense. Let me give you a sample of the marketing techniques I use to drive folks like you to my website:

- My affiliate program
- Articles posted all over the Internet
- Joint ventures with other folks with opt-in email lists
- Google®, AdWords® and other search engines
- Social website videos such as YouTube® and hundreds of other sites like MySpace® and FaceBook®
- Blogs

- Online solo advertisements in other e-newsletters
- Infomercials
- Paid live seminars
- Public speaking engagements
- Some other avenues

All of these avenues drive tremendous traffic to one of my many websites. Understand that the number one priority of each and every site published on the World Wide Web is to capture the visitor's name and email address. Once this is achieved, I have an easy means of communicating with them every day to encourage them to take the action I want them to take.

Keep in mind that close to 90% of all the people that opt in to my newsletter will never take any action I recommend. But consider that I easily capture well over 100 names each and every day. If only 1% of this number takes action...I win! Imagine that one person a day buys my book; this means that 365 people a year are receiving my message. If you have read this far, then you are encouraged by my message and you are likely to take one of the actions I have recommended in this book. You may join my club, you may make it a habit to visit *www.SpeedofWealthEvents.com* and attend webinars, teleseminars, live seminars, live workshops, packaged seminars and workshops, or you may attend my mind-boggling live three-day intensive bootcamp. And many of you will take advantage of one of our many alternative investment opportunities.

All of this adds up to revenue for me. Yes, folks, I do make a living doing this—to be honest, I make a very good living doing this. The best part is that I make a living teaching people how to explode their wealth. What a great way to make a living!

So what does all of my success have to do with you getting involved in network marketing and, more specifically, getting involved with Donna and me in the company that we promote?

I want to be perfectly honest with you. Donna and I tried our hand about twelve years ago in network marketing, promoting a vitamin company. In our first month, we were ranked number six out of all of the other recruiters in the company. Our first check was a whopping $69. It became very clear to us that the time and energy we put into earning that big check just was not worth it.

It was at that very moment that I told my wife I would never get involved in network marketing again. I have absolutely no use for what I call motions, potions or lotions. You must keep in mind that for a true networking company's downline to succeed, the product must be consumable—meaning that people must love the product so much that when they consume it, they will reorder it.

However, I have learned a lot since then. Although I still don't have a lot of use for these so-called miracle cures, I do believe in "widgets" that are used every day by people worldwide. Imagine if I could get paid just a small percentage of the money spent by these people on a product they are already using—I'd stand to build tremendous wealth.

When I introduce you to our autopilot system, it really doesn't matter what the widget is. That is because 90% of the people who join us are already pulling out their wallets before they even know what the product ("widget") we promote is. We sell the idea of owning your own business and we sell the promise of simplicity and very little lifestyle change other than having more money at the end of the day.

That being said, yes, the widget is important. It must be a product that is in high demand and used by almost everyone in the world, not just the U.S.A. It must be a product that you understand and use already. It is much easier to promote a product that you have already been using. Then if you can show people how they can make money by introducing them to a method of using the same product from a different vendor with no increased price (actually big savings, in some cases), you easily win the game.

More importantly, you want a system that introduces them to the product and the networking side of the business. I don't want one single person in my downline picking up the phone until the prospect has joined. That is the biggest no-brainer in the history of mankind. Once you are paid, then and only then do you pick up the phone to introduce yourself and introduce your new distributor to the same autopilot system you are using, and you are done. We actually take over from there.

Now, I ask you: Does that seem too complicated or time-consuming? Folks, network marketing is a legitimate business that offers you all of the same tax benefits discussed earlier.

Now, to address the other issues holding people like you back from starting your own business:

1. They think too BIG and assume it is costly and painstaking to start a business. Yes, it does cost money to start any business. The key is to find a very low entry fee. Thousands of people every year go out and enter the real estate profession. This is a business that has a perception of a low entry fee. By the time you paid for

classes to get your license, fees to take the test, license fees, business cards, basic business paraphernalia, and the big one, marketing, you are into this venture for thousands of dollars. Yet, at the beginning of this century, the average real estate agent nationwide earned barely over $30,000 per year. Today, with the current state of real estate, I would guess this is much lower. You could start a business where you go around and gather aluminum and cash it in. This, too, costs you money to enter; it costs you time and time is money. With our system, you can get involved for less than $1,000 and this includes all costs, even marketing. Do what you have to do to find that money: Borrow it, get a student loan, use a credit card, but find the money. This $1,000 could be better than any other investment opportunity I will ever share with you. On top of that, we will refer you to specialists that will guide you in the setup of your business and we will introduce you to tax specialists that understand home-based businesses.

2. They assume that they don't have enough time. Not with our systems—you just plug-n-go. In fact, I want you to get out of the way. Let the systems do all of the work. Why would you want to change a system that works, anyway? Go ahead, plug yourself into the system right now and see how well it works. Go to *www.TodayYouStart.com* and see where it leads you.

3. They assume it takes a lot of money to start a business. See number one above.

The only money that you will need is marketing dollars, which, of course, are also tax-deductible.

In introducing our co-op marketing program, I will do all the work to build your downline for you. You don't have to lift a finger, make a phone call or approach a friend or relative. You do not have to do anything but let our systems work for you.

You see, we have set up our marketing program identical to how I promote Moving at the Speed of Wealth™. We market the same way and promote the same way, primarily through the Internet. People go through our system and when they decide to join, they are signed up under you or one of our other co-op participants.

You decide at what level you want to come in. Marketing costs money, so co-op members must deposit money into the plan and they will receive leads

Secret of the Super-Rich #10

based on the contribution. You could spend as little as $50 a month or $100,000 a month—you decide.

The system is unbelievable and our goal is to produce hundreds of directors for the company. We want to help you become a director. Directors average about $2,000 a month income and we want to do all the work for you. If you are willing to commit a certain amount of money to advertising and marketing, we can take you there with us. Keep in mind that you are paid a commission every time someone joins as well—and this is over and beyond your residual income.

I have said enough about this opportunity. I didn't want to make this chapter a sales pitch—after all, this is an educational book. But I am just too excited not to share this opportunity with you. To understand how our systems work, I want you to visit *www.TodayYouStart.com* now. Once you sign up for the FREE *Home-Based Business Explosion* online newsletter, you will be in the same system our visitors will be in. Go through the action steps provided and you will see just how easy it will be for you to do very little and make a lot of money.

Once you have gone through the system, you will be able to make an educated decision about whether this opportunity is right for you. (Enough of the pitches, but now you see why self-publishing has its advantages. I can share anything I want to with you, without a publisher telling me what I can and cannot say.)

There you have two easy-to-start businesses, both of which can make you extra money or a boatload of money if you choose to take it seriously. I have news for you: You had better do something and you had better do it now because time is running short. The rich are getting richer and Middle America is fading away.

Keep in mind that, as a student of mine, you will be introduced to many other home-based business opportunities. If neither of the two I introduced to you in this chapter appeals to you, then be patient. Sooner or later I will introduce you to the one that fits you perfectly.

If you want the fast road to wealth, not only should you understand all the secrets I am sharing with you in this book, but understand Secret #10: Super-Rich People Understand that You Must Absolutely, Positively Own Your Own Business to Build Tremendous Wealth.

Chapter Eleven

Secret of the Super-Rich #11

The Super-Rich Create Tax Shelters, Pay Less Tax and Set up Tax-Free Retirement Income Streams

In the previous chapter, I shared with you what almost all Super-Rich people have in common: They all own some type of business. That isn't to say that they do not have a career or "job" outside of their own business, but they own some type of business of their own.

Now, I am not a big advocate of some of what Robert Kiyosaki preaches in his *Rich Dad* books. He has his quadrants of employee, self-employed, business owner, and investor. He makes it very clear that the only way to big wealth is to own a business and be a smart investor. This book is filled with investor strategies and investment ideas (learn of some other opportunities at *www.SpeedofWealth.com*). I agree 100% that you must use unconventional means of investing strategies if you ever plan on getting super-rich. If you read any of the *Rich Dad* books, which I do recommend, you will find that Mr. Kiyosaki and I agree on many points. He and I both agree that 401(k) plans and other qualified retirement plans are a sure path to failure for most people (you give up control of your money, but more on this in the next chapter). We both agree that real estate offers the surest path to financial freedom, although I think you can benefit passively. We agree on many topics, but I don't agree with him on a few.

I don't believe you have to own a business, in the sense that he describes a

190   *Moving at the Speed of Wealth*

business, in order to build wealth. I believe you can be self-employed and/or work for someone else and still build wealth.

The way he describes a business is an entity that you own and control that is on autopilot. In other words, it generates profits whether you are actively involved or not. Much like a franchise, the systems are in place so that you don't have to be there. A business is something you build that you can sell down the road for a huge profit.

Sure, this is ideal, but not practical in most cases. For example, my business will not survive without me. I will never be able to sell my business and walk away because I *am* the business. Believe me, I have tried to be absent and it just doesn't work. At one point, I was recruiting across the nation to have speakers present the Speed of Wealth program and all but two failed miserably. Why? Because they just don't understand it the way I do and they did not have the passion that I have. They also, in all likelihood, thought they had the ambition to make it big but did not have the work ethic to get there. I work very hard and long hours.

Important Note: *The network marketing business that I described in the previous chapter does allow me to be an absentee owner making passive income every day regardless of what I am doing or whether I am working on the business. I can also sell my entire downline, if I choose, whenever I want and for whatever price I want. When I build it up to making me $100,000 a month whether or not I even get out of bed, what do you think I could sell it for? Probably close to $5 - $10 million lump sum cash. Just more ammunition to excite you!*

Whoever came up with the phrase "work smarter, not harder" must have been broke. Do you really think that Donald Trump does not work hard? That man probably never stops. The most successful people I have seen work twelve, sixteen or more hours in a day. They do work smart but hard. So here is the real gem: "Work smarter and much harder if you have the desire to be successful." I am typing this chapter on Memorial Day, 2008. While all of my neighbors are having parties and cookouts, I am here writing my book.

Please don't get me wrong. I play very hard, too. I go on three to four major vacations a year and take time out throughout the year to get away from it all. The difference is that when I am playing hard, I have no guilt and money continues to pour into my bank account.

The point is that you can be super-rich working for someone else and you can become super-rich if you are self-employed. But whatever route you choose, you must have your own side business like we discussed in the previous chapter.

You absolutely must take advantage of the tax benefits offered by our government to business owners and you must find a good consultant that will help you maximize those tax benefits.

This is why super-rich people pay less in taxes than Middle America (in actuality, rich people pay more in taxes; they just pay a smaller percentage of their income in taxes). They understand the rules. The chances are that you knew this as well, but thought it was just too hard to set up your own business. I have teams of specialists I can refer you to that can help you set up a business in the most tax-advantageous way.

Now here is the difference between what the super-rich business owner and the wannabe super-rich business owner do. The wannabe will take all that newfound income (money saved at the end of the year due to more tax deductions) and consume it. A super-rich business owner will reinvest the tax savings (income) in either the business or another investment vehicle. Keep in mind that your business can make investments as well, and should.

Let me give you an example of what I am talking about. The following example is for illustration purposes only. I recommend that you see your local tax professional for accurate and up to date information for your area, and receive advice and guidance for your personal situation. The numbers I am going to use are calculated from the estimated 2008 tax tables and I am using a 7% state income tax rate.

In this example, I am assuming you are married with two children. The family is able to take advantage of two major tax deductions: the interest you pay when you have a home loan (see, I told you so) and a deduction for the children.

When you own your own business, your family can take advantage of one of the best tax strategies available today: hiring your children as bona fide employees for your home-based business. You may pay your children up to $5,450 per year (2008 figures) and in this example we pay each child $4,700. You choose whatever amount works best in your situation, but they must do work. Remember that even pre-school children and elementary school children have the ability to stuff envelopes. The IRS is not going to agree with you if you say your children were paid for database entry at five years old.

Let's take a quick look at what super-rich people do (Figure 63).

	NO HOME-BASED BUSINESS	WITH HOME-BASED BUSINESS
(A) Income: This includes most money that both individuals receive. This could be W-2 income, 1099 reported income, tips, interest, dividends, tax refunds, alimony, capital gains, etc.	$75,000	$75,000
(B) Home-Based Business Deductions in Excess of Income (Illustration Only): For a list of types of deductions, see previous chapter.	$0	$35,000
(C) Itemized Deductions: For our illustration, our couple is filing jointly and is able to itemize their mortgage, charitable contributions, etc. Since their itemized deductions are greater than their standard deductions, they will choose to use Schedule A to itemize their deductions.	$15,000	$15,000
(D) Exemptions: You receive $3,500 off of your taxable income for every person you have responsibility for in the eyes of the IRS (you, your spouse, two children).	$14,000	$14,000
(E) Total Taxable Income: Subtracting B, C, D from your Income (A)	$46,000	$11,000
(F) Federal Tax:	$6,097	$1,100
(G) State Tax:	$3,220	$770
(H) Total Tax Paid:	$9,317	$1,870
Amount Saved by Starting a Home-Based Business	$7,447	

Figure 63

Once again I want to stress that this is for illustration purposes only and is provided here to give you an idea. If you get to keep an extra $7,447 of your income at the end of the year (as seen in Figure 63), then this is real money to you that you can spend any way you chose to. This is money that you did not have before. This $7,447 breaks down to $620.58 of newfound money each month.

Secret of the Super-Rich #11

Our super-rich business owner will reinvest this money and not spend it. Let's assume she can get 12% in nice, safe hard money loans on this money. She will start a self-directed 401(k) plan through her newly formed business and redirect her tax savings once a year into this plan (which, by the way, gives her another tax deduction). She is thirty-five years old and will let this money grow tax-deferred and compound annually until age sixty-five. Her tax savings reinvested alone will grow to $2,012,869 in thirty years.

This isn't even counting the money earned from this new business. Even if you start a business and are self-employed, that nets you $100 per month. You are in great shape. The moral of the story is that you do not have to start a home-based business with the intent of building some multi-million-dollar conglomerate in order to build massive wealth. Set your objectives so that you can meet them. Quit trying to set goals that you will be hard-pressed to reach; this only causes discouragement and failure. I just showed you a simple plan that many super-rich people have used to build massive wealth with very little extra effort.

For crying out loud! Going around and collecting recyclables throughout the neighborhood and turning them into cash is a business and you're helping the environment. You just need to set it up as a business.

If I have not made my point by now, there is no hope so let's move on. I have shown you why super-rich people pay less tax. Now, let's talk about setting up tax shelters and creating tax-free income during your retirement years.

Despite what you may think, you do not have to be some financial whiz to set up a tax shelter. First, you have to determine what kind of tax shelter you want to create. You are not going offshore and playing that game; your government gives you choices right here in the good ol' U.S.A. to shelter your money from taxes.

Here is an important fact to remember: You are going to pay taxes on your income one way or another unless you are cheating. You are either going to pay now, or you are going to pay later. The choice is completely yours.

When setting up your plan, you have to ask yourself a few very important questions:

1. Do you want to enjoy the same standard of living in retirement, or better, as you enjoy now? If you answered yes, then it should be obvious that you will need the same amount of income in retirement as you earn now. Many financial planners will tell you that you do not need the same income for a few reasons. First, you should have eliminated debt. I've got news for you: Old debt

194   *Moving at the Speed of Wealth*

is replaced with new debt. As a couple in retirement, you should plan on spending an extra $1,000 a month on healthcare alone. Secondly, your children are likely grown up and you are no longer responsible for paying for their upbringing. Yeah, right, tell that to the hundreds of thousands of parents that still have a thirty-year-old living with them. Or tell that to the grandparents that must help the children in order for the grandkids to have a good life. Thirdly, you are not making contributions to retirement any longer so that money now goes in your pocket. It's a very valid point, so I will accept this. All in all, I will be generous and say you need 20% less in retirement income than you need now (of course, I don't believe this). Before you buy into that, keep in mind that *good* planners will tell you to expect that you will need more money in retirement. *Why?* you may ask. You are likely to spend more in retirement than you do now because you have ten extra hours a day to fill. Are you going to sit around and do nothing? No, you will probably travel, spoil the grandkids, get heavily involved in your hobby or whatever.

2. Do you think taxes are likely to be higher or lower when you retire? We really don't know but my guess is that taxes will be higher. Americans are living longer, putting more of a burden on our government in terms of healthcare costs. Social Security is projected to be upside down by the year 2012 (this varies depending on who you are listening to). Medicare is already paying out more than it collects. Pensions are going bust all over America, putting more pressure on the Pension Guaranty Benefit Corporation (PBGC), which means somebody has to pony up to pay these deficits, which typically means taxpayers. We are in a seemingly endless war against terrorism, which will not come at a small price. This is just to name a few of the problems facing our government's budget deficits. When you are running on deficits, the easy way to fix the problem is to tax more.

Our government is very good at hiding tax increases but keep in mind that most taxes are collected from excise taxes, not income taxes. Excise taxes are what you pay in addition to the price of goods. For example, there is an excise tax on gasoline. When the government is forced to increase these excise taxes, prices go up, which simply means you will probably need more money in retirement than you have now.

Secret of the Super-Rich #11

What a vicious cycle. Inflation, increased taxes, and devaluation of the dollar all add up to a massive shortfall in retirement. Oh, well, this book was intended to help you fix these problems, but you must hurry.

The government gives you the opportunity to make a decision about when you want to be taxed. Knowing the answers to the questions above can help you with your decisions.

We have already covered the fact that when at all possible, your money needs to be growing in a tax-deferred or tax-free account and compounding. You are very limited as to where you can invest your money in order to achieve this goal:

1. Real estate compounds over time and grows tax-deferred.
2. Qualified retirement accounts (your work-sponsored plans) grow tax-deferred and compound over time.
3. Traditional individual retirement arrangements (IRAs), SEPs, KEOUGH plans, simple IRAs, etc. grow tax-deferred and compound over time.

Important Note: *These qualified retirement accounts and IRAs are simply shells that allow you to defer taxes on the investments you make within them. They also allow you to fund the plan with before-tax dollars. In other words, you receive a tax deduction on your contributions. The investments themselves may or may not grow tax-free or deferred. For example, real estate grows tax-deferred whether or not it is inside one of these shells. Life insurance and annuities grow tax-deferred whether or not they are within one of these shells (you cannot have a life insurance policy within any type of IRA account). This is very important to remember as I proceed.*

---

4. Roth IRAs grow tax-free; you are not taxed on the distribution and the money will transfer tax-free to your heirs. However, you are not allowed a tax deduction on the contribution so you are funding these plans with after-tax dollars.
5. Roth 401(k)s are a new vehicle that allow a portion of your plan to grow tax-free (the money you deposit is typically treated as a Roth but your employer's contribution is treated as a traditional plan). Not all employers offer these plans.
6. Annuities grow tax-deferred and all earnings are taxed as ordinary income when you liquidate. Be very careful with annuities;

196   *Moving at the Speed of Wealth*

somewhere along the line, so-called financial specialists started selling them as a great investment alternative. I personally think they suck; again that's my opinion. Variable annuities offer so many guarantees but you must read the fine print. Fixed annuities offer guarantees as well but read the small print. I don't think they are a great investment but I think they are great for what they were intended to do: offer you a place to put your money, annuitize and receive a periodic payment over a specified period of time that you can bank on (of course, if the insurance company does not go out of business). When you annuitize, you are receiving a portion of your principal and interest with every payment, thus lowering your tax liability. One of the slicker sales tactics for selling annuities is when they say that when you annuitize, you are receiving something like 8% annually. Not once do they mention that this includes principal reduction. One other important note about annuities is that they do not have a step-up cost basis. In other words, your heirs are liable for taxes on the growth. This is not an annuity book so I will stop here.

7. Under current law, life insurance grows tax-deferred and can come out tax-free when you pull out money using policy loans, plus whatever is left over transfers tax-free. Once again, I need to point out that, like annuities, I think life insurance is a poor investment. However, the right kind of plan structured the correct way is an awesome investment tool.

8. And, finally, there are certain types of bonds for which you do not have to pay taxes on the earnings, such as municipal bonds. Again, this book is not about specific investments or all the ins and outs of them.

There you have it. With possibly one or two missing, you just saw the entire list of tax-advantaged strategies. Any investment can be tax-deferred or free if it is put into the proper shell (IRA or QRP)—which brings me to a point that is a little bit off the subject but I feel compelled to jump on my soapbox anyway…so here I go.

I am sick and tired of all these so-called financial wizards going around out there trying to get you to do something you probably shouldn't do in the first place just to earn a buck. Case in point: The only advantage to an IRA is that it allows your money to grow tax-deferred (the up front tax deductions are rarely an advantage, as you will see soon). Why on God's green planet would a so-called professional recommend that you buy an annuity within your IRA? The only advantage to an annuity is that it grows tax-deferred. You should never, ever buy an annuity within your IRA or qualified retirement account. You achieve the same goal by buying them outside of your shell.

And now for my grand finale about this point—believe me, I could go on for several pages but let me give it to you straight. There are more and more real estate gurus popping up, trying to pry money from your hands by telling you that you can and should buy real estate within your IRA shell.

This is straight up b.s. Yes, you can buy real estate as an investment within your IRA. You always could, and you can finance real estate as long as you can get a non-recourse loan (a loan that you do not personally guarantee, or they cannot come after you if you default on the promissory note, or one that you can have a non-related party take out on your behalf—again, this is for other authors).

I already mentioned that real estate compounds and grows tax-deferred. I have also pointed out that the only advantage to an IRA is that it allows the investments you choose within the shell to grow tax-deferred. So what is the advantage to buying real estate with your IRA? None. In fact, it is a huge disadvantage.

You lose the ability to take advantage of your individual or business tax deductions if your real estate is held within your IRA. Again, I am not a tax consultant but you should check with a good one to understand me correctly. Your IRA can have expenses, which will be deducted from your profitability, but expenses cost you money. Because the money growing in your IRA is not taxable, there is no ability to take tax deductions, only expenses.

If I have said it once, I have said it a thousand times: Millionaires do not buy professional sports teams for the tax write-offs. In order to receive tax deductions, it must cost you money. I would rather pay up to fifty cents on a dollar earned than save fifty cents on a dollar spent, which is a whole dollar swing.

If you are going to invest in real estate, forget about your IRA money. Use your IRA money to be the banker and control real estate. You can invest in hard money loans all day long with a self-directed IRA or self-directed 401(k). Believe me, if your IRA can consistently receive 12 - 25% returns, you win the game.

Enough of the soapbox. Let's get back to the issue at hand. Should you defer taxes and pay later or should you pay taxes now and have tax-free income down the road? Again, you must defer to the previous two questions we asked: Will you need more or less money in retirement than you need now and do you think taxes will be higher or lower in the future?

198   *Moving at the Speed of Wealth*

Once you have answered these questions, you can decide what type of account to set up because, dollar for dollar, a traditional IRA and a Roth IRA are almost exactly the same when today's factors match your retirement.

Let's assume you have $100,000 of earned income each year (while you are still working) and you believe you will need this same amount in retirement. Let's also assume you are in a 28% federal and state marginal income tax bracket. And, finally, let's assume that taxes will be the same in the future and forget about Social Security income for a moment.

If you are saving $5,000 a year in a traditional IRA, then the true out-of-pocket expense is $3,650. You save $1,350 in taxes due to your tax deduction at the end of the year. Your effective out-of-pocket cost is $3,650 but you put aside $5,000 to work for you. To have the same out-of-pocket cost in a Roth IRA, you can save only $3,650 a year because you do not enjoy a tax deduction on this contribution.

Now let's assume you could receive a 10% return compounding annually and you have thirty years to save. By looking at the chart below, you will see that your traditional IRA has grown to $904,717 and your Roth IRA has grown to $660,444.

Now, it is time to live off your savings and take retirement income. To have a net after-tax annual income of $100,000 from your IRA, you would need to withdraw $138,889. Because the money in your Roth IRA is not subject to taxation, you simply withdraw the $100,000.

Assuming your remaining balance continues to compound at 10% annually, you find that both accounts run out of money at the exact same time. At first glance it looks like your Roth IRA came out $5,000 better but don't be

Dollar for dollar contribution growing at 10% annual compounding for thirty years.					
Traditional IRA			**ROTH IRA**		
Balance	Withdraw	Balance	Balance	Withdraw	Balance
$904,717	$138,889	$765,828	$660,444	$100,000	$560,444
$842,411	$138,889	$703,522	$616,488	$100,000	$516,488
$773,874	$138,889	$634,985	$568,137	$100,000	$468,137
$698,484	$138,889	$559,595	$514,951	$100,000	$414,951
$615,554	$138,889	$476,666	$456,446	$100,000	$356,446
$524,332	$138,889	$385,443	$392,091	$100,000	$292,091
$423,988	$138,889	$285,099	$321,300	$100,000	$221,300
$313,609	$138,889	$174,720	$243,430	$100,000	$143,430
$192,192	$138,889	$53,303	$157,773	$100,000	$57,773
$58,633	$58,633	$0	$63,550	$63,550	$0

$5,000 annually into a tranitional IRA or $3,650 annually into a Roth IRA. Same tax 28% tax bracket in retirement as you are in now. Net of $100,000 after taxes income annually. Almost exactly the same!

Figure 64

fooled. You are not going to pay 28% tax on your entire IRA withdrawal; you will pay your effective tax bracket. In reality, the traditional IRA would come out slightly better in the long run. Yet, all these so-called experts are trying to convince you that converting to a Roth IRA is in your best interest. Not in every case. Remember that in this example, I assume you will need the exact same income in retirement as you need today and that your tax bracket will be the same and/or tax rates have not increased.

Very Important Note: *In our traditional IRA example above, you will note that our investor paid over $350,000 in taxes in just nine years ($38,889 each year for nine years). If you recall, he had tax deductions equal to $1,350 each year for thirty years. In other words, our investor saved only $40,500 in taxes over thirty years, only to pay out over $350,000 in taxes in just nine short years. Are you sure you are not doing it backwards?*

I do want to point out something very disturbing. In the above example, I have you contributing the equivalent of $3,650 out of your pocket into a Roth IRA or traditional IRA annually for thirty years. You are receiving, on average, 10% return on your money (don't get me started on how this is pure b.s.). You have accumulated a large amount of money, so much so that you can withdraw $100,000 after taxes each and every year…for a whopping nine years! So you have reached the ripe old age of seventy-four and you are out of money.

It gets much worse. What kind of purchasing power will your $100,000 have in thirty years if inflation holds at only 6% annually? Now, it gets really scary. If inflation is only 3%, this $100,000 a year would only have the purchasing power of $41,198 today. If inflation is 6%, you would have the equivalent of $17,411 in today's dollars!

So I have pointed out a few key lessons. First, all things being equal, it doesn't matter whether you have a Roth IRA or a traditional IRA. Secondly, you had better save more than $3,650 a year (or get a lump sum working for you). And, finally, you had better quit playing the fear game and go after better returns.

If you were only able to increase your returns to 12% in your traditional IRA, your $5,000 annual contribution compounding annually would grow to over $1.3 million. At just 15%, it grows to over $2.4 million. **GET BETTER RETURNS!**

At this point, I want to point out that a correctly structured life insurance product that creates a banking system is a lot like a Roth IRA with fewer rules and regulations and much more flexibility going by today's tax laws.

200   *Moving at the Speed of Wealth*

So just exactly what direction do you go in? Keep in mind that if your combined income exceeds a certain limit, you do not even qualify for a Roth IRA. If you have a year when you have a big dip in income, set up a Roth IRA immediately just in case. You may not be able to make contributions in subsequent years, but you have it opened.

Assuming you qualify for a Roth IRA, here is a simple guide not meant for every reader:

- If you think you will need more income in the future than today, a Roth is probably better.
- If you think taxes will be higher in the future, then a Roth IRA is probably better.
- If you think you will have higher income needs in retirement than you have now and you think taxes will be higher in the future, then most certainly set up a Roth IRA and/or a properly structured life insurance contract.
- If you believe the opposite of what was stated above, then you are better off with a traditional IRA.

Pretty simple way to determine your needs, don't you think? But if at all possible, because I preach life insurance so much, you are in the best shape if you set up a traditional IRA and a properly structured life contract that serves as a banking system.

There are entire books written on IRAs, Roth IRAs and all the other forms of qualified retirement accounts and individual retirement accounts. I am not going to go into all of the rules and regulations here, but I do want to point out a few that may sway you toward a Roth IRA as opposed to a traditional IRA. For you 401(k) holders and other work-sponsored plan contributors, I will get to you in the next chapter…and be ready to hide your head in shame.

One big difference is that traditional IRAs and the like force you to begin liquidating your plan on April 1 of the following year after you turn 70½. You may be thinking that this is no big deal since you saved this money for that purpose to begin with. Let me assure you, I have many older students facing this required minimum distribution who do not want to take out the money. They are content with the income they have.

I was working with one very frugal couple; the husband was sixty-nine years old. Their home was paid off, and they both worked for the local university for decades. Their combined pensions were just north of $100,000 a year and they were totally debt-free. On top of their pension, the husband had an

Current Plan Required Minimum Distributions

Illustration Purposes Only

Heirs Marginal Tax Bracket: 30%
Estimated Marginal Tax Bracket in Retirement: 30.00%
Estimated Rate of Return: 8.00%

Year	Age	IRA Balance	IRA RMD Divosor	Required IRA Withdrawl	IRA Balance After Required Min. Distribution	Net after Tax Withdrawl	Taxes Paid	Net to Heirs After Taxes
1	69	$700,000	0.00	$0	$700,000	$0	$0	$490,000
2	70	$756,000	27.40	$27,591	$728,409	$19,314	$8,277	$509,886
3	71	$786,681	26.50	$29,686	$756,995	$20,780	$8,906	$529,897
4	72	$817,555	25.60	$31,936	$785,619	$22,355	$9,581	$549,933
5	73	$848,469	24.70	$34,351	$814,118	$24,046	$10,305	$569,882
6	74	$879,247	22.90	$38,395	$840,852	$26,877	$11,519	$588,597
7	75	$908,120	22.00	$41,278	$866,842	$28,895	$12,383	$606,790
8	76	$936,190	21.20	$44,160	$892,030	$30,912	$13,248	$624,421
9	77	$963,392	20.30	$47,458	$915,934	$33,220	$14,237	$641,154
10	78	$989,209	19.50	$50,729	$938,480	$35,510	$15,219	$656,936
11	79	$1,013,559	18.70	$54,201	$959,358	$37,941	$16,260	$671,550
12	80	$1,036,106	17.90	$57,883	$978,223	$40,518	$17,365	$684,756
13	81	$1,056,481	17.10	$61,783	$994,699	$43,248	$18,535	$696,289
14	82	$1,074,275	16.30	$65,906	$1,008,368	$46,134	$19,772	$705,858
15	83	$1,089,038	15.50	$70,260	$1,018,777	$49,182	$21,078	$713,144
16	84	$1,100,279	14.80	$74,343	$1,025,936	$52,040	$22,303	$718,155
17	85	$1,108,011	14.10	$78,582	$1,029,429	$55,008	$23,575	$720,600
18	86	$1,111,783	13.40	$82,969	$1,028,814	$58,078	$24,891	$720,170
19	87	$1,111,119	12.70	$87,490	$1,023,630	$61,243	$26,247	$716,541
20	88	$1,105,520	12.00	$92,127	$1,013,393	$64,489	$27,638	$709,375
21	89	$1,094,465	11.40	$96,006	$998,459	$67,204	$28,802	$698,921
22	90	$1,078,336	10.80	$99,846	$978,490	$69,892	$29,954	$684,943
				TOTALS: $1,266,979		$686,886	$380,094	

Figure 65

IRA account worth $700,000. Figure 65 is the current required minimum distribution schedule for this husband

You can see that his required minimum distribution at 70½ is $27,591. This will push him into a higher tax bracket and, using a 30% marginal tax bracket, he is required to pay about $8,000 in taxes on this withdrawal, leaving him a net after-tax income of just over $19,000. This gentleman was prepared to make this withdrawal, pay the taxes and reinvest what he had left over.

It gets worse. As you can see, if his money continued to grow at 8%, his required minimum distributions would grow each year. Look at his RMD at age eighty: It is $57,883! This forces him to pay $17,365 in taxes. He will more than likely be slowing down by that age and in need of less money. Look at age ninety. He is required to withdraw over $99,000; he will never need this money.

If this student had contributed to a Roth IRA or a properly structured life insurance product with banking abilities, he would not have been forced to liquidate his plan. The truth is that the government wants its taxes. When you contribute to a Roth or a life insurance product, you are doing so with after-tax dollars.

The good news is that I showed this student how to take out his required minimum distribution, reduce his taxes or totally eliminate them altogether, and explode the growth on his money in two easy steps.

I asked this man a simple question: "If I can show you a way to take out your required minimum distribution and dramatically reduce or eliminate your taxes and at the same time show you how you could trade $6,400 for $17,000 each year, would you be interested?" I am sure you know the answer.

I can show anyone how to achieve what I just laid out but that is an advanced topic. Don't get me wrong: I can show you this strategy in minutes and you could implement it with full understanding within days, but I need to save something for members of The Speed of Wealth Gold Club™, so what are you waiting for? Become a member today by going to *www.SOWGold-Club.com* and signing up!

Most people who meet me briefly think that I am not a fan of traditional IRAs and qualified retirement accounts. Nothing could be further from the truth. I preach all the time that you must try your best to have your money growing in a tax-deferred or free environment. Make sure you understand that you do not need to put investments that already grow tax-deferred or free into an IRA or QRP shell.

What I am disappointed about with these vehicles is the pathetic returns and the absence of investment choices. Look, if you open your IRA (Roth or traditional) with XYZ brokerage house, you are limiting yourself to the investments they offer. In most cases, these choices are stocks, bonds, real estate investment trusts (REITS) and my favorite of all…those sorry-ass mutual funds. Good luck on building wealth.

Your qualified retirement plan (work-sponsored savings plan) is even worse. You are lucky if you have eight investments to choose from and they are all mutual funds except for the occasional company stock (ask those Enron employees how well that worked out for them).

At my seminars, I ask the audience who has a 401(k) or other work-sponsored plan. The majority of the hands go up. Then I ask how many feel like they're diversified within that plan. All the same hands go up. I continue by saying, "Okay, so you have large cap mutual funds, international funds, money market funds, mid-cap funds, growth funds, income funds and so on. In other words, you are not diversified at all. All of your money is in the stock market and as the tide goes, so does the ship."

I don't care what sector you are in—when the stock market is tanking, the majority of all stocks and mutual funds tank with it, regardless of the sector.

Then I will go on and ask people what they think the advantage is to these plans and here are the typical responses:

Secret of the Super-Rich #11

- **Forced savings: Yep,** the absolute best advantage to these plans
- **Tax deferral:** Good call. This is how you build wealth: tax-deferral and compounding. The problem is that these plans lose money as well. If your portfolio loses 50% of its value, you need a 100% gain to break even.
- **Professionally managed:** Give me a break. The only thing professional is the fee being charged.
- **Employer match:** This is the one that gets my blood boiling every time because this is the so-called advantage that keeps you in these plans. You think, "Hey, I cannot beat 100% returns" (if your employer is matching you dollar for dollar). Yes, you are right, but it is a 100% return on your money only one time then the money goes back to earning the pathetic returns it always has. In the next chapter, I will dispel this b.s. once and for all.

What I am appalled by is the pathetic returns these plans produce as you go about your merry way with blinders on, when it could easily be fixed. Just how easily can you fix it? First, you need to be educated about alternative investment opportunities. I have already introduced you to earning higher-than-average returns on your money, secured by real estate, by making hard money loans. Your qualified retirement plan at work or your IRA, if it is held by one of the brokerage houses, do not offer you this choice.

But you can do it! As soon as you are done reading this book, I want you to start a self-directed IRA. And if you own your own business, as I have preached, you should start your very own self-directed 401(k) plan for that.

These self-directed plans offer you the opportunity to invest in just about any opportunity that comes your way, including real estate, hard money loans, developing, fix-n-flips and so on. You can still invest in the investments your brokerage house offers as well.

You can loan money out, invest in start-up businesses—you can even invest in your own start-up business. With a self-directed 401(k), you can even loan money to yourself. Best of all, if you set it up properly, you can have check-writing abilities from your plan. In other words, whenever you come across a great investment opportunity, you simply write out a check and invest. And, believe me, when great opportunities come around you need to act quickly.

Here is an example of an opportunity that only people who could act quickly were able to invest in. We rolled out a hard money loan that was secured by real estate at less than 50% loan to value. The promissory note called for 17% annual returns paid monthly to the investor. We were making this loan on raw land in central Tennessee to a well-established developer. A $100,000 investment would have paid approximately $1,416 per month to the investor. The term was two-and-a-half years. On top of that, the developer was offering an equity warrant in his new development, which was the largest master community in central Tennessee. Basically, it was a profit-sharing agreement that was guaranteed by the equity warrant.

If you were to invest $100,000, you would have received $42,500 in return on the note over two-and-a-half years and would receive your principal back at the end of two-and-a-half years. At the end of three years, you would receive a check for an additional $140,000. This was the profit-sharing portion guaranteed. In case you cannot figure out the math, that is a total return of $182,000 in three years on your original investment of $100,000.

When you divide your return of $182,000 by your original investment of $100,000, you have a total return of 182%. To figure out what your annualized internal rate of return is, you divide the total return by three (for the three years you are in the investment) for an annualized return of 60.66%, secured by "REAL" estate!

Do you think we had a lot of takers on this investment opportunity? You bet we did, but we were only raising $3 million so it went very fast. (As a side note, you could have invested as little as $10,000. I mention this to let you know that we work with everybody, not just the rich. I am on a mission to help Middle America.)

These are the types of investments we bring to you and you need to be able to act quickly. Setting up your self-directed IRA or 401(k) plan is a must and you need check-writing abilities. To learn more about how to set up your own self-directed IRA or 401(k) with check-writing abilities and who to contact, become a Gold Club member at *www.SOWGoldClub.com* and watch the recorded webinar on this topic or listen to the teleconference.

I guess, all in all, my favorite strategy of the super-rich for setting up a tax shelter would be the self-directed 401(k) plan. If you are self-employed, own a business and have no employees, this is a perfect fit for you, your spouse and your school-age children.

Here are some bullet points on the benefits of these plans:

- Typical work-sponsored 401(k) plans do not permit direct ownership of real estate or other non-traditional investments, so indirect investment via the self-directed 401(k) is the only choice.

- When you purchase and sell real estate or other investments with your self-directed 401(k), the capital gains are deferred through the 401(k), like any other 401(k) investment. *The headaches of 1031 exchanges with real estate are never necessary.*
- Ownership of the property in a self-directed 401(k) allows you, as manager, to have direct, hands-on control of and investment decisions over all assets, including control of the checkbook. Custodian involvement and hassles are eliminated, regardless of whether the investments are in securities, real estate or other assets.
- You can use 401(k) funding as a down payment for a real estate purchase, with the 401(k) financing or borrowing the balance. The use of debt financing for real estate is not subject to UBIT tax (a totally different subject that I will not discuss here—Google® it).
- Since you control and handle all transactions and act as the "custodian," there are no expensive annual fees.
- Litigation threats, which accompany investments such as real estate, are substantially reduced. This is done by isolating the investment inside a title-holding company or trust-holding company, and away from the rest of your 401(k) funds and estate.
- The self-directed 401(k) continues to provide deferral of income and gains inside the 401(k).
- If the company sponsoring the plan generates income, then you can make contributions of up to $44,000 annually to the 401(k) plan [$15,000 for the employee (you) and $29,000 for the employer (you as well) in 2006]. These contributions are tax-deductible both for the individual and the business owner.
- A 401(k) Roth has two buckets: one Roth and the other a traditional tax-deferred bucket. You can make withdrawals of principal from the Roth side. The employee (you) can contribute to the Roth side with after-tax dollars. The business owner (you) can contribute to the traditional side with before-tax dollars.

206 *Moving at the Speed of Wealth*

- If your company has a self-directed 401(k), you must offer it to all employees. These employees should include you, your spouse and your school-age kids. Remember that your school-age kids must actually work for you and receive pay (which is something you want to do anyway), so if they are three years old, make sure their job duties are something they can handle. My kids were stamping envelopes at age three for us and they loved every minute. They couldn't do it often enough. Now that they are in high school, it's like pulling nails to get them into the office to work—unless they are out of money, of course.

There are just too many benefits to list here and I don't want to ramble on. Again, we have educational tutorials, recorded and live webinars, recorded and live teleseminars, live workshops, three-day intensive bootcamps and all sorts of cool educational information at *www.SpeedofWealth.com*. We also bring in individuals who specialize in the topics we cover. I know just enough on this topic to be dangerous; we will direct you to the right people.

Just to sum up this chapter, remember that you are going to pay taxes sooner or later, regardless of what you have heard. Unless you want brain damage, I would never suggest going offshore. Do you think the IRS hasn't figured all of that out yet? The minute that money is moved back to the States, where you more than likely need the money, it will be taxed.

The government has provided you with perfectly fine tools and incentives to set up tax shelters right here and now. Take advantage of these programs, whichever way you deem the best fit for your situation.

In the next chapter, I am going to unload on work-sponsored 401(k) plans and let you know what I *really* think. I am probably going to make a lot of enemies with traditional financial planners, but what the heck? I thrive on controversy.

Chapter Twelve

Secret of the Super-Rich #12

Super-Rich People Know How to Maximize Their Qualified Retirement Plans

Introduction to Speed of Wealth's
401(k) Arbitrage Strategy™

Many "financial experts" will give you the advice that you should "never borrow from your 401(k) plan." Their *opinion* is that you will be losing the growth on the money while you have it in your hand and that you are paying back the loan with after-tax dollars only to be taxed again when you pull it out in retirement.

Here is the reality: They are absolutely right! However, the "experts" either do not understand the bigger picture or are delusional when it comes to the returns you are achieving in your current plan. Although we at Speed of Wealth do not recommend having any qualified plan money in a "cash equivalent" type of account, most qualified plan investors do. When using Speed of Wealth's 401(k) Arbitrage Strategy™, you will find that these paltry returns are easily recouped and more, as you will see. Additionally, as I demonstrate in our seminars and workshops, most investors are lucky if their plan is growing at any more than an 8% return annually.

So, the first and foremost important point for you to understand is that the interest rate that you are being charged on your 401(k) loan *goes directly to you!* Most plans will charge prime rate or prime rate plus one percent. So let's assume that rate is 7%. If you are credited with the interest you are paying, then at minimum you are guaranteeing that you receive 7% on the money that is borrowed.

Secondly, as you make payments on your loan, this money goes directly back into *your* plan, plus the interest you paid, and starts exactly where it left off. In other words, however you have your monies allocated inside of your 401(k) at the time of taking the loan, each loan payment will be allocated in direct proportion to the money remaining in your plan (if not, then simply make a call to move the money). So the minute you make a payment, that money starts earning the same returns as the rest of your plan.

The key to remember is that, much like home equity, when you borrow the money, you are *not* taking the loan out to consume it, but rather to *reinvest the money*. More importantly, at the end of the term of the loan (i.e., five years), you have freed up a boatload of money that is no longer subject to all the rules and limitations that a qualified plan is subject to.

Now, this freed up money may no longer be in a tax-deferred environment, but if you understand the Speed of Wealth perspective on this issue, *who cares if you are receiving better returns!* However, if tax deferral is important to you (and even we agree that it should be), this money can now be repositioned into the "Family Insured Banking System"™ or directly into real estate, both of which provide tax-deferred accumulation.

Important: *The power of 401(k) arbitrage is that it allows you to borrow from your current 401(k) or other qualified account. Put that money to work in an arbitrage environment, and allow the outside investment to pay for most of your monthly payment.*

Why would anyone want to do this, you wonder. Simply put, it does not "stunt" the current growth of your 401(k)—in fact, in most cases it enhances it because you are *assuring* yourself returns based on the rate of interest you are being charged on the loan. At the end of the loan term, you have "freed" up the money that you borrowed AND you can use this newfound money to invest *anywhere* you would like without the rules and limitations associated with most of these qualified plans.

To illustrate, I have included a spreadsheet with this chapter to walk you through the logic and provide you with some real numbers. As I progress here, please follow along with the spreadsheet (it is found at the end of the chapter so you will have to flip back and forth as we go along).

Let's assume that you are "Mr./Mrs. Super Investor" and that your "current average returns in your 401(k)" (the top line of the spreadsheet) is 10%. You have a current account balance of $100,000.

Plan rules vary depending on the provider/administrator and employer, but you are typically allowed to borrow 50% or $50,000, whichever is less. In our example, because your balance is $100,000, we will borrow the maximum of $50,000. This leaves a balance inside of your plan of $50,000 that will continue to receive the 10% returns (you sure hope the market doesn't swing down, don't you?).

---

*Important Note: As of Friday, March 28, 2008, the S&P 500 Index (the broadest measure of stock market performance) is exactly where it was at this time in 1999! For people who are "math challenged," that simply means that if you had "invested for the long term," like most planners advise, and received returns equal to the S&P 500 Index, which most people did not achieve, you would have absolutely **zero growth** in your accounts! Now, that is investing for the long term—or is it? And that does not include the fees you were charged and the fees your planners charge.*

Most plans will charge you an interest rate at, or slightly above, the prevailing prime rate. In our example, we are assuming that you can borrow this money at 7.5%. Remember that this assures you that you will receive a 7.5% return on *at least that portion of funds that you borrowed from the plan.* I am being very generous in showing that you earn 10%, but even more shocking is that the average American investor believes they are earning 13.1%, according to a survey done by J.P. Morgan. This is ludicrous, but you may still believe it (if so, attend one of our seminars and/or workshops and we will enlighten you with the truth; go to *www.SpeedofWealth.com* for more information).

The typical term on the 401(k) loan is five years or sixty months, as shown in our spreadsheet. The challenge with 401(k) arbitrage is that the investment I recommend to you pays simple interest. Your loan, on the other hand, is amortized over five years. So you are not only paying back interest every month, but part of the principal as well. This means that, although I am creating arbitrage between the new investment and the 7.5% rate you are being charged for the loan, the payment back to the plan will be more than the monthly in-flow from the new investment. Don't worry, we will attack that challenge in just a moment.

Now that we know the basics, we can solve for your monthly payment.

We know the interest rate is 7.5%, the loan amount is $50,000 and the term is sixty months. Plugging these numbers into our handy-dandy financial calculator, we arrive at a monthly payment of $995.67. This is what you will have to pay yourself back each month. Don't panic! This seems like a lot but we will offset most of it in just a moment.

My recommendation to you is to take this $50,000 and invest it in hard money loans, and I can show you today how to get a safe, reliable return of 17%.

This investment pays a real return of 17% annually and is tied to deeds of trust. Remember that the primary goal at Speed of Wealth is to teach you to become *your own banker* and start a banking system. In this investment, you will receive 1.42% of your total investment on a predictable monthly schedule. In other words, you will receive a *monthly* check in the amount of $708.33 based on your $50,000 investment.

It is important to note that this income will be taxed as ordinary unearned income. In our example, I am using an *effective* tax rate of 19%. Please understand that no specialist at Speed of Wealth offers tax advice. You should, therefore, seek out competent (and I do mean competent) tax advice from a qualified, licensed practitioner. I use this for illustration purposes only.

After holding back the taxes that you will be liable for at the end of the year, you are left with a net after-tax payment of $573.75 ("Net Monthly Return" column).

In this example, I show you contributing $500 per month to your 401(k) plan ("Current Monthly Contribution"). This is of some importance later. I show your "Current Pay" being $100,000 a year and your employer contributing 6% of your pay to your plan, or another $500 per month, for a grand total, monthly contribution of $1,000.

Does this plan resemble yours? If not, it's no matter. I am simply showing you a technique but I do recognize that every individual's situation is different. *This is why it is imperative that you meet with a Speed of Wealth 401(k) specialist before trying this on your own.*

It doesn't take a rocket scientist to figure out that if your monthly 401(k) loan payment is $995.67 and your net after-tax return on your new investment is $573.75, then you are upside down each month a total of $287.34. So how do we handle this? Well, there are several ways to handle this extra expense:

1. **Start your own business:** I think I covered this sufficiently in an earlier chapter so we will leave it at that.

Secret of the Super-Rich #12

2. **Reduce your monthly contributions to the plan:** Not my favorite, but remember that you are taking control of your retirement plan. In fact, in the second section of this chapter, I will show you why you may no longer want to contribute to this plan at all. People like myself (and the likes of Robert Kiyosaki and Donald Trump) who preach that these plans are a waste of time are always bashed by the status quo "financial planner" for giving this advice. This is because traditional planners typically work with very passive investors who have little to no knowledge of how to invest successfully and will never build wealth. These people work for the masses and slowly drain their students' savings with their "invest in mutual funds for the long term and diversify" chronic advice. (Why, exactly, are you paying these guys? Just curious.)

3. **Suck it up:** Heck, you probably need to be contributing a lot more to your retirement plan anyway. With this model, you are only going to be out of pocket $17,240 at the end of five years. If you look at the second half of the spreadsheet, you will see that at year five you have paid an additional $17,240 out of pocket (see "Additional Payments" column). This equates to $287.34 for sixty months, in case you were wondering. But if you look just to the right of that number, you will see that you "freed" up $50,000. In other words, your $17,240.40 out of pocket has *grown to* $50,000 in just five years! *This is a return on your investment of 190.02% or, if you divide that number by five years, an internal rate of return of 38% annually.* I would bet dollars to donuts that your current plan is not doing anywhere near this well. In fact, if you were to contribute periodic monthly payments of $287.34 to an investment in a compounding environment with a return of 10%, it would only grow to $22,148 in five years. My method more than doubled it. If you are still questioning my approach, this one section alone should have grabbed your attention like a 100-mile-per-hour gust of wind!

After five years, you have paid back your loan. Your plan ("Current Plan" column) as is would have grown to $242,613. My "Proposed Plan" has grown to only $237,116, a whopping loss of $5,497. However, you now have $50,000 sitting on the sidelines in extra growth ("Freed up Money, Growth Compounding").

212   *Moving at the Speed of Wealth*

If I add this $5,467 loss to your extra out-of-pocket expense of $17,240, your total out-of-pocket expense of this proposed plan is $22,737, for a gain of $50,000. That is a gain of $27,263 divided by your out-of-pocket expense of $22,737, for *a total five-year return of 120% on your money*. Again, divide this by five years and you come up with an IRR of 24% per year. This means that if you go back to day one, you received 24% on your money (this, of course, is the time value of money).

Ask yourself, and answer honestly: Do you really think that your current plan is going to more than double your money in five years? Using the Rule of 72, we know that if you are receiving a 10% return in a compounding environment, it will take 7.2 years to double your money (seventy-two divided by ten). My plan *more than doubled* your money in only five years.

The key is that your 401(k) plan is almost entirely intact at the end of five years (after repaying that loan), but you now have $50,000 sitting outside of this qualified environment, so you can invest it anywhere *you* choose. I would recommend that you continue investing in this hard money loan that is paying 17%. Even though the gains are taxable, at the end of the year your net return, after taxes, is still a whopping 13.6%. In my spreadsheet example ("Freed up Money, Growth Compounding"), I show that $50,000 growing at a compounded annual rate of 13.6% compounding will be worth $1,211,793 by year thirty.

The bottom line is that by year thirty, using just *one* 401(k) arbitrage maneuver, your money in aggregate has grown to $5,397,519 compared to your current plan of $4,263,065. *You have $1,134,454 more money at retirement and it cost you a whopping $17,240.* That is truly Moving at the Speed of Wealth™!

If the light bulbs are going on, it should be apparent that if this maneuver works once, it would work a second time and a third time and so on. In other words, you should be paying back the loan and pulling it right back out as another loan, right? The second time you will have $100,000, earning you 17%. So you will not have to come up with any spread. In fact, you will have positive cash flow in your second round. Assuming interest rates remain the same and you are paying 7.5% on your second loan, you know your payment will be the same $995.67. Now, however, you have $100,000 working at 17%, or a net after-tax monthly in-flow of $1,133. You have a positive monthly cash flow of $137.66 and you are going to free up another $50,000 at the end of the tenth year (five more years).

So the only real question becomes: Do you believe you can get 17% on your money? Of course you can, and now that you are a student, I will show you where. This plan is only for people who think BIG and do not believe that "if something seems too good to be true, then it probably is." That is an unfortunate frame of mind and some deeply entrenched propaganda handed down by the rich for centuries. In fact, rich people won't accept anything less than 15% on their money while the middle class slowly seeps into obscurity over time. Are you really willing to allow your paradigms and conditioning to lead you to financial ruin?

So as not to overload your circuits, understand that I only showed one loan on the included analysis (spreadsheet). The fact is that once you understand the power and strength of this plan, you are going to want to pull out a new 401(k) loan every *five years*. As I said earlier, you will have no out-of-pocket expenses on the second go round, as well as any subsequent loans. The growth is mind-boggling.

There is one disadvantage to this strategy that you must be aware of. Of course, I do not think of it as a disadvantage but you may seem to think so.

If you were to leave the place where you are employed, either by your own choice or by the choice of your employer, then the loan may become due and payable in full. The investment I recommend is not liquid for three years so you won't have the ability to pay off the loan. Many plans will simply allow you to continue on and keep your current plan in place, but some may call it due.

The bottom line is that if you choose not to pay back the loan, the IRS will call it an early distribution and you will owe taxes on the loan amount plus a 10% penalty if you are under the age of 59½. In our example, you may owe an additional $14,500 in taxes if the loan is called at the end of the year. This may sound like a negative but if you are a Speed of Wealth student, you may come to realize that it's okay to roll these plans out and pay taxes and penalties—especially if you can gain control of your money and receive better returns on it.

I assure you that there are investments available that will blow away the returns that you are receiving from your mutual funds within these plans. You just need to be educated and that is the whole purpose of becoming a Speed of Wealth Gold Club™ member: to teach you what you don't know and teach you the strategies of the super-rich.

Maybe You Shouldn't Contribute to a Qualified Plan at All!

Just for kicks, what are the advantages of contributing to one of these plans? Let me take a stab at what you may be thinking:

1. Tax deductions
2. Tax-deferred growth
3. An "automatic" savings plan
4. Employer matching contributions

214   *Moving at the Speed of Wealth*

Did I answer that question correctly for you? Was I right on the money? The truth is, in my opinion, only one of the four reasons above is legitimate: the automatic savings plan.

Let's explore the other three so-called advantages for a moment.

Tax deductions

This is without a doubt the dumbest advice a planner or CPA can give to a person. I have to assume that you will want to have the same or better standard of living in retirement as you enjoy now. If you earn $100,000 today and you do in fact want the same standard of living, won't you need that same $100,000 a year into retirement as well (this, of course, does not factor in inflation). The so-called experts will argue that you will not need as much money in retirement as you need in your working years. They will argue that your kids are moved out and that you have paid off most, if not all, of your debt. This is pure hogwash. The fact is that you will *probably need more money in retirement than you need now*. What are you going to do with the newfound ten hours a day that you didn't have during your working years? Are you going to sit around smoking cigarettes and watching Captain Kangaroo? Of course not. You are going to stay active. You will need to fill up that time with activities and I have bad news for you: Activities cost money. Golf is pretty darn expensive, as is traveling. I guess you can sit around and play cards all day—who am I to judge? On top of that, old expenses will be replaced with new expenses. My parents, for example, spend over $750 each month on medicine alone, and this is over and above their retirement entitlements.

The major healthcare expenses faced by retired households include premiums for Medicare Part B (which covers physician and outpatient hospital services) and Part D (which covers drug-related expenses); co-payments related to Medicare-covered services; and healthcare services that are not covered by Medicare. In 2007, the Centers for Medicare and Medicaid Services estimated that Medicare out-of-pocket expenses amounted to $3,800 per year for a single individual. *For a couple, the amount would be $7,600.* In addition to the Medicare expenses are expenditures on items not covered by Medicare, such as dental care, eyeglasses, hearing aids, etc. These items may amount to another $500 for a single person, $1,000 for a couple. These figures are averages; healthcare spending can vary significantly by individual and households. Those who have bad health habits and/or chronic illnesses likely incur higher costs, while those who have good health habits and/or few illnesses would, ideally, spend less.

Let's look at this from another angle. Assuming that we round the number to $10,000 per year for a couple, and assuming a twenty-five year retirement, you can expect to pay *$250,000 of your own money on medical expenditures alone!* According to Ibbotson, the average Middle American thinks he can retire on an accumulated nest egg of only $499,999. Whoops! Half of that is wiped out on medical expenses alone and that's *if* your health is good.

And, no surprise, these annual healthcare costs are projected to grow over time. The Centers for Medicare and Medicaid Services publish annual premiums for the various components, from which growth rates can be calculated. The growth rate is projected to average 5.9% per year for the next twenty years and 4.9% thereafter. Personally, I think these are very low estimates because we know inflation is much higher than what is reported to us.

As for long-term health needs, I haven't even addressed this issue yet. According to numerous studies, *more than two-thirds of those over age sixty-five will require long-term care at some point in their lives.* Of this group, 40% will require care for two years or more. With an average daily rate of $213 ($77,745 a year) for a private room in a nursing home in 2007, nursing home care can be financially devastating. Even those lucky enough to remain in their homes will find that home health aides are expensive. In 2006, the average hourly rate for a home health aide was $19/hour.

There are certainly a couple of expenses that will go away once you retire. First, you will no longer be making contributions to a retirement plan. Secondly, you will no longer have the expenses associated with work; this would include transportation, clothing, meals, etc. Assuming that you can relax knowing that you can survive on 20% less money than you make now, do you still think you will be in a lower tax bracket?

I have already asked you if taxes are going to be higher, lower or the same in the future. I am not even going to go into my opinion because it could be another complete book. The truth is that we do not know, but my guess is that with all the baby boomers retiring and healthcare costs going nowhere but up, there is a very good chance that taxes will be (much) higher.

All of this was discussed again to make a very important point: If you think your income needs will be lower in retirement than they are now, then you have been severely misled. Sure, you may start slowing down when you hit seventy-five years old, but that's a few years away from the day you retire.

So, today you make $100,000, and I concede that you can probably maintain the same standard of living on 20% less or $80,000 a year (of course, I really don't believe this, but I will go along with the "professionals" for the moment). Once you understand that true inflation is closer to 6 - 8%, then you will realize that this $80,000 today equates to the same as $143,268 per

216   *Moving at the Speed of Wealth*

year at a meager 6% inflation rate in ten years. In other words, if your standard of living requires an $80,000/year income today, you will need $143,268 in annual income in ten short years at only a 6% inflation rate. Understand that the government currently adjusts taxes for inflation, *but* they adjust them by the government's *published inflation rate*, which has been around 3% for quite some time. Things are looking worse with every word I write, but don't worry—we can fix it. But only if you are prepared to *play to win*.

What does all of this mean? It means you are extremely unwise if you believe you will be in a lower tax bracket in retirement than what you are in right now. Your tax bracket is likely to remain the same or may even be higher. So let's look at this advice to "take tax deductions now."

Let's assume that you are in the 33% marginal federal and state tax bracket (do not attempt to debunk me by bringing up "effective" tax brackets; taxes are taxes, and what I am about to show you remains a fact). As you know, when you contribute money to a qualified retirement plan, such as a 401(k), the money deposited is tax-deductible. This, of course, was one of your arguments in favor of these plans.

Let's assume that you contribute $6,000 each year for the next thirty years and your money grows at 8% on average. At the end of the year, you deduct the $6,000 from your tax return and it comes right off the top of your income. You "save" $2,000. In other words, this is $2,000 you do not have to send off to Uncle Sam and ordinarily have to deposit with the United States Treasury Department. Money not sent to Uncle Sam is real money in your pocket; it is savings. In thirty years, you "saved" $60,000 in taxes. Not bad—and, again, this is real money to you.

Now it's time to live off of your savings and accumulated earnings. Your money at $6,000 a year growing on average at 8% has grown to $734,075. Good for you; you are one of the few Americans who actually saves money. Your biggest fear is running out of money before you die so you make the mistake most Americans make and decide you can live off the interest alone and not touch principal (this is a mistake because, once again, you are not factoring in inflation). You decide to take the interest you earn each year, 8%, as a withdrawal to live on: 8% of $734,075 is $58,726. Don't worry—you probably have another $24,000 coming in from Social Security, so you are up to the $82,726 that you think you need to keep the same lifestyle. (Of course, this is thirty years down the road and this $82,726 at a 6% inflation rate is the same as $14,403 in today's dollars, but that's for another discussion.)

You withdraw this $58,726 and, lo and behold, you are in the same tax bracket in retirement as you were during your working years (as discussed above). You are taxed at 33% on this money because it is last money in and your tax bill equals $19,380. Your net withdrawal is $39,346 (are you feeling sick yet?).

I stated above that in thirty years of taking the tax deductions, your total savings equaled $60,000. In the very first year, you paid back over $19,000 of this savings to Uncle Sam. *In three short years of retirement, you have paid back all of the tax savings you enjoyed over thirty years.*

I know what you are thinking because your planner planted this seed. "Okay, Wayde, I understand that I shouldn't take the tax deduction now. I would probably be better off opening up a Roth IRA or Roth 401(k)" (if your employer even has such a plan).

Apples to apples, folks. There is absolutely no difference, dollar for dollar, between a Roth plan and a traditional plan, providing you are in the same tax bracket at retirement and in the exact same investment.

The truth is that a Roth is better if you think you will be in a higher tax bracket at retirement and a traditional plan is better if you think you will be in a lower tax bracket at retirement. It really is that simple. This is an argument I will take on with anyone and win every time. A Roth does provide the added benefit that you are not required to take out distributions at the age of 70½—nice to have, but still not optimal.

The plain truth is that the only way you are going to keep that lifestyle is to get better returns on your money and use the techniques I teach to build wealth. *You need to quit trying to beat the system and understand the system if you expect to win.* If you are afraid of risk today, just wait until you reach retirement with only $499,999 saved, then talk to me about fear. You will live in fear every day for the rest of your life—just ask my parents.

So much for the benefit of tax deductions!

Tax-deferred growth

Without a doubt, tax-deferred growth is a major plus. In fact, I always preach that you should only invest in a tax-deferred or free compounding environment so I have to agree with this one…to a certain point. After all, since I have already debunked the tax deductions advantage, wouldn't *tax-free* compounding growth be better? Not necessarily. As I stated before, it depends on the tax bracket you will be in down the road. Because you have no way of knowing what this will be, it really doesn't matter much at this point. With any luck, you will be in the highest tax bracket possible at retirement (this means you are making a lot of money).

You want your money compounding tax-free or deferred if at all possible and a qualified plan is one of the few places you can achieve this phenomenon.

The problem is not tax deferral; the problem is that your returns are pathetic. I mean, come on! Do you honestly believe you are going to win the game earning 4% returns? Chances are, you are earning less than this in your plan, whether you believe that or not.

The problem with these plans is that you are limited as to where you can invest and you are not truly diversified. Stop your screaming. I know you *think* you are diversified, but are you really?

Let's see: You are in large cap stocks, small cap stocks, bio-tech, utilities, foreign, etc. Are you really diversified? No, you are *in the stock market and as the tide goes, so does the ship.*

Three weeks ago I was flying on a plane and watching CNN as the stock market tanked. The funny thing was that almost every single stock was red. It didn't matter which sector it was in—the entire market was down. Some sectors may be down less than others, but the point is that the *entire* market was down. When was the last time your qualified plan gave you the option to invest in real estate? I'm betting other than maybe an REIT, never!

The good news is that as member of The Speed of Wealth Gold Club™, not only will I show you what business to start and how to save money on taxes, but I can show you how to set up a self-directed 401(k) plan as well. You really need to see this! Now, we can start to get you real returns.

You see, I am not opposed to 401(k)s and other qualified plans; I am opposed to your limitations and puny returns. To sum this up, tax deferral is great, bad returns are not so great!

Automatic savings plan

I have no argument here. This is the greatest advantage to qualified plans. You know the old saying, "Out of sight, out of mind." If you cannot touch the money, it makes it very difficult to spend. My only rebuttal would be to convince you to get more disciplined because in just one moment I am going to show you why you probably don't want to contribute to these plans at all.

Employer match

Do I ever get an earful on this subject! "*You cannot beat 100% returns.*" That is, if you put in $500 a month and your employer matches your $500 with another $500. This is, of course, a return of 100%. The problem is that it's only a 100% return *for that one instance* then the money goes into the investments that are providing you with low returns.

Are you ready to be enlightened? Let's go to our second spreadsheet at the end of this chapter. This will not take very long.

Secret of the Super-Rich #12   219

You can see on this sheet that you have a $100,000 balance ("Current Balance"). This is not relevant, but I had to choose some number. The next line indicates that you are contributing $500 per month to your plan AND that your employer is matching you with an additional $500 for a total monthly contribution of $1,000. You are receiving an average of 8% return inside your plan, which, based on lots of case studies, is probably laughable. If you really believe you are doing better, then we need to talk. (I know those Enron employees were doing better than that.)

The next line ("Monthly Payments Minus Matching Contributions") shows you making contributions of only $500 to an outside plan with no matching contributions, but in this investment, you are receiving a 13.6% after-tax return ("Outside Investment Returns"). In other words, you are actually earning 17%, but after paying 20% in taxes, your *effective* return is 13.6%. So, as you see the money grow, understand that it has already been taxed and you will owe no more taxes on the growth.

Column one shows the year of the plan stretching out for thirty years. Column two shows you how your plan ("Current Plan") will grow compounding tax-deferred with your $500 contribution, plus a match of $500 from your employer for a total of $1,000 per month. Remember that we started with a balance of $100,000 and you are receiving an 8% average return. Column three ("Current Plan After Taxes Owed") shows your current plan after paying 20% tax on your growth—in other words, the true worth of your plan. The "Cumulative Tax" column shows the deduction that you get to keep out of the hands of Uncle Sam at the end of the year. This is important if we are comparing apples to apples.

The next two columns illustrate my point and, to lay that out, here is the point of this section: ***The matching contribution does not mean squat if you can GET BETTER RETURNS ON YOUR MONEY!***

Remember that I am now showing you starting with a balance of $100,000 and only making a ***$500*** monthly contribution—no employer match, but you are receiving a *13.6%* after-tax return on your money as opposed to 8%. The "Proposed Plan" shows growth of $120,869 in the first year, *but* you still owe a 20% tax on your original $100,000. This is illustrated in the next column, "Proposed Plan After Taxes Owed." So you will see a total of only $100,869 in year one. This is all your money after taxes have been paid.

By contrast, in the very first year with my proposed plan, I beat your plan, *with a 100% matching contribution,* by $4,202.79 (as illustrated in the last column, "Difference Accounting for Tax").

That's right. In the very first year, my proposed plan beat yours without the

220   *Moving at the Speed of Wealth*

matching contribution all because you received better returns—the type of returns that are *not* available to you within your current qualified plan because your choices are severely limited.

Although I do not show the following in this analysis, it's important to note that even if you were able to squeeze out a 10% average return, my proposed plan beats your current plan in year one by $2,355.82. If I were very generous and assumed you could average a 12% return, my proposed plan beats your current plan by year four by $475.62.

Going back to the spreadsheet, where you are receiving an 8% average return, you will see at the bottom right hand corner that my proposed plan beat your current plan, with matching contributions, *by over $6.1 million*. If you were fortunate and/or sophisticated enough to receive an average return of 12% over those same thirty years, my proposed plan would still beat your current plan, with matching contributions, by over *$2.5 million*.

Keep in mind that not only did my plan beat yours hands down, but if you take advantage of my proposed plan (a.k.a., get better returns), then you were not handcuffed by a bunch of rules and regulations telling you what you could and could not do with *your* money! How's that for power and control?

But this still all boils down to one simple question: Do you believe you can get better returns? The answer must be a resounding yes! And you can do it safely and securely with real collateral by investing in hard money loans and becoming the banker.

So what is the moral to this story? Don't believe everything you have been told. Conventional wisdom is failing you and you are a victim of other people's greed unless you make a decision to empower yourself and take control. Continue to educate yourself and a whole new world of wealth-building opportunities will reveal themselves to you.

Conclusion

In this chapter, I have shown you how to explode your current qualified plan by using Speed of Wealth's 401(k) Arbitrage Strategy™ and I hope I have dispelled the myths associated with the benefits of qualified plans and especially matching contributions.

Whether you take my advice and implement these plans or not is entirely up to you, but I bet you are much wiser and, at the very least, considering the realities and possibilities of what I've just shared with you. The investment world is not at all what it seems to be. Do you think that there may be some benefit to large brokerage houses and mutual fund companies to spend

Secret of the Super-Rich #12

millions in advertising dollars to keep you convinced that you are doing the right thing? Do you think fee-based financial planners and/or commission-based financial planners may stand to gain something from you believing the propaganda passed down from generation to generation?

It's too bad I don't have the marketing budget of a big mutual fund company because if I did, I would spread this message far and wide. Of course, these large companies may have me "quieted" for turning people against them, but let's be real: Only one in ten people who read this are going to understand what I just taught them, much less take action.

For those of you who *are* ready to take action, here is what I recommend: Become a member of The Speed of Wealth Gold Club™ today! *Not tomorrow, today!* The next step is to become a Super Affiliate (*www.SpeedofWealthAffiliate.com*) and help me spread the word and share these ideas with people you care about—and watch your wealth flourish in a multitude of ways!

Once you become a member of the club, it is at that point that I can speak freely to you and be completely transparent about our investment opportunities, including trust deeds that pay a very nice return. You must be a member first and join us on teleconference calls, attend a seminar and workshop in your area, or join in on webinars, etc. As a member, you can view all of my educational material right online immediately.

When you are ready to take action, you can simply sign up as a member at *www.SOWGoldClub.com*, complete the application, and a Speed of Wealth specialist will contact you directly. It's important to know that we do not accept all applicants. We are very picky about whom we choose to work with. I learned my lesson a long time ago to only work with people who truly want to build wealth and people who take action.

401(k) Arbitrage

Current Average Returns in 401(k):	10.00%	
Current Balance in 401(k):	$100,000.00	
Maximum Loan Amount:	50% $50,000.00	50% of current balance or $50,000.00 maximum
Remaining Balance:	$50,000.00	
Loan Interest Rate:	7.50%	Typically Prime Rate
Term:	60	Typically Five Years Maximum
Monthly Payment:	$995.67	
Reinvest:	$50,000.00	
Trust Deeds at Rate of:	17.00%	
Monthly Return:	$708.33	
Effective Tax Backet:	19.00%	
Net Monthly Return:	$573.75	
Current Monthly Contribution:	$6,000.00 $500.00	$500.00
Current Pay:	$100,000.00	
Employer Monthly Match:	6.00%	
Employer Match in Dollars:	$6,000.00 $500.00	
Current Overage:	-	
Difference in Payments:	$287.34	
Difference in Contributions:	$287.34	

Estimated Returns in Side Bucket: 13.60%

End of Year	Current Plan	Proposed Plan	Additional Payments	Freed Up Money Growth Compounding	Total Return on Difference in Payment	IRR Difference in Payment	Current Plan	Proposed Plan
1	$123,142	$80,521	$3,448				$123,142	$130,521
2	$148,706	$114,030	$6,896				$148,706	$164,030
3	$176,948	$151,047	$10,344	*Real Estate,*			$176,948	$201,047
4	$208,149	$191,940	$13,792	*ROTH IRA, FIBS*	190.02%	38.00%	$208,147	$241,940
5	$242,613	$237,116	$17,240	$50,000			$242,613	$287,116
6	$280,688	$274,511		$56,800			$280,688	$331,311
7	$322,750	$315,821		$64,525			$322,750	$380,346
8	$369,217	$361,457		$73,300			$369,217	$434,757
9	$420,549	$411,872		$83,269			$420,549	$495,141
10	$477,256	$467,566		$94,594			$477,256	$562,160
11	$539,901	$529,092		$107,458			$539,901	$636,550
12	$609,106	$597,060		$122,073			$609,103	$719,133
13	$685,558	$672,146		$138,675			$685,558	$810,820
14	$770,015	$755,094		$157,534			$770,015	$912,628
15	$863,316	$846,727		$178,959			$863,316	$1,025,686
16	$966,387	$947,956		$203,297			$966,387	$1,151,254
17	$1,080,251	$1,059,785		$230,946			$1,080,251	$1,290,731
18	$1,206,037	$1,183,324		$262,354			$1,206,037	$1,445,679
19	$1,344,995	$1,319,800		$298,035			$1,344,995	$1,617,834
20	$1,498,504	$1,470,565		$338,567			$1,498,504	$1,809,133
21	$1,668,088	$1,637,118		$384,612			$1,668,088	$2,021,731
22	$1,855,428	$1,821,112		$436,920			$1,855,428	$2,258,031
23	$2,062,386	$2,024,371		$496,341			$2,062,386	$2,520,712
24	$2,291,015	$2,248,915		$563,843			$2,291,015	$2,812,758
25	$2,543,585	$2,496,971		$640,526			$2,543,585	$3,137,497
26	$2,822,602	$2,771,002		$727,637			$2,822,602	$3,498,640
27	$3,130,835	$3,073,728		$826,596			$3,130,835	$3,900,324
28	$3,471,345	$3,408,153		$939,013			$3,471,345	$4,347,166
29	$3,847,510	$3,777,597		$1,066,719			$3,847,510	$4,844,316
30	$4,263,065	$4,185,726		$1,211,793			$4,263,065	$5,397,519

Figure 66

Secret of the Super-Rich #12

Rolling 401(k) Arbitrage Loans

Current Average Returns in 401(k):	10.00%	
Current Balance in 401(k):	$100,000.00	
Maximum Loan Amount:	50% $50,000.00	50% of current balance or $50,000.00 maximum
Remaining Balance:	$50,000.00	
Loan Interest Rate:	7.50%	Typically Prime Rate
Term:	60	Typically Five Years Maximum
Monthly Payment:	$995.67	
Reinvest:	$50,000.00	
Trust Deeds at Rate of:	17.00%	
Monthly Return:	$708.33	
Effective Tax Backet:	19.00%	
Net Monthly Return:	$573.75	
Current Monthly Contribution:	$6,000.00 $500.00	$500.00
Current Pay:	$100,000.00	
Employer Monthly Match:	6.00%	
Employer Match in Dollars:	$6,000.00 $500.00	
Current Overage:	-	
Difference in Payments:	$287.34	
Difference in Contributions:	$287.34	

Estimated Returns in Side Bucket: 13.60%

End of Year	Current Plan	Proposed Plan	New 401(k) Loan	Additional Payments	Freed Up Money Growth Compounding	Current Plan Before Tax Growth	Proposed Plan Before Tax Growth	Before Tax Difference
1	$123,142	$80,521	$(50,000)	$3,448		$123,142	$130,521	$7,380
2	$148,706	$114,239		$6,896		$148,706	$164,239	$15,532
3	$176,948	$151,487		$10,344	*Real Estate,*	$176,948	$201,487	$24,539
4	$208,149	$192,635		$13,792		$208,147	$242,635	$34,488
5	$242,613	$188,092	$(50,000)	$17,240	$100,000	$242,613	$288,092	$45,479
6	$280,688	$233,074		$17,240	$113,600	$280,688	$346,674	$65,986
7	$322,750	$282,766		$17,240	$129,050	$322,750	$411,815	$89,065
8	$369,217	$337,661		$17,240	$146,600	$369,217	$484,261	$115,044
9	$420,549	$398,304		$17,240	$166,538	$420,549	$564,842	$144,293
10	$477,256	$415,297	$(50,000)	$17,240	$239,187	$477,256	$645,484	$177,228
11	$539,901	$484,070		$17,240	$271,717	$539,901	$755,787	$215,885
12	$609,106	$560,044		$17,240	$308,670	$609,106	$868,714	$259,608
13	$685,558	$643,974		$17,240	$350,649	$685,558	$994,623	$309,065
14	$770,015	$736,692		$17,240	$398,337	$770,015	$1,135,030	$365,014
15	$863,316	$789,119	$(50,000)	$17,240	$502,511	$863,316	$1,291,631	$428,314
16	$966,387	$897,036		$17,240	$570,853	$966,387	$1,467,889	$501,502
17	$1,080,251	$1,016,253		$17,240	$648,449	$1,080,251	$1,664,742	$584,492
18	$1,206,037	$1,147,954		$17,240	$736,683	$1,206,037	$1,884,637	$678,600
19	$1,344,995	$1,293,446		$17,240	$836,872	$1,344,995	$2,130,318	$785,323
20	$1,498,504	$1,404,172	$(50,000)	$17,240	$1,000,687	$1,498,504	$2,404,859	$906,355
21	$1,668,088	$1,576,493		$17,240	$1,136,780	$1,668,088	$2,713,273	$1,045,186
22	$1,855,428	$1,766,858		$17,240	$1,291,383	$1,855,428	$3,058,241	$1,202,812
23	$2,062,386	$1,977,157		$17,240	$1,467,011	$2,062,386	$3,444,168	$1,381,781
24	$2,291,015	$2,209,477		$17,240	$1,666,524	$2,291,015	$3,876,001	$1,584,986
25	$2,543,585	$2,694,409	$(50,000)	$17,240	$1,943,171	$2,543,585	$4,359,295	$1,815,710
26	$2,822,602	$2,416,124		$17,240	$2,207,443	$2,822,602	$4,901,852	$2,079,250
27	$3,130,835	$3,001,835		$17,240	$2,507,655	$3,130,835	$5,509,490	$2,378,654
28	$3,471,345	$3,341,452		$17,240	$2,848,696	$3,471,345	$6,190,148	$2,718,803
29	$3,847,510	$3,716,631		$17,240	$3,236,119	$3,847,510	$6,952,750	$3,105,239
30	$4,263,065	$4,131,097		$17,240	$3,676,231	$4,263,065	$7,807,328	$3,544,262

Figure 67

224   *Moving at the Speed of Wealth*

So You Say Matching Contributions Makes All The Difference in the WORLD!

Current Balance:	$100,000.00
Current Monthly Payment with Matching Contributions:	$1,000.00
Current Returns Inside Plan:	8.00%
Monthly Payments Minus Matching Contributions:	$500.00
Outside Investment Returns:	13.60%
Marginal State and Federal Tax Bracket:	20.00%

Both In Tax Deferred/Free Compounding Enviroment

End of Year	Current Plan	Cumulative Tax Deductions	Current Plan After Taxes Owed	Proposed Plan	Prposed Plan After Taxes Owed	Difference Accounting For Tax
1	$120,833	$1,200	$96,666	$120,869	$100,869	$4,202.79
2	4143,395	$2,400	$114,716	$144,760	$124,760	10,044.24
3	4167,829	$3,600	4134,264	$172,111	$152,111	17,847.16
4	$194,292	$4,800	4155,434	$203,422	$183,422	27,988.16
5	$222,951	$6,000	4178,361	$239,267	$219,267	40,906.08
6	$253,989	$7,200	$203,191	$280,303	$260,303	57,111.65
7	$287,603	$8,400	$230,082	$327,281	$307,281	77,198.54
8	$324,007	$9,600	$259,205	$381,062	$361,062	101,856.18
9	$363,432	$10,800	$290,746	$442,630	$422,630	131,884.38
10	$406,130	$12,000	$324,904	$513,114	$493,114	168,210.24
11	$452,371	$13,200	$361,897	$593,804	$573,804	211,907.48
12	$502,451	$14,400	$401,961	$686,179	$666,179	264,218.75
13	$556,687	$15,600	$445,349	$791,931	$771,931	326,581.20
14	$615,424	$16,800	$492,340	$912,995	$892,995	400,655.80
15	$679,037	$18,000	$543,230	$1,051,591	$1,031,591	488,361.13
16	$747,930	$19,200	$598,344	$1,210,256	$1,190,256	591,912.06
17	$822,541	$20,400	$654,033	$1,391,897	$1,371,897	713,864.18
18	$903,344	$21,600	$722,675	$1,599,840	$1,579,840	857,164.82
19	$990,854	$22,800	$792,683	$1,837,895	$1,817,895	$1,025,211.58
20	$1,085,627	$24,000	$868,502	$2,110,421	$2,090,421	$1,221,919.45
21	$1,188,267	$25,200	$950,614	$2,422,411	$2,402,411	$1,451,797.85
22	$1,299,425	$26,400	$1,039,540	$2,779,579	$2,759,579	$1,720,039.03
23	$1,419,810	$27,600	$1,135,848	$3,188,467	$3,168,467	$2,032,619.36
24	$1,550,187	$28,800	$1,240,149	$3,656,565	$3,636,565	$2,396,415.59
25	$1,691,384	$30,000	$1,353,107	$4,192,445	$4,172,445	$2,819,338.15
26	$1,844,301	$31,200	$1,475,441	$4,805,925	$4,785,925	$3,310,483.92
27	$2,009,910	$32,400	$1,607,928	$5,508,240	$5,488,240	$3,880,311.51
28	$2,189,265	$33,600	$1,751,412	$6,312,254	$6,292,254	$4,540,842.04
29	$2,383,505	$34,800	$1,906,804	$7,232,694	$7,212,694	$5,305,889.51
30	$2,593,868	$36,000	$2,075,095	$8,286,419	$8,266,419	$6,191,324.60

Figure 68

Chapter Thirteen

Secret of the Super-Rich #13

Super-Rich People Thoroughly Understand the Effects of Inflation and Use it to Their Advantage

The more people I talk to about building massive wealth, the more I come to understand that Americans, in general, just do not have a clue about the destructive effects of inflation. I think the problem is that during your working years, you really do not feel inflation so much because, until recently, incomes tended to increase at the same rate of inflation. But, mark my words, when you reach retirement and start living on a fixed income, you will quickly come to realize the true danger of inflation.

If you have a true wealth builder mentality, you would never, ever put your money in any investment that was not outpacing inflation. Before I go into this, I must first awaken you to the reality of inflation. As you may or may not know, inflation rates are reported to the American public by our federal government. The government doesn't hide the fact that inflation exists—that would be insane. Rather, it manipulates the rate of inflation to its own benefit.

Do you think that your government would have any reason at all to manipulate this figure or any other statistic? Let's dive into this a tad bit more.

For years the government has been telling us that inflation is between 1 - 3% annually. In August of last year (2007), the Department of Labor's Bureau of Statistics reported a low inflation rate of only 1.7%. I don't for a second think that you believe this, especially when everything you buy keeps going up in price. As I write this, a gallon of gasoline costs over four dollars and there is no end in sight. You are lucky if you can walk out of a grocery store with two bags for under one hundred bucks. Taking a family of four to a movie costs me well on the north side of $50 (I happen to love to go to the movies and, yes, I always buy refreshments). It just doesn't pay to get sick; healthcare costs are through the roof. And heating and cooling your home just keeps costing you more and more (not only because of rising energy costs but we are also buying bigger, albeit more energy efficient, homes).

So how does the government compute inflation? Inflation is based on the Consumer Price Index (CPI). This is a complex government statistic created in the 1920s to track the costs of a basket of goods and services. During the Carter administration, the government started to tamper with this basket of goods and services by removing expensive items that had erratic price movements, such as energy and food (how clever of them). Food and energy were removed from this basket of goods and services, leaving us with "core inflation." The rationale behind this is that because energy and food tend to fluctuate and spike erratically, they must be removed in order to give us a "truer" picture of real inflation.

Now, I don't know about you, but I still have to pay for gas and food like every other American out there and it has a big impact on my wallet whether or not the government wants to count it.

The original standard for measuring inflation was really quite simple and straightforward. They would take the goods and services in the basket of goods and price them out. Each month from that point forward they would again price them out. This is a very easy method to see how prices are going up or down.

Alan Greenspan, along with other so-called geniuses, argued that if a steak dinner got too expensive, the American public would simply replace the steak dinner with a hamburger dinner. If this were the case, he argued, then we are not truly seeing an accurate picture of inflation.

This, of course, just represents a lower standard of living and is total hogwash. So what was the solution for the government during the Clinton administration? Geometric weighting. Simply put, the CPI would give less importance to goods and services rising in price and more weight or relevance to goods and services that were declining in value. For example, during the most recent housing appreciation boom, the relevance put on these increases was devalued or ignored altogether. They could do what they wanted, but housing prices were still escalating, affecting the purchasing power of every American.

Another great way to manipulate inflation is by hedonic adjustments. I love this one. The government rationalizes that some prices go up due to enhanced benefits. For example, a computer may go up 10% in price but only because it has a new, faster chip. The government ignores this 10% increase because of the perceived benefit you enjoy. When a gallon of gas goes up ten cents because of a federally mandated additive to the gasoline, it is not included in the inflation rate because of the added benefit you will enjoy from this new additive. Keep in mind that the government imposed this ten-cent increase; you did not get to choose if you wanted it or not. Whether the government wants to include the ten cents in its inflation number or not does not change the fact that you are paying ten cents more per gallon for gasoline.

Removing food and energy from "core inflation" because of spikes in costs does not change the fact that these goods have been increasing dramatically over time. Keep in mind, when inflation numbers are released, that core inflation removes food and energy—yet Americans spend approximately 23% of their incomes on these two items.

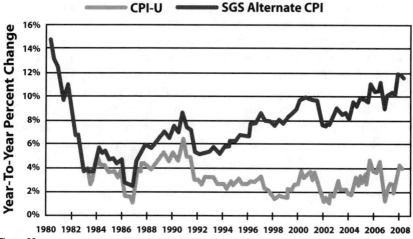
Figure 69

From www.ShadowStats.com: *The CPI chart on the home page reflects our estimate of inflation for today as if it were calculated the same way it was in 1990. The CPI on the Alternate Data Series tab here reflects the CPI as if it were calculated using the methodologies in place in 1980. Further background on the Alternate CPI and Ongoing M3 series is available in the archives in the August 2006 SGS newsletter.*

According to Walter J. (John) Walters, on his website *www.shadowstats.com*, if you go back to pre-1980s and use the old formula for analyzing inflation, you

228   *Moving at the Speed of Wealth*

could find the true rate of inflation simply by adding 7% to what is being reported today.

You can find the chart above at Mr. Walters' website. I highly recommend that you peruse his site and possibly join his newsletter. Mr. Walters makes a compelling case about true inflation.

According to this chart, "true inflation" today is closer to 12%! That should grab your attention. Now we know a few things that we need to be aware of when it comes to building wealth. We know that:

- True inflation is much higher than what we are being told.
- Inflation compounds.
- Inflation erodes purchasing power over time.

For my argument, let's not go overboard. I don't want to believe that true inflation is 12% but I am not foolish enough to believe that true inflation is the mere 3.5 - 4% we are being told it is. I am inclined to think that inflation is closer to 8%. For the following exercise in wealth building, you can use any number you are comfortable with but I strongly urge you to follow my example.

If we believe inflation is 8%, then what returns must we receive on our money in order for one of our dollars today to have the exact same purchasing power ten years down the road? If you answered 8%, you are partially correct.

We know that inflation compounds so you must receive at least 8% in a compounding environment. We also know that inflation numbers are not subject to taxation so not only do you need at least 8% in a compounding environment, but it must be growing in a tax-free environment in order for our one dollar today to have the same purchasing power ten years from now.

I have preached throughout this book that you are lucky if you are receiving 5% over time on your money.

Are you saving your entire paycheck? Well, if you are only receiving an average of 8% return on your money in a tax-free compounding investment, then you know that to keep the same standard of living in retirement you enjoy now, you must save all of your money. The only other solution is to get better returns on your money.

That paragraph above is very profound and shocking. You had better pay close attention to it because it is make or break time. Let me show you what I mean. First of all, you can go on covering your eyes and ears and believing what the government is telling you or you can let the truth rush into your brain.

If you are going to go on believing the government, then just skip this next part and proceed to the next chapter. If you are fairly convinced that inflation

Secret of the Super-Rich #13

may be truer to 8%, then follow closely. Let me assume that you are better than the average investor and you average 10% returns on your money. Let's also assume that you are unlike most Americans and are actually saving money; however you derive the money you are saving $1,000 each and every month like clockwork. You started at thirty-five and plan on retiring at age sixty-five. Your money is growing in a tax-deferred account such as a 401(k).

If you are receiving 10% and it is compounding annually tax-deferred but inflation is 8% (we know it compounds tax-free), then your true effective return is only 2%. Your contributions will grow to $492,075 after inflation is factored in.

Most Americans believe they can retire on $500,000, not factoring in inflation; this is ludicrous. This is also important. Your bank account will show $2,079,293 but your money only has $492,075 in purchasing power in today's dollars.

Unfortunately, most Americans are so concerned with what their bank account looks like that they totally ignore the most important part of the equation: What is that money truly worth? Obviously, if your goal was to have over $2 million in your retirement account by age sixty-five, then you met your goal. However, when you set that goal, you were delusional because you could only envision today's dollars. In reality, when you factor in inflation, you were short of your goal by over $1.5 million.

This is not your fault; it's just how we are programmed as humans.

So where are you if you have the $492,075 in today's dollars saved and it is time to live off of your savings? You are now in retirement. You, like most Americans, have one big fear: You are afraid of outliving your money. So you come up with a plan. You will live off the interest alone and never touch your principal.

However, you are pretty comfortable with your current living standards and don't want to have a lifestyle relapse. You are probably going to be fairly active in retirement and more than likely spend more during your first ten years of retirement than you did during your working years.

You are under the impression today that you will not need as much in retirement as you do during your working years but we already laid that b.s. to rest.

The bottom line is you don't have to buy into anything I say. Your bank account shows over $2 million but has the equivalent purchasing power of $492,075 in today's dollars. The only way I can make my point is to bring everything into today's dollars for you.

You have done pretty well in your investments, averaging 10% annually and allowing it to compound, so you instantly figure that to ensure you do not outlive your money, you can live off of the interest alone. Your rationale is that

230 *Moving at the Speed of Wealth*

if you just pull out your interest, you can never outlive your money because your principal will stay intact.

Before I get to the flaws with this stinking thinking, let me point out that you will be able to pull out $207,929 a year to live on ($2,079,293 times 10% returns). In your mind today, you're thinking, "Wow, I pulled it off and it wasn't that hard." But, remember, we have to contend with "true inflation." So to keep everything in perspective, the purchasing power in thirty years will be $49,208 ($492,075 true growth after inflation times 10% returns).

Now, I ask you: Are you going to keep your same standard of living on $49,208 a year, or just $946 a week before taxes? To add injury to insult, let me throw this tidbit of news at you. Just because you decided to retire does not mean that inflation stops happening.

If "true inflation" is at 8%, as we have determined for this example, then your annual withdrawal will lose 8% of its purchasing power each year. In other words, if you just take out the interest that you earn and leave your principal intact, your lifestyle is taking a turn for the worse with every year.

Many of you are thinking, "So what? I'll be old, can't do anything. I'll slow down." Folks, I don't care how decrepit my body becomes. I will still want to go on cruises even if I am in a scooter. The reason seniors slow down is because they are running out of money.

Now, I don't claim to be a financial planner (I prefer to be called a financial opportunist), just someone with a lot of common sense. But a true financial planner will make it clear to you that if you want to ensure that you do not outlive your money and maintain your same standard of living, you can only withdraw from your account the difference between your returns and "true inflation".

So what does that mean? It means that if "true inflation" is really 8% and you are receiving 10% returns and want to keep your same standard of living, you can only pull out 2% of your total accumulation during retirement (10% returns minus 8% inflation). I am just full of good news, aren't I?

Let me show you an example on the following chart. Once again, I know that there are a lot of numbers to absorb here but just understand the principles.

In Figure 58, I show that you have true purchasing power of $500,000 after thirty years of diligent savings. You are receiving 10% annual returns and "true inflation" is 8%. You are in the 20% effective tax bracket and you think you can pull out your interest each year and never deplete your principal, ensuring you will not outlive your money.

Your first withdrawal is $50,000 and you are left with $40,000 after taxes. You will notice that right off the bat your end of year balance has dipped

Secret of the Super-Rich #13

Inflation erodes your wealth Withdrawls Taken at Beginning of Each Year

Balance: $500,000
Returns: 10%
Tax Rate: 20%
Inflation Rate: 8%
Dispersment Rate: 2%
Withdrawl: $50,000

Year	Balance	Withdrawl	Taxes	Net Withdrawl	End of Year Balance	Present Value of Balance
1	$500,000	$50,000	$10,000	$40,000	$495,000	$495,000
2	$544,500	$54,000	$10,600	$43,200	$490,500	$454,167
3	$539,550	$58,320	$11,664	$46,656	$481,230	$412,577
4	$529,353	$62,986	$12,597	$50,388	$466,367	$370,217
5	$513,004	$68,024	$13,605	$54,420	$444,980	$327,073
6	$489,478	$73,466	$14,693	$58,773	$416,011	$283,130
7	$457,612	$79,344	$15,869	$63,475	$378,269	$238,373
8	$416,096	$85,691	$17,138	$68,553	$330,404	$192,788
9	$363,445	$92,547	$18,509	$74,037	$270,898	$146,358
10	$297,988	$99,950	$19,990	$79,960	$198,038	$99,068
11	$217,842	$107,946	$24,589	$86,357	$109,895	$50,903
12	$120,885	$116,582	$23,316	$93,266	$4,303	$1,845
13	$4,733	$4,733	$947	$3,787	-	-
14	-	-	-	-	-	-
15	-	-	-	-	-	-
16	-	-	-	-	-	-
17	-	-	-	-	-	-
18	-	-	-	-	-	-
19	-	-	-	-	-	-
20	-	-	-	-	-	-

Figure 70

because you withdrew $50,000, leaving you a balance of $450,000 that earned 10% the following year. In the final column, you will see that the remaining balance of your account is losing value rapidly because inflation is eroding the true purchasing value away. Again, don't get too caught up in these numbers; just bear with me.

You withdrew $50,000 and you were fine with that but if you look at year two, you must withdraw $54,000 to have the same purchasing power as you did just one year earlier if inflation is at 8%. You will notice that to ensure you maintain the same standard of living, your annual withdrawals must increase each and every year to keep up with inflation. This causes you to deplete your entire account by year thirteen.

Now, for you critics out there, I understand that inflation is not constant and it fluctuates. I also understand that receiving a 10% return on your money year in and year out is true fiction as well. I use numbers to make a point and the chart above holds true to this erosion of wealth or depletion of standard of life.

Let me make it simple: If you pull out only $50,000 each year during retirement, you will find that every year you can buy fewer goods and services with this money. If this is the reality, then your standard of living is dropping with each passing year. I cannot make it any clearer!

In their book *Die Broke: A Radical Four-Part Financial Plan,* authors Stephen Pollan and Mark Levine preach that you should accumulate your assets and convert all your assets to annuities that will pay you a monthly stream, or annual stream, of income during retirement. Now, if you don't wish to leave money to your heirs, that's entirely up to you. I, for one, intend to leave my heirs a boatload of money and a financial education to go along with it.

This strategy is exactly what annuities were designed to do. They are not the great investment so-called financial planners and insurance reps make them out to be. They do not beat inflation. Annuities were meant to annuitize so that you have a steady, reliable source of income during retirement.

Here again lies a problem. If you annuitize an annuity, the payouts will not keep up with inflation. Some annuities have inflation riders (the payout increases each year) but it is b.s. The initial payout is lowered and the inflation rider is based on the "false inflation" that the government reports.

Not to go too deep into annuities, but this *Die Broke* idea is fine and dandy if you can predict inflation and if you are willing to reduce your standard of living each year during retirement.

Hopefully by now you are letting my message sink in. Inflation is unpredictable and ugly and because we think in terms of today's dollars, we are doomed for a shortfall of cash. So how do you beat inflation when it comes to building wealth? It's simple: Get better returns on your money and start playing the damn game to win.

Using the same example we have been using throughout this chapter, underscoring that "true inflation" is closer to 8%, what happens if you could just get 14% consistent, safe and reliable returns by making hard money loans? Remember that you are saving $1,000 per month in a 401(k) on which you will never get 14%, but we already covered that. The net return on your money after "true inflation" is now 6% and you save $1,000 each month for thirty years.

Now your money has grown to $4,599,621, or $979,256 adjusted for today's dollars. This is more like it. Knowing that, to ensure you do not outlive your money and keep the same standard of living, you can withdraw 6% each year (14% returns minus 8% inflation rate). You can now withdraw $58,755 each year before taxes, adjusted for today's dollars, or $275,977 in future dollars.

Don't live and breathe by the numbers I have used here because calculations can vary widely with just one small change. To get an idea of the present value of money and the effects of inflation, visit this site: *http://www.money-chimp.com/calculator/present_value_calculator.htm.*

Once there, plug in how much money you think you will have saved in retirement, plug in how many years it will take you and then plug in what you think "true inflation" will likely average over that time period in the discount rate field. Hit "calculate" and bingo…time to get depressed.

So there you have it—a shocking dose of reality. You know inflation exists, you probably just never knew the true death grip it has on you. My wife and I recently ran an insurance illustration showing us putting in $50,000 a year for five years with no more premiums. Keep in mind that this is the most aggressive plan I could build using the product I demonstrate throughout this book.

The final result was that I could pull out $124,882 starting at age sixty-five, tax-free—forever (if all parameters hold up, and they won't). My wife got very excited! Until, that is, I brought her to the money chimp calculator and plugged in the numbers.

When I used an 8% inflation rate, I pointed out that this $124,882 would have the same purchasing power as $26,793 today. She got really depressed. Even when I used the more conservative number (like the government uses) of 4%, this money would only buy $56,994 worth of goods and services in today's dollars.

I tell you this story to show you that even an educated woman like my wife, who lives with me every day, can be delusional about future dollars. I also use this to point out that life insurance, as well as mutual funds and 401(k) plans, are not a good investment. It is what I can do with that plan as a banking system that makes the difference.

In summary, I will state it for the third time. To beat inflation, you must play to win and get better returns on your money!

Chapter Fourteen

Secret of the Super-Rich #14

Super-Rich People Understand the Reality of Money

Super-rich people understand that money, as in cash, is fiat. That is to say that it is fake. Cash in hand does not represent true wealth. True assets equal true wealth.

We need cash to exchange for goods and services every day and a true asset will produce this cash in hand, but cash in hand is worthless unless it is used.

Remember that assets produce income and liabilities cost you. To provide yourself with financial independence, you must understand the difference between paper assets and true assets.

Paper assets are absolutely worthless. What you think you are worth is a delusion. I hear the following statement from my students all the time. "I lost 'X' amount of dollars during the freefall the market took between 2001 and 2003." You didn't lose anything because you never cashed it in or converted it into a true asset.

Let's use some common sense here. Assume you have a car with a book value of $20,000 and you owe no money on it. On paper, this is a $20,000 asset. In reality, it is nothing more than a liability because, although you probably want your car in order to get from A to B, it costs you money every day to maintain and operate this so-called asset—not to mention that it is a depreciating asset.

I will go one step further and revisit an earlier chapter. Assume your home is free and clear and you have $300,000 in equity. On paper, this adds $300,000 to your net worth, but it is a paper asset. In reality, your home remains a liability. Every month you shell out property taxes and homeowner's insurance premiums, and the maintenance bills are staggering. You need a place to shelter you and this asset over time will appreciate. This $300,000 asset will never produce any income for you unless you remove it.

To remove it, you must sell and find another place to live, which means shelling out cash or refinancing. If you can create a spread on your money (the difference between what you are paying to borrow this money and what you are receiving by reinvesting this money), then this $300,000 creates income and is a true asset. When you remove this equity and reposition it, the $300,000 still shows as an asset on paper for the exact same amount. The difference is that once you reposition it and earn spread, this asset produces income.

Owning rental properties, commercial or industrial real estate is a whole different animal. These are true assets. Let's say you own a commercial building worth $1,000,000 and it is free and clear. Sure, you still have maintenance costs, taxes and insurance but if it is rented out, it produces income.

Make no mistake: Hard assets can lose value just as easily. The value of your real estate holdings can go down but, historically, will continue upwards. The nice thing about real estate, unlike stocks and bonds, is that there will always be some kind of intrinsic value to it. Stocks and bonds can lose all value.

Intellectual property can be a hard asset. Look at what Microsoft® has done. They license out the intellectual property they own to make income. I sell this book. It is nothing more than my intellectual property yet I produce income from its sales. This book, and all subsequent products that I make available to my students, makes me more money than any investment I could ever be in.

I write this book once and it generates income for me in many different ways: residual income.

So what is the purpose of making this statement? It is simple: While most of you do everything you think you should be doing to save and build wealth, super-rich people do it more easily. Do you think it would take me more time to write this book or save $500,000? It would take me much longer to save $500,000, yet this book will produce more lifetime income than my $500,000 of savings ever will.

You, too, need to tap into your intellectual property and create income. Every person reading this book is very good at something.

School was very easy for me. I am not saying I was a straight A student, but I was always a solid B student. Yet, I could get straight B's in my courses and only attend class once a week. While my buddies were cramming for finals, I would be out dancing and partying the night before and still get a good grade. My buddies hated that about me.

The thing is that I thought everybody should be able to do as well as I did with as little dedication as I had. I was pretty good at football, too, yet never worked out off of the field. It just came naturally to me.

Here is the point: Everybody has a strength. To figure out what you're exceptional at, just ask yourself one very easy question: What is it that I do that I think everyone should be able to do well but they don't? You see, you are so good at what you were put on this Earth to do that you never give it a second thought.

I made it clear that each and every one of you should own a business. A thriving business is a hard asset in that it earns you income and it saves you taxes (which is income). Find your strength and make it a business because there is someone out there who wants to have what comes very easily to you.

There is one big difference between my wife and me. She can talk to anybody. She has the gift of gab (one of my daughters has this same gift). I am not as social and never have been. I can speak in front of thousands of people but when I am forced to talk to someone one-on-one, I am very uncomfortable. I get this trait from my father. I have always disliked this about myself but "I yam what I yam," as Popeye would say.

I think one of the best attributes to have in life is the power of gab, the ease to walk up to just about anyone and strike up a conversation. My mother is very good at this but never realized it as a strength; she never gave it a second thought.

If you have the gift of gab, what better business to be in than the network marketing business? Some people can just handle rejection and go onto the next person; these people make the greatest salespeople in the world. Others, like me, take rejection very hard. I can be complimented 99 times but when someone says something bad about me, I dwell on it for weeks. Network marketing is a poor business for me—however, I developed systems that allow me to build a huge downline without ever speaking to a single soul.

The point I am trying to make is that super-rich people discover and embrace their strengths and put them to use while at the same time accepting their weaknesses and working to overcome them.

The greatest hard asset you own is you! I can teach anyone how to achieve greatness, but only when we discover their true hard asset. Not the one you fabricate in your mind or aspire to be, but your *true strength*.

Super-rich people harness this asset and build a fortune. If you are a poor negotiator, don't do real estate unless you can partner up with or hire someone who negotiates on your behalf. People will charge you thousands of dollars, saying they can make you a better negotiator, but if it is not in you, chances are you will never make a good one.

I get so frustrated when I watch people spend tens of thousands of dollars to watch Tony Robbins or some other motivational speaker. What you paid for this book was less than thirty bucks! Here is all you need to do: Look in the mirror, straight into your own eyes, have a piece of paper and a pen next to you and, for the next hour, write down your true strengths and weaknesses.

Those of you who aspire to be super-rich will start to find ways to harness your strengths and hire people or partner up with people who are strong where you are weak. Now you know how to unleash the lion within, the way rich people do.

The reality of money is that it ain't worth squat if you are not happy, and you will never be happy doing something you were not born to do. I was born to educate and that's what I do. I was born to raise money for real estate developers, not to be a real estate developer. So I find trustworthy, upstanding, strong developers with my same objectives and I raise money for them and let them do what they were born to do: develop. The developers I work with are not great at raising money but are great developers. Doesn't it just make sense to partner up?

Why would I want to raise money and be a developer? I suppose over the next ten years, I could become a good developer…but why? I would hate the day-to-day grind of it.

Super-rich people understand the reality of money: It is not the money; it is the game! Money is just a scorecard. Find the game you want to play and find a way to excel at it; the money will come. I don't care if your only talent is flying remote-controlled airplanes. There are scores of people that would love to tap into your knowledge of flying these planes. I do mean scores of people! And they will pay you money to learn from you.

I knew a guy who, in his own eyes, had absolutely no talent whatsoever. So he settled into doing labor to make a living. He worked for contractors and hauled off their trash. I made one simple suggestion. I told him to buy a beat-up truck and go around neighborhoods offering to haul away their trash. I said that he could do it very simply, and here was the plan I gave him:

Pick a neighborhood about one square mile in size, then go around and leave a flyer that reads:

Secret of the Super-Rich #14   239

I Want to Haul Away Your Trash! I will be in your neighbor-hood on April 1 between 7 a.m. and 4 p.m. Leave your trash in your driveway and I will pick it up and haul it away.

I charge $30 for a normal-sized pickup load. I have left a self-addressed envelope attached to this flyer. Once I have hauled away your trash, I will leave a note telling you how many loads. When you are satisfied, place a check for $30 per load into the envelope and mail it to me.

Thanks for your business in advance,
John Smith
johns@xyz.com

He told me that he was overwhelmed with work! All he could afford was to borrow a friend's pickup truck, which he drove into town on April 1. On one block alone, there was a pile of trash in every third driveway. Almost everyone sent in the check. One year later, he had three dump trucks and six employees. Not bad for a guy that thought he had no talent!

He didn't even have to grow his business; he could have easily made $100,000 a year on his own, doing what he enjoyed. He actually liked hauling trash for the most part. He later started going through the trash and learned how to sell some things on eBay®.

For this guy, I define $100,000 a year and being happy as a lark as being super-rich. You may not agree, but then you are missing the point of this entire book. Sure, I told you some great ways to invest your money and some uncon-ventional strategies to build wealth, but what good does it do you if you do not understand the reality of money? For the record, this guy was an African-American who grew up with nothing. He thought he had three strikes against him coming into life and that he would leave with the same. Nothing could be further from the truth. This man found his strength, capitalized on it then began to educate himself as time went on. Once you are happy and a bit more comfortable, you will find the time to continue to open your mind and learn from others.

The reality of money is exactly what you make it out to be! The guy mentioned above made so much money that he started to invest; he used the strategies of the super-rich and bought hard assets. Every investment he makes is collateralized by something tangible or real.

Super-rich people understand that it is not how much you accumulate; it is how much income it produces that you keep after taxes. Super-rich people understand that your intellectual power is a true asset and paper assets are fake. I could lose it all tomorrow and gain it all back in a matter of years because of what I know. I never worry about layoffs or losing my money—that would be a waste of time. Losing money once in a while is just part of the game.

Chapter Fifteen

Secret of the Super-Rich #15

Super-Rich People Do Not Invest Where You Do; They Do Not Accept Returns Below Twelve to Fifteen Percent

Super-rich people have a totally different mindset when it comes to investing their money. They simply will not accept returns of less than 12 - 15%. Super-rich people play to win—all others are not even in the game. A typical Middle American investor is happy to receive a puny 8% average return on his money and, as you have read in the chapter on inflation, this just won't cut it.

By now you should see some solid rhyme and reason in this book. Super-rich people invest in themselves first and once they have achieved success, they turn to unconventional techniques, strategies and investments to allow their money to grow larger, faster. While this money is stockpiling, they continue to invest in themselves. They attend seminars, they listen to people who have what they want, they read and read some more. Super-rich people are never content with the knowledge they have gained; they always hunger for more.

I have mentioned time and again that super-rich people own their own business. The problem with most Americans is that they think this is just too big of a challenge, when nothing could be further from the truth. Americans always think on a BIG scale and never understand that small steps can get you to the same place as big steps can—it may just take longer (unless, of course, you find shortcuts…and that is why super-rich people are always investing in gaining more knowledge).

242   *Moving at the Speed of Wealth*

All those self-proclaimed self-help gurus preach the same thing: Set goals and set them big. Write down your goals, review the progress toward your goals daily, and restructure your goals, yada, yada, yada! I am sure you have heard all this b.s. before.

Let me give you my point of view. I set objectives—*daily* objectives. You see, I learned long ago that all this goal setting is crap. Let me explain.

Let's say you are sitting at a dinner table and you are strapped to a chair. Your arms are free but you can only lean forward just about five inches. Somebody sets the salt at the far end of the table (this would represent you setting big, lofty goals). You really want some salt on your food but the salt is way out of reach. You will not even reach for the salt. You know you cannot reach it so you give up before you ever try, no matter how badly you want that salt.

On the other hand, let's say that the salt is just barely out of your reach. You will try over and over again to reach that salt. You will stretch and contour your body in any means you can think of to reach that salt. You may not succeed the first ten or fifteen times, but it is just outside your reach so you keep trying. This is how you need to set your objectives: just barely out of reach.

The next thing you need to do is ask for some help, whether it is for ideas or tools to reach that salt. What if, before that salt was placed on the table, someone put a tablecloth underneath it? Your plate of food and the salt are sitting on top of a tablecloth and you are still sitting there strapped in.

The tablecloth now becomes the tool and with just a little bit of contemplation, you figure out the solution. You will grasp the tablecloth with your hands, pulling it toward yourself little by little. You will then use your nose to inch your plate forward. Eventually, with small steps, it won't matter where that salt sits on that table—you will reach it.

Of course, there is always the easiest way: Just find someone nearby to pass you the salt and be done with it. Someone may be nearby, but you may have to look. Super-rich people use all three methods to reach the salt:

1. They use tools.
2. They use ingenuity.
3. They use help (mentors).

It has been my objective throughout this entire book to get you to have a complete change in the way you think about things. I hate to use the cliché to "think outside of the box," but it is very appropriate here.

The title of this chapter is "Secret #15: Super-Rich People Do Not Invest Where You Do; They Do Not Accept Returns Below Twelve to Fifteen Percent"

Secret of the Super-Rich #15

and I am positive that the first thing to grab your attention was the 12% returns on their money, and you assumed it was in some sort of investment. This is partially true, but super-rich people understand that the word "investment" means a whole lot more than what the average Joe thinks.

Here are a couple of examples:

I attend seminars, workshops and bootcamps, read books, listen to tapes, watch educational DVDs, spend big money on personal trainers and mentors, and listen intently to every word that comes out of the mouths of successful people.

I recently hired a successful Internet marketer to mentor me on his techniques and strategies. This thirty-year-old and his wife are nothing short of Internet marketing machines. I hope my mentor doesn't mind me spilling the beans on how much I paid him, but it was more than $24,999 and less than $25,001.

You can ask my mentor himself (hopefully you will meet him soon because he is part of my team of experts). When the price was quoted to me, I did not hesitate for one second nor did I negotiate. I simply said, "I will be in your city in two weeks. Can we do it then?"

My mentor knows from experience that my quick response without hesitation proved I was a winner and super-rich. Here is the point: I knew for a fact that the $25,000 I would be spending for two days with him would at least return $28,409 to me in personal revenue (for you non-mathletes, that is a 12% return on my money).

The reality is that this $25,000 will probably return millions of dollars to me over the course of time, but I was willing to accept just the $28,409 every day. You see, I did not invest in an investment opportunity; I invested in the ability of my mentor to teach me how to make at least 12% on the money I paid him.

I think the world of my mentor, but I also know that he is not the only Internet marketing guru I can learn from. I also paid another mentor by purchasing one of his courses to teach me how to promote this book. Both of these men are millionaires because they think differently and invest in themselves.

Be careful whom you pick as a mentor. Just because they claim to be successful doesn't mean it's true.

I will spend thousands and thousands of dollars on seminars, workshops and bootcamps if I can learn just one thing. If I can sit there for three days and walk away with an idea that will make me at least 12% on the money I paid for the event, it is well worth every single dime and I will do it over and over again.

Instead of spending thousands and thousands of dollars on self-help gurus, why don't you redirect that money and pay someone who is very successful in the area you want to succeed in to mentor you? Quit thinking that a return on your money is all about investments. The number one investment is YOU!

I have waited until the later chapters to share these true secrets of the super-rich with you. You thought this was all about investment opportunities, techniques and strategies.

The most important strategies I have shared with you are what you have read in the previous chapters, this chapter, and in upcoming chapters: starting your own business and creating your own banking system. Once you understand, adopt and implement those ideas, you will be well on your way to implementing everything else I have shared with you.

Here is some simple arithmetic to make my point. Let's say you start a business and your easily attainable goal is to produce an extra $1,000 a month in income part-time. I am about to show you just how easy it is when you put it in proper perspective.

You spend $500 to join a network marketing company that you truly believe in (I have already mentioned the program we are involved in). If your strength is talking to people, then go out and talk to them. If talking to people one-on-one is a weakness, then learn how to recruit using the Internet. Either way, it is part-time work.

Most of you will give up within three months because "it's too hard," "it just doesn't work," "I cannot seem to find the extra time" or whatever your doomed-to-be-poor excuse is. Many of you will hang in there and listen to successful marketers until you find an approach that you are comfortable with.

Let's just say it takes you two years to reach a point where you can count on an extra $1,000 a month part-time income.

If you are like most "boxed in" Americans, you will invest in mutual funds, bonds, money markets, CDs, or some other nonsense. I have already shared with you the types of returns you can expect and seeing as how the market is exactly where it was nine years ago, good luck with any positive returns at all.

A typical American with his "well-balanced" portfolio generates an average 5% return on his money. This typical American will have to save $240,000 to generate $1,000 per month, which will typically be taxed as ordinary income. Just how hard is it today to save a quarter of a million dollars? I'll bet dollars to donuts that it was more painful and took a heck of a lot more time to save $240,000 than it took our network marketer. Remember, our network marketer took two years of part-time work to produce this residual income.

Here comes my biggest confession of all time. Many of my past and

Secret of the Super-Rich #15

current students don't even know this. I only confess this to make sure that everything I have shared with you sinks in and a light goes on in your head.

I have to take a deep breath. This is going to be hard for me.

My investments make me well over $100,000 in income each and every month. Now here comes the confession: I have less than $500,000 saved! In other words, I have less than $500,000 of my own saved money in any investment opportunities (of course, what little I have is invested where I recommend that you invest).

I don't have an IRA, I don't have a 401(k)—though I'm thinking about starting a self-directed one soon—I don't have anything that you probably have. I have less than $500,000 of my saved money invested yet my investment income exceeds $100,000 each month. My family lives very luxuriously. We spend almost every dime we make and enjoy our lives.

The investment that generates me over $100,000 each month is my systematic business that I have built over the last four years. I have more shocking news for you. Yes, I make a commission on most investment opportunities that I present to you but this commission is not the bulk of my income. The bulk of my income comes from the systems themselves and teaching others how to implement systems to build wealth.

Here is another shocking confession. I don't think I could sell my business for one red cent. My business revolves solely around me. If I am not around, it won't fail, but it won't grow, either. But here is the kicker: I could be a paraplegic in a wheelchair and still do what I do for income.

Wait a minute, Wayde! Robert Kiyosaki writes in his books that to be very rich, you must invest your money in good investments and own a business that you can be absent from and sell for a price.

Well, he is wrong and you guys are being led down a path that most of you can probably never live up to. Owning and operating a large-scale business is hard work and requires special talents. Being self-employed can get you just as rich.

There you have my personal wealth secret. Isn't it reassuring that you can do the same thing I have done? I will gladly let you pay me and I will spill the beans on just how easy it is to do (just start attending my workshops, and especially my intensive three-day bootcamp; you can learn of upcoming events at *www.SpeedofWealthEvents.com* or *www.SOWBootcamp*). What, you don't think I deserve to get paid to show you everything I have done to get to where I am within four years?

If you think I was born rich, you are sadly mistaken. I tell every student that

I have made a ton of money and lost it all two times over. Before I learned *this* chapter's secret four years ago, I was falling apart. I was literally climbing on roofs after hailstorms to sell replacement roofs (a far cry from being in the financial fields for twenty years, but I was sick and tired of being sick and tired so I did whatever was necessary).

The physical work was very good for me (if you don't think a six-foot-four, 250-pound, forty-year-old man, beat up from years of football, climbing and walking on roofs is physical work, you are insane!). The money sucked but I had plenty of time to think and reflect and learn the true secret.

The true "secret" is not that law of attraction crap. The "true secrets" are as follows:

1. Determine your strengths and weaknesses.
2. Invest in making your strengths stronger and ignore your weaknesses.
3. Believe in yourself and be focused on a *realistic* objective.
4. Implement and don't quit (you will never quit once you accomplish the first three secrets).
5. Surround yourself with people who are strong where you are weak (either hire them or make them a limited partner).
6. Repeat over and over again!

Thinking you're super-rich is not going to attract wealth. Do you really buy into that crap? "Work smarter, not harder" is a bunch of bologna, too. The four-day workweek is pure fantasy if you really want to be super-rich (just ask Donald Trump).

No, folks, super-rich people work smarter and harder and longer, and they play harder and enjoy life!

Keep in mind that you don't know what you don't know. Literally hundreds of thousands of people across the country are convinced they want to build their wealth by doing fix-n-flips or buying rental properties. Are you absolutely sure? It takes a special breed of person to be successful at these ventures. I, for one, have no interest at all in these two wealth-building arenas.

Sure, you have heard great success stories, but you seldom hear about the failures. There are multiple failures to every success story. I am not trying to dissuade you from doing these things; I am simply saying that you don't know what you don't know.

I currently have less than $500,000 invested and it is primarily invested where I recommend you invest your money: a real estate related investment. The difference is that I chose to invest passively and could do without the hassles. Now for the rest of the story…

I am quite confident that within the next five years, I will save more money. I am just running out of places to spend it so I might as well save it for my kids' benefit. You, too, should save money so that you can have the financial freedom to chuck it all in when you are good and ready, if ever.

For you egotistical, red personality types, you may want to ignore what I am about to say, but you would do well to listen: **You Are More Powerful as a Group Than You Are as an Individual!**

Here is the sad truth for many of you readers: Many of you are not permitted by our government to invest where rich people invest. The government figures that if you, as an individual, have not accumulated at least $1,000,000 in net worth, excluding your house, or are incapable of earning $200,000 a year, year in and year out, then you are an unsophisticated investor.

My goodness, what a blow to people just starting out in life! If you do not meet the above qualifications, you are not an accredited investor and you are limited as to where you can invest. After all, it is the government's job to protect you from yourself. On top of that, people in the financial fields are mandated to discover what a suitable investment is for you. Go figure! How in the hell am I to know what is suitable for you if I haven't known you for years? Heck, I still am not sure of all the things that are suitable for my parents.

Take a person sixty-five years of age, who is considered a senior citizen (what a joke!). Let's say this person has a whopping $100,000 saved to last him through retirement. The job of a financial professional is to recommend a suitable investment, one that does not put that money at risk. Well, that pretty much leaves bonds.

My opinion is: *What the hell is the difference?* This $100,000 won't do squat for this so-called senior citizen; he might as well go for big returns. This person is doomed to pull ticket stubs the rest of his life and live off the government or your tax dollars to make ends meet (of course, a sixty-five-year-old "senior citizen" can implement anything in this chapter, perhaps better than a person in his or her twenties).

Let this person with $100,000 make up his own mind as to where to invest his money. The problem is that people in America do not take personal responsibility for their own actions. If people were to lose money in a recommended investment, you can bet one out of ten losers will sue or threaten to sue the person who made the recommendation.

Don't believe me? Then who do you think is taking all the heat from all those people facing foreclosures due to adjustable subprime loans? Very seldom do you hear that the borrower is at fault. I have heard all kinds of excuses like "I didn't know it adjusted" or "I didn't know I could create negative amortization." Give me a break! If you refinanced your old loan, then you had at least three days to review all the documents. If it was a purchase loan, these folks had every opportunity to ask for the closing documents in advance and review them or have an attorney review them on their behalf.

The point is that any legal document you sign should be reviewed thoroughly and if you feel you are not competent, have a family member or an attorney help you out.

Every week you read about some person who bilked others out of millions in some investment scheme. Sadly, this is the reality of life, but it is nothing more than criminal. It is no different than someone robbing your home of everything you own. But not everyone has criminal intent.

In fact, what you do not hear about is the scores of people out there that bring solid investment opportunities to investors who succeed. There are much more success stories than criminal stories. It is your job to do some due diligence.

As you know, the bulk of my investments are hard money loans, where I am secured by a promissory note tied to a deed of trust or mortgage. I have collateral. If the borrower fails, and sooner or later some will, I can take possession of the property and dispose of it in any way I deem fit. The nice thing about real estate is that you can get very creative when it comes to making the asset perform.

Here are a couple of rules that the super-rich understand thoroughly:

1. You will lose money.
2. Your better-than-average returns will make up for the losses.
3. Always be patient when you lose money.

Losing money does not sound pretty but what you are looking for is a blended rate of return. If all you do is hard money loans, have enough diversification so that in the event that one goes south, the others will keep your overall returns strong. And remember that you are stronger as a group than you are as an individual.

Let's say you have $100,000 to invest. Alone, you may be able to find one hard money loan to make. If that one deal goes south, you are in trouble. Now, let's say that there are ten of you, so you each put $10,000 into that one deal and

Secret of the Super-Rich #15

go out and make nine other loans. If that one deal goes south, you don't panic. The other nine loans will hold you up while you are patient and deal with the one going south. And when you are patient and have time, you can almost always turn the situation into a moneymaking proposition.

People talk about diversification all the time. I agree, but it doesn't have to be different investment classes. Should you take your $100,000 and invest some in hard money loans, some in mutual funds, some in stocks, some in bonds and so on? Only you can decide the answer, but as for me, I am just as diversified if I am in ten different hard money loans that meet my criteria. At least I will earn a minimum of 12% returns on each loan and if one fails, I may make a better return when I take possession and liquidate the property. I may lose some money on one of my loans but the most it may do is pull down my blended return from 12% to 11.5%. For some reason, I have had trouble explaining this to my students in the past: All that matters is your blended rate of return.

I put together an investment club a couple of years ago based on the current investment environment. As you know, investment environments change. I have a handful of club members bitching because a few of the investments within this club are losing money—never mind the fact that the blended rate of return is north of 10% while the stock and real estate markets are both tanking simultaneously!

The complainers will be washed out and never be allowed to work with me again. They just don't get it.

You see, Americans will complain when they lose money in mutual funds, but nowhere near as loudly as they complain if it is in a non-traditional investment.

If you have what it takes, if you understand this book to this point, if you are ready to play to win, then pay very close attention. If you understand that you are stronger as a group than you are individually, you will want to take a hard look at The Speed of Wealth Gold Club™.

First of all, I want to make you aware of investment clubs. Investment clubs have been around for years and many of them specialize in different investment classes. Here are the basics:

- They are a group of like-minded individuals who come together for a common cause.
- The primary focus is education.
- A secondary focus is pooling their money together to diversify and spread the risks of a particular investment class and to invest.

250 *Moving at the Speed of Wealth*

I don't want to get into the rules and regulations of how they operate but there are several ways of achieving these common goals. The Speed of Wealth Gold Club™ is such a club where our primary focus revolves around continued education and passively investing club members' money in investments that are collateralized by real estate. Basically, I put together something I wish I had years ago.

I'll be the first to admit that I have gone through some learning curves but I am confident I have the perfect model now. Here is a short list of the benefits you enjoy as a club member:

Monthly Educational Newsletter: Each month you will receive my hard copy newsletter, *Wayde's Pearls of Wisdom*, delivered to your mailbox. Each issue will keep you updated on current events, techniques, strategies, investment opportunities, financial issues and more. We include some humor and trivia. Members can run their own classifieds and/or announce their own investment opportunities to other members (must be approved by Retirement TRACS, LLC). To see a very small list of some of the topics covered, keep reading. You will anxiously await this newsletter each and every month. We will even show you moneymaking opportunities, so if you are starting with no money saved, we can show you how to generate more income immediately. You will also read articles from other specialists in their areas of expertise, including, but not limited to, tax issues, self-improvement, home-based business opportunities, investment techniques, IRA expertise and so on. This monthly newsletter alone is worth the price of membership, but there is more...

Monthly Educational Audio, Video or Computer CD: Each month you will receive at least one audio CD, DVD or computer CD. These CDs are educational and cover various topics. We try to keep them to an hour or less in length so you can gain your education in the relaxing atmosphere of your home, car or office. Many of our webinars and/or teleseminars are recorded and sent to you along with your newsletter each and every month. Make sure you take the time to retrieve the information on these disks...just one of them may provide the information that you have been waiting for that will make you rich!

Monthly Member Teleconference with Wayde McKelvy: If you are trying to build tremendous wealth sooner than later, why on God's green Earth wouldn't you want to ride the coattails of someone who has done it? Mentorship is the most valuable thing you can reach out for. Successful people will take you on

Secret of the Super-Rich #15 251

their coattails once a month to provide you with proven techniques, strategies and investments that have brought them to the Promised Land. Once a month you will be invited to a mentoring session with what I consider a true "guru" in his or her field. You know by now that I don't fall for most of these self-proclaimed experts, but some do exist and you will get your chance to listen as they share their infinite wisdom with you. On top of that, you will have the chance to ask questions specific to your needs. In his book *Think and Grow Rich*, Napoleon Hill makes it very clear that anyone who wants to achieve great wealth must belong to a "Master Mind" group. Simply by becoming a member of The Speed of Wealth Gold Club™, you are automatically in this group. Can't make a session? Don't worry, we record all sessions but the replays are only available to members of the club.

Priority Notice of All Investment Opportunities: This perhaps could be the biggest benefit of all. As many of my current students will testify, I personally research and find some of the greatest alternative investment opportunities available today. Believe me when I tell you that right now, during these uneasy financial times, is the best opportunity to grow filthy, stinking rich—it is a better opportunity than you have ever had before. In fact, you may not get these opportunities again in the future. The problem is that most of these opportunities are limited as to how much money they require and need to raise. As a member of the club, you are notified first (before all of my non-club member students) of any and all investment opportunities. Essentially, you get first right of refusal. This doesn't guarantee you a spot because other members may take action faster than you do, but it gives you a leg up. For example, about eight months ago we announced a hard money loan secured by real estate that was paying a 50% return in just eight months (that's a 75% annualized return). I was only allowed to raise $5.5 million and we had over $8 million committed within six hours. We had to turn down $3 million. As a club member, you would have had first right of refusal. By the way, we just paid off all of the investors and, yes, they received 50% returns in just eight months (don't worry, we have opportunities like this all the time). If I were you, I would not hesitate. I would join the club right now to ensure that you do not miss any more of these great opportunities.

Affiliate Program: Although membership dues are very affordable, as a club member you have the opportunity to earn much more than you will ever pay in dues. Only club members are invited to join The Speed of Wealth Super

Affiliate Program™ (you can be a Basic Affiliate without joining the club, but Super Affiliates make a whole lot more money). This is your chance to earn huge commissions and fees simply by referring people to one of our many educational websites. You can earn a commission on every product we sell to the people you referred, and you can earn BIG finder's fees on selected investments if the person you referred opts into one of these opportunities. In this program's first month alone, I paid out over $200,000 in these finder's fees.

Discounts on all Products and Bootcamps: With forty-five years of knowledge and twenty years of financial experience floating around in my head, it is imperative that I make it available to my students. I have many products for sale to the general public, including club members. Keep in mind that once you are a club member, your education begins…but it takes some time. If you want to jumpstart your wealth building, you may want to buy one of my many products or attend our intensive three-day investor survivor bootcamp. You don't need to make any purchases, but if you do you will enjoy discounts of up to 50% over non-members. The savings on the bootcamp alone will pay for an entire year of club membership.

24-Hour Back Office Access to All Previous Webinars, Teleseminars, Teleclasses and Articles: Although I make many of my educational pieces available to the general public, it is nowhere near what will be available to you. Keep in mind that if you are a club member, I am allowed to speak more freely to you. After all, this is essentially an investment club (remember that you are more powerful as a group than you are individually). You have access to all of my reports, articles, recorded webinars and teleseminars, and more. When we announce an upcoming webinar, you can relax if your schedule will not permit you to attend because you can go to the back office at www.SpeedofWealth.com at your leisure and view or listen on your own time. This is priceless because we know just how hectic your schedules are today, especially if you have kids or grandchildren.

Personally Assigned Wealth-Building Coach: As a club member, you will be assigned a Speed of Wealth Building Specialist™. These specialists are personally trained by me and are on top of the game. They can direct you in the right direction, answer your most pressing questions and just be there whenever you want to ask something. Don't take this lightly. These folks are trained to help you acquire riches you only dreamed of. Many of them started out just like

Secret of the Super-Rich #15 253

you and decided to make a career change. They learned about my specialist program, believed strongly in what I teach and jumped on board with both feet. Today, many of these specialists earn very, very good incomes helping you become richer. If you would like to learn more about our specialist program, visit *www.SOWSpecialistProgram.com.*

Enhanced Returns on Selected Investment Opportunities: As a club member, you are entitled to a higher return on many of our investment opportunities. When non-club members may make 16% on hard money loans, you may be entitled to 17% on the same note. The reason is simple: I do not charge a management fee to club members; your fees are paid in the form of dues. This 1% enhancement on $100,000 will pay for your club dues for three years, but you receive this enhanced return every year, year in and year out. This alone makes the club worth its membership in gold.

Free Weekly Stay at One of Our Fractional Resorts: We are currently developing three fractional ownership resort clubs. They are located in central Tennessee, Granby, Colorado, and Neiva Puerto, Mexico. As a club member, you can reserve time to have up to a week's stay in one of our properties at absolutely no cost to you (you can deduce that this is a first-come, first-served opportunity due to supply). You are not required to sit through any presentation but we do ask that you have dinner, on us, with a representative toward the end of your stay. In many cases, we pick you up at the airport and deliver you to the site, where you may be provided with a vehicle. It is important that you take advantage of this because Moving at the Speed of Wealth™ provides unparalleled opportunities for you to grow rich with our fractional ownership programs.

Limited Time Offer

Private 30-Minute One-on-One Session with Wayde McKelvy Each Month: The granddaddy of them all! As a club member, you are entitled to a private one-on-one mentoring session with me. You receive thirty minutes each month and this is a limited time opportunity. My schedule is becoming more demanding daily and I cannot hold this open to everyone. Believe me when I say that people want to talk to me personally. You may want to present an investment opportunity, receive guidance on your current plan, learn more details about a subject we have talked about or just talk about your kids. You will receive this access only as a club member. Remember that you must reach out to me—I will not call you. I prefer to work with people who truly have the mindset to build tremendous wealth in the shortest amount of time possible. This club was officially launched in August of 2008. You can imagine that I cannot keep this offer open for very long so you must take action today! You can learn more and join at: *www.SOWGoldClub.com*.

You do not have to have money to invest or ever have to invest in any of the opportunities that we present to you to be a Gold Club member. The education alone is worth the meager monthly dues. Let me ask you a question: How much do people pay in college tuition each year? Is it safe to say that with room, board, books, fees and tuition, it is close to $40,000 on average each year? If you are a college grad, did you ever receive the education that I provided to you in this book? Well, I have a business degree and never learned one-tenth of a percent of what I presented to you while I was in college.

The monthly dues to belong to The Speed of Wealth Gold Club™ are only twenty-nine dollars per month. Think of it as better than a book of the month club. It would cost you 115 years' worth of membership dues to equal one year's price of a college education.

Here is the skinny: If you think this book was well worth the money, then you need to join the club. You just ain't seen nothing yet! If you think this book is a load of crap, then it probably is not in your best interest to join…see ya, wouldn't want to be ya!

If you think this is a sales pitch, then you are very astute. You're damn right it is a pitch—it's a pitch to help you better your life and give you a reasonable and affordable way to receive not only my expertise but that of dozens of my associates, from all angles of wealth building, to mentor you. Do you think that a meager twenty-nine dollars per month is worth monthly coaching from someone who earns over $100,000 per month on his investments? I don't hold anything back because here is the deal: I want to get super-rich *with* you, not in spite of you!

Remember that you must invest in yourself. Membership would only cost you about $348 per year, so how much money do you need to make to make this worth it? All I have to do is show you how to receive an extra $390 per year and you will have made a 12% return on your money. If you cannot do that with all of the things I will be sharing with you, then you are not taking any action whatsoever.

So here is the deal for you non-action takers: If you don't want to continue with your membership, just quit! I only charge monthly, no annual dues, so if you don't think you are getting your money's worth, simply email us and quit, no questions asked. However, after the sixth month, I will not refund any money you have paid up to that point, but you will know within a couple of months if this club is right for you.

Listen, I don't want your money if I cannot help you. I sincerely mean that. My current students will tell you that with all of my faults, I truly care about them. My wife thinks I am generous to a fault.

Enough of the sales pitch. Let's see how much you are buying into what I have been preaching throughout this book. If you are ready to build wealth, if you are ready to take action, then go to *www.SOWGoldClub.com* and sign up. If you are not ready by now, quit reading and give this book to someone else. If you do, please email me and I will refund you the cost of this book, no questions asked, and I don't want you to return it...just give it to someone else (this is the honor system).

By joining the club, you will learn boatloads about building wealth. You will also learn some strategies just by moving on to the next chapter...

Chapter Sixteen

Secret of the Super-Rich #16

Super-Rich People Own Nothing but Control Everything; They Protect Their Assets

It's no secret that we live in a predatory environment. If you have something, you can bet that somebody else wants to get his or her hands on it. I read once that the United States has more lawsuits annually than all other countries combined. I don't know if that is true or not, but suffice it to say that people sue on a whim here.

We are one of the only countries that allow attorneys to charge on contingency, meaning they receive payment if they win the lawsuit. There are a whole lot of starving attorneys out there. I also read once that there are currently more law students than active attorneys. Again, I don't know if this is true or not, but most attorneys barely get by. Like in every other profession, there is the top tier and everybody else. This being the situation, many lawyers will take on a case on contingency in hopes of winning and making a name for themselves. I can't say I blame them, but it causes a whole lot of frivolous lawsuits.

On top of that, there are people out there who actually make a living suing people like you and me; they go by the name of "consumer advocates." They purposely try to put themselves in harm's way so they can sue. Why not, when it is so easy? Again, I don't want to go into statistics but let's just say that when you are "perceived" to have money, you can bet that you will be sued at some time in your life.

258   *Moving at the Speed of Wealth*

This chapter is not about the good, bad and ugly of our legal system, however; it is about what super-rich people do to protect their assets from these predators. I want to break it down into a couple of short parts. First, I want to talk about some actions that super-rich people take to protect their money. Secondly, I want to introduce you to one of the greatest legal entities of all time and show you how you can make a boatload of money using it.

First off, I am not a lawyer nor do I profess to know even a fraction of what specializing lawyers know about protecting one's assets. I know just enough to be dangerous because I employ some of the techniques. If you really want and/or need to know about asset protection, there are volumes of books and courses you can order to get started. Just go to amazon.com and search for "asset protection," and you will be overwhelmed with the results that are returned.

I will attempt to give you a very abbreviated idea of things you can do to protect your assets, but please consult a competent attorney or asset protection specialist before taking any action.

In a nutshell, in order to protect your assets from lawsuits and, consequently, from judgments, they simply cannot be your assets. You actually have to give your assets to another entity in order to protect them. So what does this mean? Well, it doesn't mean you give up control and it doesn't mean you cannot use the assets. It simply means that you, as an individual, no longer own the asset.

So what do I mean by "another entity"? You, as a person, are defined as an entity. The following is the definition as outlined at *www.wikipedia.com*:

> *In law, an **entity** is something capable of bearing legal rights and obligations. It generally means "legal entity" (such as a business entity or a corporate entity) or "artificial person" but also includes "natural person."*

Put another way, corporations, partnerships and trusts are considered "legal entities" with a pre-defined lifespan, which could be indefinite. To protect your assets, you must move control of them from yourself to a legal entity. The good news is that you generally control the legal entity. Here is a quick warning: If you are about to be or are being sued and you have not moved your assets prior to the knowledge of this, it is too late.

In other words, you must move your assets into another entity well before the fact, not after. If you are caught trying to hide assets and move them for the

Secret of the Super-Rich #16 259

sole purpose of protecting them from a lawsuit, the judge will not allow the protection these entities provide.

Let me try to put this in layman's terms. Here is how it plays out for the non-educated American. You are tired, driving late one night, and hit a motor-cycle driver, killing him. Forget for a second the sorrow and guilt you will feel. You can bet your first-born on the fact that the family of the deceased will sue you. Of course, you have car insurance with $500,000 protection and a two-million-dollar umbrella policy to protect your assets in an event just like this one…or so you think. You have $100,000 in home equity and another $500,000 in mutual funds outside your IRA or 401(k). You have $500,000 in your IRA and $200,000 in your 401(k) plan at work. How much do you think the family will sue you for? On first impulse, you may say $2.5 million (the total of your umbrella policy and your car insurance). You would be wrong. They will sue you for everything you have and add on some more money just in case. You will be sued for over $3.8 million (everything you own plus the value of your car and umbrella insurance).

Of course, you will lose, but the plaintiff will not be able to get his or her hands on your IRA or 401(k); they are both protected from creditors. Well, not really. Assume the plaintiff wins the case and now has a judgment against you for $4 million. You are forced to sell your home (this is another reason you never want to have equity in your property) to pay that $100,000. You will be forced to liquidate your $500,000 in mutual funds. The insurance compa-nies will pay but your car insurance will be dropped for good and you will not be able to get another umbrella policy. All that's left is the $500,000 sitting in your IRA and the $200,000 in your 401(k). You feel a little bit relieved because you still have $700,000 after that long and tedious nightmare.

Don't feel so relieved! The minute you start taking withdraws from your IRA and/or 401(k), the plaintiff will attach those proceeds and the money will go right into the plaintiff's pocket. At this point, it is way too late to reposition your assets to protect them.

All those years of planning and saving, doing what you thought was right! All those years of listening to your financial planner, gone with one accident. The worst part is that this could have easily been avoided with education. Let's take a look at a very simple approach that super-rich people take.

Keep in mind that this is just the tip of the iceberg to get you thinking. I would be happy to refer you to a specialist or an attorney who can educate you more thoroughly, but for now I will give you a snapshot of what you could have done to prevent this financial implosion.

You, of course, are you: an entity. You move all of your assets to a limited liability company (LLC) called XYZ. XYZ, LLC is also an entity that now controls your money. You own stock in XYZ, which is, of course, an asset. Here is a simple example of how it would work.

You form XYZ, LLC and divide the stock any way you deem fit. You could hold 100% or split it with your spouse or split it with as many people as you would like to. Instead of XYZ, LLC, let's call this newly formed entity John Smith's Investments, LLC (you being John Smith).

The first thing I would do is pull out the equity in my home and reposition it into my newly formed LLC. Then I would change the ownership of my mutual funds to the name of my LLC. Now your LLC owns the mutual funds. You cannot have another entity other than you individually own your IRA or 401(k), which is just another reason these plans are not my favorite places to build wealth.

In our lawsuit scenario, you have a judgment against you for $4 million. The insurance companies still pay (which means you lose your car insurance, etc.) but they cannot touch your $500,000 inside your LLC because the LLC— *not you*—owns the mutual funds. They could attach your stock certificate, which is what gives you control over your assets, but you are going to create layers of protection (again, use a specialist).

If your LLC disperses dividends to you, they can attach those dispersals, but since you control the LLC, you decide when a dividend is to be made. If you declare a dividend and keep it back as retained earnings, then the creditor (plaintiff, if they attach your LLC) will be liable for the taxes due even though they do not have the money. This is why most creditors or collection agencies will not attach an LLC.

The point I am trying to make is that you do not own anything. The LLC you created owns everything—but *you* control the LLC. A better approach may be to create a foundation or a family limited partnership. This is not an asset protection book; I just want you to think ahead so that if you ever do have any problems, you are protected. Super-rich people own nothing but control everything.

Another myth spread around by so-called gurus is that if you put your assets into a trust, they are protected from creditors. This is true and false, depending on the type of trust. Just to be clear, let me give you a Trust 101 education in layman's terms.

Trust arrangements have been in common use for centuries and are used for a variety of reasons. There are literally scores of types of trusts, but all have one common element. A trust is a legal document that involves three parties:

Secret of the Super-Rich #16

- The person placing assets into a trust, called the trustor
- The person en*trust*ed with the assets, called the trustee
- The person who receives benefits from the trust, called the beneficiary

The document that clearly explains each of the three parties' roles is called the trust or trust agreement.

By creating a trust, a person is essentially giving up ownership of the assets but can still keep the use and benefits of the asset. A very strong characteristic of a trust is that it provides privacy. In fact, when Walt Disney was buying up land around Orlando, he didn't want the sellers to know it was one person buying because he didn't want them to start raising prices. By allowing his trust to buy the land, nobody really knew who was doing the buying; at closing, it was a trust that was buying.

It is important to note that the trustee generally directs all activity within the trust and handles all administration. This is known as a trustee directed trust.

Here is where I have a problem with all of those seminars, less than ethical lawyers and non-lawyers running around preaching the merits of creating a living trust (or whatever type of trust) and charging you an arm and a leg to create it for you. Most of the types of trusts they recommend to you allow you to act as all three parties: the trustor, trustee and beneficiary. This is not illegal and is done all the time; it is called a grantor trust. My question is: Why bother? You can achieve most of the same goals with simple documentation from a bank or by creating a corporate entity (which would be my preference). Grantor trusts usually have no anonymity, no creditor protection and no tax benefits. So, again, why bother to pay that kind of money and create the headaches for something of little value?

There are two types of trusts: a revocable trust and an irrevocable trust. Take the name to mean exactly what it says. If you create an irrevocable trust, you cannot change your mind later without taxes or other consequences. You are essentially giving your assets away and giving away control of your assets, limited to what is written out in your original trust documentation. An irrevocable trust offers you the absolute largest amount of creditor protection, anonymity and tax benefits of any entity. The problem is that once you make this decision, you must abide by it…and we all know things change in life.

A revocable trust can be created, dissolved, changed, manipulated, and so on all you want, and you have the flexibility to make more decisions as life throws curve balls. Unless planning for estate transferring, you will probably stick with a revocable trust (one again, this is a generalization).

I have mentioned that a trust can have all the assets and administrative duties handled by the trustee (trustee directed trust) or the trustor (grantor trust), but there is still one other person who can handle the assets of the trust: the beneficiary. Now, it is important to keep in mind that you, the trustor, may well be the beneficiary.

In this type of trust, you have an independent trustee handle all directions and administration but only as directed by the beneficiary, which could be you.

Because I am a firm believer in real estate investing and this book is primarily about building wealth, not protecting your wealth, I want to introduce you to one of the greatest trust structures available today. If you have not heard of a revocable land trust, then you are missing the boat because this trust can not only be used to protect your real estate assets but can make you outright rich quickly.

I believe that all of your property should be held in a land trust but not just any type of land trust—an Illinois land trust (this is the style of trust; it doesn't mean you have to form it in Illinois). However, the bigger picture is that when it is used and structured properly, you can buy and sell real estate easier and, regardless of whether you are the seller or the buyer, you can benefit greatly. Here is a very short list of the advantages of using a land trust:

- Avoids property being probated
- A judgment against the trustor does not attach to the beneficiary
- Not a partnership, so it is much easier to manage when you have multiple owners (This is a great way to sell homes on a fractional basis, which is one of Speed of Wealth's favorite current investment types. It is able to fracture interests of multiple owners without being partners.)
- Legal and equitable property interest in trustee's name (Simply put, a land trust is much better than selling a home on a lease with an option to buy, which I personally would never recommend because it can be argued that you have given the renter an equitable position, meaning you would have to foreclose on him/her to evict.)
- Avoids the due on sale clause (This is perhaps the strongest benefit of a land trust and I will discuss it in greater detail.)
- Privacy of ownership

Secret of the Super-Rich #16

- Keep sales price private
- Ease of operating across state lines
- No recordation of the trust agreement
- To avoid "seasoning" problems (a better alternative to fix-n-flips)
- Great way to negotiate the sale and purchase of a property
- To provide non-recourse financing (never do seller carry without this trust)
- Avoids state regulations that apply to corporations and LLCs

I could go on and on about the benefits of a land trust, but suffice it to say that you can use them to create a real estate empire for yourself. I don't want to go into too much detail here because we have an entire course at *www.SpeedofWealth.com* that you can order regarding land trusts and their uses…but I want to give you a sneak peek by telling you a hypothetical story.

This story takes place in 2008, during a time when real estate inventory is through the roof, prices are dropping, people are being foreclosed on in record numbers and sellers cannot sell their properties because there is a credit crunch and too much inventory on the market. The homeowner in our story, Mary, can no longer afford her payments and has her home on the market for what she owes on it. Mary's home is worth $200,000 and she owes $200,000; if she were to sell traditionally using a real estate agent, she would have to come to the table with close to $15,000—that is, if she could even find a buyer.

You are a Speed of Wealth student and understand that in a time when foreclosures are high, the inventory for renters is growing larger. You don't have a lot of money and the credit crunch is just as real for you as for everyone else. You cannot get a home loan for two reasons: You already have one other investment property loan and you do not have the required 20% down payment (yes, folks, in the year 2008, investors need a substantial down payment).

Mary's current mortgage payment, including taxes and insurance, is about $1,500 per month. You like Mary's home and are positive you can rent it out for $1,500 per month so you approach her with an idea. You suggest that you create a land trust together and that Mary makes both you and her the beneficiaries to the property. You suggest that you will simply take over the payments and be responsible for all costs and maintenance. You tell Mary that according to a land trust agreement, she can evict you from the property for non-payment, but you will make it easier for her.

You recommend that the trustee hold three months' worth of rent in escrow with instructions stating that if you do not make your payment, she can make the payment out of the escrow and evict you immediately. If she is forced to evict you, she can keep the remaining money that is sitting in the escrow account.

Mary is a little uncomfortable because she does not understand the concept and if she moves out, she will have to take on another payment to live somewhere else. If she is forced to evict you, she will be responsible for payments on two properties and she will only have enough money to cover three months.

You agree and can empathize with her. You ask her if she would be more comfortable if she had a year's worth of payments in escrow. Mary gets excited and agrees. This is no problem for you because you are taking control of a piece of real estate with no new loan and can use your IRA money. You will escrow $18,000.

You and Mary come to an agreement as to the current fair market value of the property. This is the value that Mary will ultimately sell the property to you for. You both agree on $200,000. You give the land trust a life span of three years, in which time you have full use as the owner and share beneficial interest in the property with Mary.

You and Mary agree that if you both decide to sell the property to a third party (you are both beneficiaries, so you must agree to this up front), you will share the profit, if any. You also spell out that you have the right as one of the beneficiaries to rent the property to a third party.

Okay, so that is a very simple illustration of how you put this thing together, but let's see how each of you benefits from this transaction.

The seller (Mary): Most astute real estate investors know that whenever possible, obtaining seller financing is preferable because the terms can be negotiated. As far as selling a property is concerned, using seller financing puts the negotiating ball right on the seller's home court. If the above example resembles a seller-financing sale with a wraparound mortgage, then read on. As many of you may know, a wraparound mortgage is when the seller keeps the underlying mortgage, the buyer makes payments to the seller, and, in turn (and, of course, in theory), the seller sends off the payment to the lender.

Every home loan has what's called a "due on sale" clause, which simply means that if you sell the home (transfer the deed), the entire loan is due and payable immediately. Wraparound mortgages are essentially fraudulent and break the contract. Seller financing, unless the home is owned outright by the seller, is very dangerous and, in most cases, fraudulent.

So why would Mary go along with this land trust?

Secret of the Super-Rich #16

- The co-beneficiary can take over the mortgage payments without triggering the due on sale clause. A land trust offers a legitimate way to "take over" the existing mortgage obligations without assuming the loan by qualifying.
- If Mary were on top of her game, she would realize that she could have probably asked for a higher "selling price" because of the benefits offered to the co-beneficiary.
- A faster sale and shorter closing period. This transaction can be completed within days of agreement, getting the seller on her merry (no pun intended) way.
- Avoidance of IRS' imposition of a tax on debt relief. What most people do not realize is that if Mary would have been foreclosed on or the lender would have settled for a "short sale" (accepting less than is owed), Mary would owe a tax on the amount below the remaining loan balance. Remember that Mary was very close to foreclosure and in today's market, it is very likely that the bank would have to accept less than what Mary owed, thus triggering a tax on the difference when Mary can least afford it.
- Mary was freed from the mortgage obligation as well as homeowner's insurance, taxes and maintenance.
- Mary, the seller, has protection from a third party (if she had to rent the property out). The seller is protected from any tax liens, lawsuits, bankruptcies, judgment liens or marital disputes that might arise in the co-beneficiary's life.
- Ease of payments and of collection of payments by the co-beneficiary. The trustee handles all of the administration.
- Unlike a lease with an option to purchase, this land trust ensures that Mary can evict the co-beneficiary with ease and typically within thirty days. On top of that, if she is forced to evict the co-beneficiary, she keeps all the money that is in the escrow account. In many ways she almost hopes the co-beneficiary will default. Keep in mind that the seller could ask for any amount of money she wants to be held in the escrow account. If the co-beneficiary buys the home with new financing, then the seller has to apply the escrow to the purchase, but Mary doesn't care. She has sold her home at the price she wanted.
- Mary can easily sell her home without the use of a real

266   *Moving at the Speed of Wealth*

estate broker. Not that I am against real estate brokers (my wife owns her own real estate company), but you should not even consider using an agent if you decide to sell your home through a land trust unless that agent thoroughly understands what a land trust is. If you are a real estate broker or agent, this is your opportunity to specialize and make a killing. Specialization in any field will make you super-rich. I have not talked to one real estate agent in my entire professional lifetime who thoroughly understood the uses of a land trust. Maybe you should be that person. On top of that, if you have considered becoming a real estate agent or are looking for another career, you could become a land trust specialist and make very good income. There is no special licensing required; you do not need a real estate license to specialize in land trusts. If this were something I was interested in doing for part-time or full-time work, however, I would still apply and obtain my real estate license; the education you receive during pre-licensing alone is probably worth it.

- Participation in the upside of the market. Mary has agreed to sell the property in the future to the co-beneficiary at a set price. However, if both parties agree to sell to an outside third party, they can both receive a portion of the newly created home equity due to appreciation (if negotiated up front).

As you can see, especially in today's market, this is a winning deal for Mary. Everything she was trying to achieve—and more—has been achieved. As we move on to the advantages for the co-beneficiary (you), you will clearly see why this is a win-win situation.

The buyer (you): Compared with traditional forms of financing a home to purchase (or, more importantly, to control) or with seller assisted financing, the use of a land trust provides all the benefits with less effort and maximum safety. The land trust is very convenient and easy to use; the toughest part is helping the seller understand the benefits. Once again, I am just touching the tip of the iceberg and you can purchase an entire course complete with contacts, forms, trustee information, people willing to structure the contract for you, etc., at *www.SpeedofWealth.com* under "land trust." The land trust is an

Secret of the Super-Rich #16 267

unbelievably awesome structure, especially in today's high default rate market with real estate prices dropping. However, and this is big, it can be used in any real estate market and should be a staple in your arsenal of techniques and strategies if you plan on being a real estate investor.

Let's take a look at some of the overwhelming benefits a buyer receives when using a land trust to purchase real estate to either live in or as an investment property.

- No need to go through all of the bank's "red tape" to qualify for a loan. The seller determines whether or not you are credit-worthy and all payment arrangements are made between you and the seller only. The two of you come to an agreed upon payment structure. Obviously, as the buyer, you would want to negotiate for better terms but the key is that it is open to negotiation and not set by the lender. You could actually create a tiered payment schedule: higher payments now, lower payments in the future, or just the opposite. You could create any payment structure that you and the seller mutually agree upon.

- The down payment requirements, if any, are negotiated between you and the seller. Once again, you are not subject to the lending institution's rules. The days of zero-down traditional financing are over for a while (this created the sub-prime mess we are currently in), especially for real estate investors. When purchasing a home utilizing a land trust, you and the seller negotiate on and agree to a down payment. This down payment is held in escrow to ensure that payments are made and a reserve is held for repairs. As a buyer, you could negotiate a no down payment purchase if the seller is willing. If you just don't have any money for a down payment, keep looking for a seller until you find one that is very motivated and will accept a no down payment plan. I typically like to make the seller comfortable and give in on the down payment so I can negotiate stronger terms on the payment. I do this because I know that if I go through with the purchase, the down payment is credited back to me. In other words, it is not as if I lost the money (however, the escrow does not typically earn interest); it is there to be applied at a later date. The key is that I have negotiated a better payment plan for myself to help create positive cash flow when I rent the property.

- Perhaps this is one of the strongest advantages to purchasing a home using a land trust, as opposed to buying on a lease option plan or renting a home: When you use the land trust as your vehicle when purchasing the home, you (the buyer) receive the income tax deductions on the mortgage interest paid and the property taxes. The seller, of course, loses these benefits but you as a buyer are treated just as if you had a "true" mortgage. There has been a lot of case law to prove this, and each time the buying co-beneficiary has won the case. (Our course explains in great detail why you receive these benefits even though you are not taking out a new loan.)

- As the buying co-beneficiary, you receive the equity built up as the current underlying mortgage principal is paid down. The older the loan is, the more principal is applied on each payment.

- On top of equity build-up through the reduction of principal on the home loan, you also benefit from any appreciation that the property receives. Again, depending on how you structure the deal with the seller, you could benefit from all appreciation or just a fraction. To persuade the seller to sell you the property through a land trust and allow you to rent the property to a third party, you may want to split any or a fraction of any appreciation when the property is ultimately sold. Your imagination is the key when negotiating a deal with the seller. I am a big proponent of win-win situations and I do not believe I need to make a fortune on any one deal—but, hey, you do what you feel is right.

- I learned the hard way about this next benefit. I recently had a tax issue with the IRS and they placed a lien on my primary residence. I could not refinance my home until the taxes I owed were paid. If the property were in a land trust, it would have been shielded from judgments, tax liens, lawsuits, bankruptcy or claims in a marital dispute.

Secret of the Super-Rich #16

It is so important that I will state it again: If you own any real estate at all, you need to investigate land trusts much more thoroughly. You will more than likely want to put each property into its own land trust. (Again, our course explains this in further detail or you can search "land trust" using Google®.)

- Instead of being a renter, you can purchase real estate and enjoy the pride of ownership without all the constraints of traditional real estate financing and acquisition. Instead of just pissing your money away renting, you can now enjoy all the benefits of home ownership without all the hassles and constraints of traditional financing. As a side note, if you are a renter and have decent, but not great, credit, you should still probably apply for FHA financing. The down payment requirements are minimal and the terms are very favorable.

- As a buyer, you can shield this entire transaction from your financial statement, unless, of course, you want to show any equity you may have. If, as a real estate investor, you were forced to apply for traditional financing, the land trust does not show you as having another investment property loan. For you real estate investors reading this, you understand that lenders will cap how many outstanding investment properties you can have at any one time. Today that number has come down quite a bit. In fact, I have students with stellar credit, great income, and a 20% down payment that are having difficulties being approved for more than one investment property loan. I am sure that will loosen up in the future, but for now the land trust allows you to have as many rental properties as you can handle.

- The land trust protects the buyer (co-beneficiary) from illicit acts of the "other party" (seller). In a traditional wraparound mortgage type of transaction, other than being fraudulent, the seller collects payments from you and you pray they make the payment to the lender. If the seller does not pay the lender, you are in deep trouble (this is called equity skimming and it is very much illegal—but at this point you have already committed fraud). With the

270 *Moving at the Speed of Wealth*

land trust, the trustee collects your payment and makes the payment directly to the lender. You must have a reputable trustee and I would not typically use the seller's "best friend." (The course offered at *www.SpeedofWealth.com* will point you to very reputable trustee who handles land trusts all the time.) Also, the property cannot be attached by any action the seller commits. In other words, a judgment or lien against the seller would not attach to the property. Remember that the property is shielded from these problems (which, of course, is the basis of this chapter anyway).

- You, as a buyer or real estate investor, no longer have to keep postponing your transactions due to lack of money. You no longer need to find an equity partner if you are low on cash to begin your real estate investing plan. Remember that you can walk into a property with no money down and receive all the benefits of home ownership today so long as you negotiate the terms that meet your needs. Today's real estate environment provides the perfect timing to jump into the game and start playing to win when you use a land trust. No more excuses—you need to order the course and understand the land trust thoroughly, and then get out there and start building wealth.

- If you as the buyer decide to purchase the property, you will need to apply for traditional financing. However, you are not going to apply for "purchase money" financing; you are going to be refinancing your home. Refinancing is always easier and quicker with fewer hoops to jump through. Some lenders are starting to treat the land trust as purchase money, but many are still treating the financing as a refinance.

Well, there you have it. As promised, I delivered another strategy of the very super-rich. I realize this chapter is about protecting your assets, but this book is about Moving at the Speed of Wealth™ and building wealth as quickly as possible.

Some of you reading this book may already have accumulated substantial assets. If you have not looked into protecting those assets through various

Secret of the Super-Rich #16 271

means, you need to find one of the many books or courses available to you tomorrow and start honing your knowledge.

I will be honest with you: Protecting your assets using any one of the methods described here or in any other course or book is a pain in the ass. It will take time and you will need to constantly review your position. Consider that you create one of these entities and put your current assets inside. If you continue to accumulate assets, and you should, they more than likely will be outside of this entity. You must always review your situation and ensure that your assets are protected.

Although it is a time-consuming process, it is very important to protect your assets. You are one car accident away from filing bankruptcy and bankruptcy will not solve the problems. I bring this up because I hear this from lazy people all the time: "If I am sued and lose, I will just file bankruptcy to protect my assets."

Folks, it just doesn't work that way. If you are sued and lose and you have substantial assets, you will more than likely be forced to file a chapter 13 bankruptcy (personal reorganization). If this is the case, you will be obligated to make monthly payments, which will dramatically affect your lifestyle.

I cannot say this enough: DO NOT PROCRASTINATE...IT COULD COST YOU A FORTUNE!

With that final sentence, I believe it is time to move on to the final chapter of this book and the seventeenth closely guarded secret of the super-rich. In fact, this one is not a secret at all—it is more of a way of life for super-rich people.

Chapter Seventeen

Secret of the Super-Rich #17

Super-Rich People Do Not Procrastinate; They Take Immediate and Decisive Action

Lead, follow or get the hell out of the way! "Rich people play to win; poor people play not to lose" (from T. Harv Eker's *Secrets of the Millionaire Mind*).

I am quite confident that many readers have a favorite sports team. Now, although I played offensive line through college and loved football as a young man, I am not much of a sports fanatic today. I am not one to sit around and watch sports and build my schedule around it, unless, of course, the Denver Broncos are playing.

So what does this have to do with anything? I am a Broncos fan, not like I was ten or twenty years ago, but still a fan. I don't buy the team's paraphernalia or have season tickets but I like to see them win. I am very competitive by nature and, thank goodness, I am seeing that in my children. The point is that when John Elway played for the Broncos, many times they would build what seemed to be an insurmountable lead against their opponents. Football fans will know exactly what I am talking about. They would instantly go into conservative mode and start playing the game not to lose. You know, they would start running the football on every down and go into that God-forsaken "prevent defense."

I cannot tell you how many times I watched my team go from what seemed like an easy win to a loss because of this mindset. I would say to myself, "Man, when you've got them down, go for the kill." So, again, what does this have to do with anything? It has to do with the way you approach life. Sports are a great mirror of the type of person you are or will grow to be—in fact, not only sports but any type of competition. As a kid, if you had little or no interest in anything, the chances of you becoming super-rich are nil to none.

As you know, I have twin teenage daughters and I watch as many of their friends just float through life, sleep until the late afternoon, and do not participate in any type of sport, hobby or club. What do you really think the ambition levels of these kids are? Maybe it's because we have become too soft as parents and spoil our kids to death.

Hey, my kids are very spoiled but they are both very competitive and want to win. By the way, when did they stop keeping score at little league games? When did they make the rule that all kids get to play? This is bull! What are you teaching kids—that it is okay to go through life half-heartedly because you are a winner anyway? Look, if your kid isn't good at football, help him or her find something he or she is good at. Every kid is good at something (just like every adult is good at something). You just need to find out what it is…and it is really easy to discover: ASK YOUR KID!

The point is this: There are nine indisputable golden keys to becoming super-rich and the very first key is: Understand that life, and especially building wealth, is a game!

The Nine Indisputable Golden Keys to Becoming Super-Rich is going to be the title and subject of my next short book, so I don't want to go into too much detail here, but I do want to explain.

You grew up as a kid competing in whatever you did. I don't know one kid who likes to lose at something they are good at. Somewhere along the line, we lose that competitive spirit. All of life is a game and you need to continue to compete. You need to fight to keep your health. You need to fight to instill good values in your children. You need to fight to get better pay at your place of employment. You need to fight to keep your marriage strong. You need to fight to understand and love your own parents at times. You need to fight to understand and love your siblings.

And you need to fight to build tremendous wealth. The funny thing is that building wealth is a game and you keep score by how much money you accumulate. I am not talking about building tremendous wealth to show off; I am talking about knowing internally that you are winning the game of financial independence. I am talking about taking a 45 - 0 lead in a football game by half-time. If you have ever played any sport, you know what a feeling that is! In fact, on the rare occasions a team I played for had that kind of lead, it allowed me to relax and I actually played much better and reduced my chances for injury.

Life is a game and you need to play to win. People who invest in money markets or certificates of deposit because of the fear of loss are never going to become financially secure. Don't get me wrong. Once you have accumulated the wealth that you believe you need (always add a little more), then and only then is it okay to get conservative.

If you are playing the wealth-building game to win, then you will, without a doubt, lose money on some of your investments. The trick is to minimize those losses and to think in terms of your blended rate of return. Just like playing in a football game, there is a strong possibility that even if you win, you will surrender points to the other team. It is inevitable that you will lose money in some of your investments.

I have a handful of students who forget this indisputable golden rule to building wealth. It's funny; they will invest in a hard money loan that eventually needs to be foreclosed on. Of course, when you have to foreclose, it means you are not receiving your monthly payment from the borrower. I actually had one student come out and say that he lost all of his money. How quickly we forget. At the first sign of adversity, we forget everything we have been taught.

I had to remind this person that although the monthly income stream had dried up, there was a very good chance that when all is said and done his internal rate of returns would be much higher. I had to remind this student that he had collateral and we would simply have to foreclose to take control of that collateral. I had to remind him that although he had to pay the costs of foreclosing, this amount is added to the overall balance owed to him. I had to remind this student that once he had control of the property, he would own a piece of real estate at wholesale and all kinds of options would present themselves to him to recover the principal. Long story short, the student ended up with a 21% annualized rate of return on his money rather than the 12% the note called for—all because he had to foreclose.

Does it work this well every time? Hell, no! When you are playing the game to win, you will eventually surrender some points to the opposition.

The thing is that people will have their money sitting in mutual funds, watching the value go down, and they don't give it a second thought other than a little moaning and groaning. Average people are happy just to recover their principal; super-rich people play to win! You are not playing to win if you have $500,000 saved up for retirement. You want to talk about fear? Wait until you have to budget $500,000 plus your miserable 4% returns against 8% inflation over twenty years of retirement.

Here is another great story that actually just happened yesterday. A new student of mine attended a live webinar where I introduced an opportunity to earn 51% annualized returns over the next three years collateralized by real estate (deeds of trust). This person called and stated that she was a very conservative investor and was a bit skeptical and nervous. I asked how much money she had saved to this point. Her answer was a little over $30,000 and she was in her mid-fifties. After reading this book, you can probably imagine what my response to her was, but I will leave that to your imagination!

The point is: Do not become a student of Speed of Wealth if you are not ready to start playing to win and accept the fact that you will lose money in some investments. Out of all of the investments I have recommended, we have only lost money on one (the students involved did not lose all of their money, but they lost some). My good students grumbled and complained but kept playing the game to win. Receiving 12 - 50% returns on the majority of your money will overcome a loss. You should only be interested in your blended rate of return and the final score at the end of the game (retirement).

Important Note: *Who on God's green Earth said you needed to end the game at age sixty-five? Is that all that work means to these folks who count the days to retirement? If that is the case, you need to re-evaluate your life and even if it means a temporary pay cut, get involved in something you love to do. Life is too damn short to be counting the days until you turn sixty-five. I will do what I do until the day I die. I may slow down a bit but I love what I do and cannot imagine not doing this. Truth be told, you can make money doing anything you love to do. There may not be a market today for what you like but you can begin to create a market. I'll bet that in this world of over six billion people, if you reach out you can find at least 100,000 people who love to do what you love to do.*

Whatever you do, when you put this book down at least pick a side. Either you are going to play not to lose (which means you will eventually lose) or you are going to play to win. Get off the fence, make a decision and run with it. Don't sleep on it for the next year. DO NOT PROCRASTINATE EVER AGAIN IN YOUR LIFE!

DON'T ALLOW YOUR CHILDREN OR GRANDCHILDREN TO PROCRASTINATE EVER AGAIN IN THEIR LIVES. I am as guilty as you are. My children will put off their homework until the last minute and I let them

Secret of the Super-Rich #17

get away with it because they are both straight A students. But what values am I teaching them? I am teaching them to put off decisions and actions until the last minute. You and I both know that as adults, these last-minute decisions can cost us a job or a boatload of money.

Another golden key is that you must think BIG! Quit thinking small when it comes to building wealth. Why would you settle for less than you are worth? Is it because you have no self-worth? What makes you believe that you do not deserve $10 million? Other people are accumulating that kind of money at record paces.

I told you in the chapter on starting your own business that it is perfectly fine to start small and to take baby steps. First off, when you start your own business, regardless of the size, you are thinking BIG. You have taken a scary and massive step toward financial independence.

When you are investing in real estate, why would you settle for two rental properties or one fix-n-flip a year when I have shown you how to do an unlimited number of these transactions? If real estate developers are making all the money, then why are you not a developer? I am sure your response is "Because I don't have the time, knowledge or expertise to take on this BIG task." You don't have to. Developers need your money, so negotiate an equity position to loan it to them and let them do all the work. You can still build tremendous wealth sharing in the profit, even if it is a small percentage.

Sure, you may lose a little money, but think of the upside. If you are fifty-five years old, have a whopping $100,000 to your name and will settle for 8% returns, you lose! That will create a whopping $8,000 in income a year before taxes, not factoring in inflation. You can probably save that much in taxes each year by starting your own business. You can probably earn that much in two years if you would commit to a good network marketing company. You might as well take the plunge and try to win the game because, if you are like most people I talk to, you are more than likely losing.

You need to start thinking bigger than yourself. When my friend who picked up garbage at construction sites finally understood that there were over 300 million people in America, all with garbage, he stopped looking at his self-perceived "limitations" and started making a hell of a good living.

Folks, winning the investing game is not very hard. Here are some of my golden keys:

1. Invest only in something you understand. If you do not understand a certain type of investment, start studying. My primary investments have been hard money loans. I have done very well

with them and have tried to educate you on them as well. Maybe this isn't your thing. Find your thing and learn all you can about it. I know a handful of people who have made a ton of money on oil and natural gas. I know more people who have lost money on oil and natural gas because they never took the time to educate themselves. The losers saw people making money and figured it must be a good deal...wrong! It is a good deal when you understand it. I do not invest here because I do not understand it well enough. If I ever get the urge, I can and will educate myself thoroughly before I invest a dime. Despite what many financial planners may say, you do not have to be as diversified as they claim. Almost all of my money is in hard money loans. Does that sound like I am diversified? Well, I am because at any given time I may have ten or fifteen loans on my books and that diversifies me. Sure, real estate can take a plunge (and it has recently) but it will always bounce back. This brings me to my next golden key.

2. Be patient when you invest. If you thoroughly understand what you are investing in, then you know the absolute worst thing that could happen to you before you invest one red cent. Do you recall my story about the student who panicked because he had to foreclose? Do you recall the outcome? I am not one to preach about putting your money in the stock market for the long term. What I am saying is sometimes you just need to be patient.

3. Don't be afraid to take your losses and run. I think I covered this pretty well already. You will lose money in investments occasionally. Don't panic. Re-evaluate and take a hit if it is warranted then move on. Surrender the field goal, get the ball back and drive down for a touchdown. I had a student who owned an annuity that was growing at a snail's pace. It was averaging about 5% over the last five years. He had a fifteen-year decreasing surrender charge and did not want to liquidate the annuity because he "perceived" he would lose money. I don't remember the exact amount but let's assume he had a 10% surrender charge and his balance was $100,000. I showed him how he could make hard money loans and receive 17%. Do the math: 17% minus the 10% surrender charge minus the 5% he was averaging. He still would have been ahead of the game by 2% in the first year and by 12% starting the second year. (In reality, he would have broken even his

first year but you have absorbed enough math by now. Suffice it to say that the 17% would have been on $90,0000 instead of 5% on $100,000).

4. Never, ever, ever make investment decisions based on the tax consequences. This is very simple. I have had scores of students who wanted to get into the hard money loan business and get out of the landlord business. As miserable as they were as landlords, they refused to liquidate their properties because they didn't want to pay the capital gains tax (which is currently very low) and recapture of depreciation. Folks, the government is going to get its share of the money. Let me ask you a question: Would you rather pay twenty-five cents on a dollar gained or save twenty-five cents on a dollar spent? I am not saying not to plan to reduce your taxes; I am saying do not make investment decisions based solely on tax consequences. If you do not like the investment, or would rather invest somewhere else, pay the taxes and move on.

5. Never let fear rule your decisions. Remember rule number one: If you understand the investment, fear should never come into play. I mentioned in this book that I evaluate dozens of investments a month and, truthfully, I could find a reason to reject every single investment if I let fear dictate my decision-making process. The funny thing is that you probably do not even know what you are fearful of when it comes to investing. That's why you must start with my very first rule.

6. Finally, **GET INTO THE GAME AND PLAY TO WIN**. Super-rich people are decisive and make decisions quickly. Once they understand the type of investment they are comfortable with, they know exactly what to look for. They go straight to that issue, complete their due diligence and ACT! Super-rich people do not procrastinate; they understand that they will make mistakes occasionally but also understand all the other rules. When you do not quit, you will almost assuredly overcome your mistakes in life. When you quit, your mistakes win. My definition of being "broke" is that I see it as an opportunity. I know that whatever I was doing did not work so I try something different.

It's all about the human spirit; it is about the spirit within you. There is not one person reading this book who cannot become financially independent if you

280   *Moving at the Speed of Wealth*

will just listen to and put into action the techniques, strategies and ideas that other super-rich people have achieved. If you are reading this book, especially if you have made it this far, there is no doubt in my mind that you are already halfway to wealth. You welcome new ideas and are willing to listen. Think of the few people who will ever even pick up a wealth-building book. What are their chances of success?

I have told you many times that, although I present the ideas in this book in my own way and have formulated and applied my own opinions, I did not *create* anything you have read about. I may have tweaked or twisted some ideas but I had mentors, just as you should.

I would like to apply for the job of being your mentor. I want to help you achieve financial independence, but not if you are not ready to listen and hear what I have to say. I never want you taking what I say on blind faith. I want you to hear me, absorb what I say, and look for different opinions. Then I want you to formulate your very own opinion.

What I teach is not right for everyone and you can bet that the financial community, as a whole, is not very fond of me. It would do them good to listen to me, do their own research (not what was passed down to them from some financial planning class), and formulate their very own opinions.

Although I am not a fan of some of the nationally recognized financial "gurus," I will sit and listen to what they have to say. I will then do my own research and formulate my own opinions (you have probably guessed that).

All I am saying is to quit listening to the mainstream and start building wealth. If you are ready to join in my movement and become a student, then your first step is to join The Speed of Wealth Gold Club™. You can do this by visiting *www.SpeedofWealth.com* and clicking the "join" button. After you have done that, you must stay involved. Make sure you attend as many webinars, teleseminars, live seminars, live workshops, and bootcamps as possible.

When I present ideas that appeal to you, do further research. For example, I am not the world's most respected authority on hard money loans. I don't know who is, but there are other people out there providing educational material on hard money loans. Learn from them all, provide to all the people you care about, and enjoy life!

Now is the time to act. Super-rich people do not procrastinate! Either you are ready to become my student or you are not. Get off the fence. I am waiting with open arms. I also want you to know that I have hundreds of students from whom you will learn as well. Each and every student of mine has his or her own unique skills and traits. We are a group of like-minded *individuals* looking for the same outcome: financial independence. That includes you.

www.SpeedofWealth.com
www.SOWGoldClub.com
www.SpeedofWealthEvents.com